W9-AXO-248

A book should ideally be dedicated to the person or people who helped the author produce the work. There are many friends and associates who have helped in ways too numerous to mention. But this book had its beginnings in the days of my self-discovery. My most sincere thanks to Dr. Edward P. Rubin who helped me recognize and direct my emotional energies in a productive and satisfying fashion. And it is to you, Dr. Rubin, that this book is dedicated.

This publication is designed to provide accurate and authoritative information in regard to the subject matter covered. It is sold with the understanding that the publisher is not engaged in rendering legal, accounting, or other professional service. If legal advice or other expert assistance is required, the services of a competent professional person should be sought. *From a Declaration of Principles jointly adopted by a Committee of the American Bar Association and a Committee of Publishers.*

Library of Congress Cataloging in Publication Data:

Bernstein, Jacob, 1946–
The investor's quotient.

Includes index.
1. Investments. 2. Investments–Psychological aspects. I. Title.

HG4521.B444 332.6′78 80-17127
ISBN 0-471-07849-2

Printed in the United States of America

10 9 8 7 6 5 4 3 2 1

The Investor's Quotient

THE PSYCHOLOGY OF SUCCESSFUL INVESTING IN COMMODITIES AND STOCKS

Jacob Bernstein

Publisher, M. B. H. Weekly Commodity Letter

JOHN WILEY & SONS New York • Chichester • Brisbane • Toronto

The Investor's Quotient

"We learn more from error than from confusion."

Novum Organum, or True Suggestions for
the Interpretation of Nature, 1620.
Francis Bacon (Lord Verulam)

The Investor's Quotient

Introduction

Since the early 1950s stock and commodity trading have increased by 200 percent. As volume records are set almost yearly, the desire and interest to trade and/or invest in the markets becomes more common. Activity on the major exchanges has, however, outpaced the growth in overall investment success. Brokerage houses would have us believe that knowledge is the key to speculative profit. "Investigate before you invest," we are told. "Know corporate management, earnings reports, long-term debt, and projected sales," we are cautioned. The emphasis is, and has long been, on *market knowledge*. Yet, despite the voluminous output of market information, financial reports, advisory publications, and brokerage-house material, there are still many individuals who fail to profit from their investments. In fact, an overwhelming majority of public investors are net losers, year in, year out.

Some speculative markets such as commodity futures are well-known for their ability to relieve traders of their funds in relatively short order. And yet, there are those who have managed to profit handsomely from their speculative and investment ventures in the marketplace. Paradoxically, our computerized technology and lightning-fast communications may have actually inhibited investment success. With our economic forecasting ability as well developed as it has become, market winners should be in the overwhelming majority. But they are not. The question naturally arises as to why. To one who is familiar with the basics of human psychology, the answer is quite simple. However, remediating the underlying problem is complex. For it is the individual who stands in his or her own way. It is the speculator who takes sophisticated market tools and uses them to create losses rather than gains. And it is the average investor who feeds the market with losses through his lack of self-knowledge, self-control, and self-discipline.

In our frantic race to outpace and outdate even the most advanced technology, we have overlooked the human variable. People are the strongest link in the chain and at the same time the weakest. Without people there would be no technology. And without people there would be no market. Paradoxically, human beings have removed themselves from the very situation they sought to improve for their own benefit. They have therefore become the limiting factor in a highly complex system. Such anomalies are common in highly advanced societies. The same situation is predominant in the investment world. In developed countries, people have fooled themselves into believing that knowledge of economic events will lead almost directly to financial success. In so doing, they have overlooked the very basic fact that knowledge can lead to success only if those who use it do so appropriately. For many reasons, unknown to most, the emotional workings of each individual can be the determining factor in trading success or failure. This has long been common knowledge among successful investors.

The time has come to rekindle knowledge of the self and how it relates to the marketplace. It is now necessary to return to the most basic of basics–the human mind. It is to this end that I will strive.

> The speed and efficiency of transportation by superhighway and air in many ways restricts freedom of travel. It is increasingly difficult to take a walk, except in such "reservations for wanderers" as state parks. But the nearest state park to my home has, at its entrance, a fence plastered with a long line of placards saying: NO FIRES. NO DOGS. NO HUNTING. NO CAMPING . . . change is in some sense an illusion, for we are always at the point where any future can take us! (Watts 1966, pp. 38–43)

Today, more than ever before, it is important for the average investor to acquire and implement effective market strategy skills. The 1970s witnessed a marked increase in economic instability and price fluctuation. The tame markets of yesteryear are gone. It is no longer possible to approach investing casually. The net result of an undisciplined or unstructured strategy will, today, be even more catastrophic than it might have been in the early 1950s. At the same time, it has become necessary for most of us to invest our funds in places other than saving bonds or savings accounts, if only in an effort to keep pace with the runaway rate of inflation. Frequently, monies kept in banks tend to earn interest rates lower than the rate of inflation. While our buying power is decreasing at the rate of more than 10 percent per year, our savings accounts may be growing at a much slower pace.

Many individuals have, in effect, been forced into the security and commodity markets, in a frantic effort to lessen the erosion factor. Paradoxically, a majority have become victims of the vehicle they sought to use as a means to financial independence. Why has this happened? How is it that the average investor is, more often than not, a net loser in the equity markets? What can be done to counteract the ever-increasing rate of investment failure? Are the answers to be found in better technical trading tools? Is there any salvation in the use of computer technology as an investment aid?

It appears that we have entered an age during which knowledge of one's self can be more productive than acquisition of so-called facts, news, theories of economics, or political motivation. During times of worldwide instability emotion reigns supreme. Facts fall by the wayside and there is no wrong or right. He who has mastered the self and its behavioral extensions typically emerges as the survivor. When the dust has cleared, and most investors have nothing to show but losses, those in command of their emotional self will emerge victorious.

The psychological state of humankind appears to have passed through several stages as it has evolved from the cave to the computer room. Whereas life was, at one time, a series of struggles for survival, the development of sophisticated technology in agriculture and electronics has liberated people to pursue ends considered more lofty. Certainly this is not true throughout the world. But today more than ever before there is a higher worldwide level of need satisfaction. We have at our command the skill required to eliminate human starvation and much disease. And yet political involvements, financial expediencies, and bureaucratic confusions prevent us from realizing this humanitarian cause. Technology is not to blame. Humanity itself is the culprit.

Perhaps awareness of our personal limitations has itself awakened an era of self-study in modern man. Increasingly there has been a move toward self-discovery, self-awareness, self-improvement, self-analysis, and self-motivation. The self has become a central issue in our modern world. Note the revival of religious consciousness so evident throughout the United States in the last five years. It represents, rightly or wrongly, a return to basics. After attaining a highly advanced technology, we are coming to the end of our current disposition to sit and ask in wonderment (or even in horror): "Is that all there is?" The exponential growth of applied science has far outpaced the ability of humanity to implement its full potential. And now the human psyche must move quickly to catch up with the sciences–otherwise their fruits will be wasted, abused, or both.

The investment sciences are no exception to this general rule. We have the tools to forecast with a relatively high degree of accuracy. Price trends can be determined with reasonable success. Yet their ultimate realization may, in many cases, result in profit for very few. In order to rectify this phase shift or lag it becomes necessary to reeducate ourselves in the basics of human psychological functioning. Regardless of technique, forecasting method, trading system, or econometric analysis, it has become evident that the prerequisites to technological methods are human factors. The success or failure of current investor technology is, more than ever before, almost exclusively a function of human input. The investor acts as a filter in the total picture. This is in no way any different from what his role has been at any time in investment history. It is, however, necessary that he fulfill this role more effectively than ever before owing to the profound change witnessed in the price climate. It is for this reason that I propose prerequisite personal analysis by all investors. I have, to this end, devised the Investor's Quotient, a questionnaire designed to highlight the personal strengths and weaknesses of each investor or speculator. By combining this with the accompanying text of this book, all readers should benefit.

Whether involved in stocks, bonds, commodity futures, capital-intensive business, or real estate, all investors, prospective and aspiring, should become totally familiar with the topics covered here. This work should serve as a stepping-stone to more advanced reading. What, precisely, is meant by Investor's Quotient? How do I propose the use of this concept in the investment scheme? Why do I believe that it is the ultimate key to profitable trading?

The work of French psychologist Alfred Binet led to development of the Intelligence Quotient, late in the 1890s. The IQ, as it is called, is a measure of intellectual ability derived from a standardized test score. The concept of mental age is based on the results achieved on a given IQ test, divided by a person's chronological age. An IQ is thus a measure of intellectual ability relative to age. Up to a certain point in time a person's IQ score tends to climb. Thereafter, it stabilizes and then, as old age sets in, declines. IQ score is more a measure of achievement than of innate ability. In the same way, I suggest the eventual use of a similar concept in the investment area. The Investor's Quotient, as I have coined the term, represents trading readiness or ability.

The Investor's Quotient is, in some respects, an emotional qualifying test. The intended function of this assessment technique is to permit a relatively objective evaluation of your psychological trading or investing readiness. The term "readiness" means "preparedness." In other words, are there any clearly limiting psychological predispositions, attitudes, or conflicts that could result in significant financial loss? The answers to these questions can be obtained by comparing your present response tendencies and attitudes to those that are known to be either profit or loss producing. If, for example, you have internalized the attitudes and responses associated with investors whose performance in the market is poor, then it is very likely you will not be successful. On the other hand, attitudes, responses, and opinions characteristic of successful investors will most likely bring you positive results as well. But much more important than the analysis of your trading readiness skills is the treatment that can then be applied to those areas shown to be lacking.

Although the state of investment science permits many technical methods, there is not, to my knowledge, any technique that attempts to assess the psychological readiness or emotional ability of an investor. Hence there is a glaring deficit in the investing arena. We are expected to do well in our trading, yet we have not been taught how best to implement the trading systems that predominate. By obtaining our individual Investor's Quotient Profiles, we could arrive at an evaluation of where we stand and what remains to be achieved. Thus far no standardized test or assessment method accomplishes the goals I believe necessary. Perhaps none ever will. People are slow to act when it comes to self-evaluation, particularly when it may contain information that is not pleasant. The attempts of this initial work are in the direction of such an assessment tool. The evaluative tools contained in this book mark only a very small step in the direction of a psychological methodology for investing.

In the case of Intelligence Quotient, it is possible for an individual to score high and yet perform low in actual life. There is frequently a great gap between ability and achievement. The Investor's Quotient, I propose, will provide a more pragmatic score, one designed to give equal weight to ability and achievement. What is said here, however, is intended to be only the first step in a series of efforts.

My focus in the following discussions is twofold:

1. I will attempt to provide a framework within which to evaluate your own Investor's Quotient. This will not necessarily be done through use of a standardized test. Rather, I will familiarize you with some basic psychological concepts that relate to investment. You will then find it possible to determine where you stand and how much help, if any, you require.

2. In addition to the determination of your ability and standing in the investment scheme of things, you will also be given a variety of procedures for changing those behaviors as well as attitudes that may be inhibiting your progress.

3. Suggestions regarding various corrective techniques, including reading references, will be provided. All of the above will be done in a pragmatic and realistic fashion, one that employs true-to-life situations and examples.

1 Some Personal Background

As a college student I became interested in stocks. One weekend, while reading a weekly financial publication, an advertisement for commodity futures attracted my attention. The ad, seductively done, depicted a rocketship on its way to the moon. Inside the rocket was a basket of eggs. A caption on the ad read: "Will Egg Futures Hit the Moon This Year?" The ad was rich in psychological and symbolic appeals, so much so it lured me into requesting more information. Lo and behold, several days later a fast-talking and very smooth commodity broker called me. His technique was expert, but alas it was wasted on me since I had only $1000 to my name. Being very persistent, as brokers are likely to be, he called time and time again until at last he hooked me. My last few dollars went his way.

By now you're probably sure you know the outcome of this little story: a small loss, some margin calls, and a bigger loss. But you're wrong, for I was more fortunate–at least initially. Luck was on my side. Within several weeks my friendly broker (let's call him Joe) phoned to tell me that my $1000 had turned into $3500. My original $1000 was being returned. But the story gets even better. Within several months the original investment grew to over $6000. And as the days passed, the profits grew fatter. All the while, I knew nothing about the commodity market, but each day I received sheets in the mail–"We have today for your account and risk bought 5 Sep 69 EGGS. . . ."

As far as I was concerned, the game was easy. The commodity

market struck me as just the right thing, particularly for a young Jewish kid who grew up in a poor home with parents who had instilled in him a high degree of motivation. The commodity game soon pushed my studies in psychology into a back seat as I got hold of a textbook on the markets. After some hours of study and a little creative thought, I developed a system. I gave it dry-run tests on several markets, and soon I was ready for the "acid test."

After some calculations based on my system, I concluded that the day had come to double my money in pork bellies. I called Joe to place an order just before boarding a commuter train–I wanted to be there when the market went up. "Joe," I said in a self-assured voice, "buy 15 Feb bellies on the open with a stop 10 points from limit down. Place an order to liquidate at limit up and an OCO order." (I was proud to show off my market knowledge in such a professional way.) Aghast, he replied after regaining composure, "Jake, you don't want to trade the belly market, stick with eggs, we know the market here at Klutz Kommodities, if you trade bellies you'll get creamed . . . besides that you've never even traded before, don't buy 15 right off the bat!" I refused to listen to reason. "Just buy them bellies," I commanded. "But Jake, you don't know the market. You think that just by reading one book and having a system you'll profit. Believe me, it's not that easy, or I would have done it myself. Don't do it . . . you'll be sorry . . . OK, let's just buy a few bellies, not 15; or better yet let's open a second account with some money from this one. Then you can lose it slowly." But his pleas fell on deaf and overconfident ears. I had allowed a large percentage gain, none of which came from my own efforts, to get in the way of logic and good sense. "Joe, if you don't buy those bellies, I'll close my account. I know what I'm doing. I have a trading system. I know I can double the money today . . . so just put in those damn orders and I'll be down there in about an hour to watch the fun." He hesitated a bit, then replied: "OK, Jake, but you'll be sorry, very sorry."

I boarded the train from Chicago's northern suburbs to downtown. With a copy of the *Wall Street Journal* in hand and wearing my best pair of blue jeans, I sat and observed around me the businessmen in suits. All looked alike–unhappy, going nowhere in their humdrum jobs, void of excitement and potential. As for me,

I was a modern Jesse Livermore. Visions of compounding profits danced in my head. "What a dull life these people must lead," I said to myself as I glanced over the commodity section. "No need for me to wear a suit. I'm making money in the market. All I need worry about is how to spend it. . . . What color should my Jaguar be?"

Before long, the train chugged its way into Canal Street station and I boarded a taxi to–the Chicago Mercantile Exchange. As I entered this realm where, or so it seemed, higher-class peasants labored, I felt more at home and my anticipation was beyond control. This game was so very easy, once you knew the ropes. It was almost boring, I thought.

A quick ride up to the Klutz Kommodities office and into the "boiler room" to see Joe. But Joe didn't look so good. "What's up, Joe," I quipped. "Not bellies," he answered as he handed me a buy/sell slip showing where I had bought my bellies and where I had been sold out. In disbelief I looked at the sheet several times; finally I realized that all my money had been lost.

The story ends here. But it also begins here. For this was the beginning of my commodity education. How much I made or lost was clearly not the important thing. Indeed, what was significant was the lesson itself. I was much more fortunate than many stock and commodity traders. For I, at least, had lost back only what I had made. There are countless others who daily lose much more than they can afford. And despite their charts, graphs, inside information, tips, systems, and news, their losses keep rising.

Having no speculative funds left, I fortunately had no choice but to stay out of the market. This was a blessing in disguise. In my thirst for knowledge and in my efforts to intellectualize the loss, I was driven to the writings of Bernard M. Baruch, Jesse Livermore, W. D. Gann, Burton Pugh, Aurthur Cutten, and others. The resulting education was *not in technique,* which is, of course, very important, but in *self-awareness.* My experience did not teach that technique itself was at fault, but rather that attitude was at the base of this loss, as it is at that of virtually every loss. Had I traded only one contract, I might have had many other opportunities to prove the system. But the system did not get a valid test because of my personal shortcomings. By being overconfident, by overtrading, by ignoring the basics of "know thyself," I became an instant loser. In the sense that we are all subject to emotion, we are all vulnerable to losses. The system is an inanimate scheme that cannot win or lose. A car without a driver is only a shell of metal and parts. It can go nowhere. It can only stay in one spot and look attractive. A car with a destructive driver becomes an instrument of death. It can be driven into a brick wall, and despite all its beauty and mechanical perfection it has served no one well.

WHAT THIS BOOK IS ALL ABOUT

Since the first days of recorded history, the urge or need to speculate has been a driving factor in the development of humankind. The cultural growth and technological advancement of civilizations have had a freedom-producing effect that has liberated people to pursue speculative ventures. But the tugs of the primordial roots of chance taking remain basic. In all ages, the farmer who sets out seed is constantly engaged in a gamble with nature. Should he plant early? Will there be sufficient moisture to support a crop of corn? Will there be an early frost? Are prices now best for marketing his crop? The struggle and anguish of winning our daily bread is now refined into the lofty and romantic undertaking called "speculation."

By nature, we are speculative beasts. Living as we do in a world of constant change, instability, aggression, and uncertainty, we must be willing to accept the very ephemeral nature of our existence. To drive an automobile, fly in a plane, or even walk on the streets, we must be willing to speculate on the outcome of our actions. Some of us seek an even higher quantum of chance. Driven by a variety of needs–emotional, physical, and financial–some of us attempt to increase without limit what we have, knowing all the while we thus risk losing some, or all, of what we possess. For many, these freely accepted challenges provide a high-risk game of financial life and death. For some, they offer a profession providing steady and above-average income. For a few, they provide a mighty engine to create vast wealth and financial empire.

What are the motivating factors that drive individuals to speculate? What are the traits that differentiate successful speculators from those destined to failure? Are there, indeed, ways in which speculative performance can be improved? What, if any, are the psychological forces that underlie success or failure in the world of stocks and commodities? Can the necessary and appropriate behaviors be learned? Is successful speculation more a product of the *speculator* than of the *system* he or she is employing? How can one determine his or her standing in the speculative world?

As a clinical psychologist who is also a commodity futures trader, I have come to recognize a very close relationship among speculation, success, and emotional stability. After spending considerable time in the study of human behavior and personality, I was attracted, quite fortuitously, to the commodity futures and stock markets. At first I saw little, if any, relationship between my profession as a clinical psychologist and my market hobby. But as the days passed and my losses increased, I reached an awareness that changed not only my life but my fortune as well. Once I recognized the close relationship between these two seemingly diverse fields–psychology and trading–the road to personal and financial success was considerably easier to travel and well marked. Until then, I felt like most traders–a small and anxious child attempting to be heard above the loud voices of traders in the pit.

Regardless of education, background, intellectual ability, and effort, there are some individuals who are extremely successful in the markets. And there are those who spend virtually every free moment studying the ups and downs of prices only to fail time and time again. I have personally known traders who had little or no understanding of the fundamentals behind price movements but who, despite this seeming liability, have acquired considerable wealth through trading the markets. I have known traders who similarly had no understanding of the markets and who were repeated losers. What differentiates loser from winner? The question is not only intriguing, but also highly valuable in the lessons it can teach us. Why did such legendary speculators as Livermore, Baruch, and Gann place great emphasis on personal development, self-control, and emotional stability? Were these assets the true reasons for their success? Is it possible to be a market winner without thorough knowledge of the market?

Invariably there will be those one-time winners who strike it rich in the markets or in real estate ventures. But such victors are few and far between. If you want to play with these odds, go buy a ticket in some state lottery. In the following chapters I will devote considerable attention to *gambling* versus *speculation.* In the meantime, suffice it to say that luck versus skill is not an important factor in anyone's long-term success or failure in the financial markets.

After years of watching traders beat themselves, and after years of watching myself become my own instrument of destruction, I have finally decided to write down the lessons learned. The chapters that follow are intended to provide a roadmap of the self. The Bible says "know thyself," and in this sense my writings are designed to be a trader's bible to self-knowledge of his or her own weaknesses and strengths. For, by knowing where we stand psychologically, we will know how to get where we want to be financially by the most direct and successful route.

2 Basic Facts about the Marketplace

MAKING WINNERS OUT OF LOSERS

In writing this book I have found it necessary to ignore most of the golden rules held so dearly by so many in the marketplace. I have made numerous statements and reached a number of conclusions that may arouse controversy, anger, and fear. But as in the case of most new ideas, these responses are normal. Yet my ideas are anything but new; in fact, they are among the oldest known. Back in the Garden of Eden, Adam and Eve chose to speculate on the wrath of God and paid dearly for their poor judgment. I do not intend to lead speculation and trading into the realm of the divine; nor do I intend to stifle my feelings about the fallibility of humankind. In saying things the way I believe they are, I have taken risks that may or may not pay off. In a sense, I am speculating on human nature as I write these words. For I see speculation and life as so intimately bound together that *not* to speculate means *not* to exist. The true success of the words I write can be measured only by their ability to awaken in others those sleeping giants waiting to express themselves. Let but one loser rise up and become a winner and my work will have been done.

Knowledge is power, according to a well-worn truism. In and of itself this statement is too general. It is more meaningful to say that *self*-knowledge is power. It is self-knowledge that I will discuss in detail throughout this book. If you believe that I or anyone else can provide you with a sure-fire formula for wealth and success in the markets, then you are wrong. If you believe that those who have acquired vast fortunes in the marketplace have done so through well-protected secrets, then you are also incorrect. If you believe that you can attain market success through a positive, self-confident attitude, through emotional control and appropriate motivation, then you are on the right track and are likely to find some very meaningful answers in the pages that follow.

In placing only minor emphasis on the basics of trading, market fundamentals, and economic factors, I am not by any means discounting their importance. I am, however, departing from the old tradition of technique and placing major emphasis on the individual person who must act upon the information. We are not all fortunate enough to be Baruchs, Wykoffs, or Livermores. We must learn *how to* rather than *why to.* Economics can tell us why things happen. Indeed, economics may tell us *that* things are going to happen. But it won't tell us how to make the future work for us. Knowing how to make the future into a reality that is beneficial financially requires the type of education not offered heretofore between the covers of a single book. True, knowledge of the masters has been available in bits and pieces, but a work devoted exclusively to the psychological aspects of trading and investment has had to wait its time. That time is now.

BRIEF OVERVIEW OF THE MARKETS

The underlying principles of all markets are similar. Whether involved in stocks, commodity futures, real estate, or even retail marketing, individuals must respond to many of the same economic influences. Most market variables, however, have no direct relationship to the field itself. Instead, traders are coping with forces inside themselves. For those who are new to the marketplace, let me first briefly define precisely some of the "markets" to which I will be referring. Since I will concentrate almost exclusively on the individual person rather than the market, only a general overview of market terminology is necessary.

THE MARKETS—SIMILARITIES AND DIFFERENCES

To comprehend this book, one need know only that the stock market, like any market, consists of a central location where individuals (traders) gather together to buy and sell, in this case pieces of ownership in corporations. These portions of companies, which are called shares, rise and fall in value as a function of what buyers and sellers at any one time and place are willing to pay and to receive for them. Economic conditions, company sales, management ability, government policy, and corporate profits are all believed to influence the movement of stock prices up and down. If a stock is bought at $15 per share, for example, and then sold for $20 per share, the buyer has made a profit of $5. If 100 shares were owned, then the profit amounts to $500.

The real estate market, one to which many more individuals can relate, is basically no different from the stock market. One buys and sells pieces of property either to make a profit or to avoid a larger loss. Instead of a single, central exchange, these properties, either vacant land or some kind of construction, are bought and sold through real estate brokers whose offices are found throughout the world. The real estate market moves slower than the stock market, but in most other aspects the two are similar. In the stock market one can borrow money from one's broker in order to purchase a stock. This loan, called a margin, allows a purchaser of stock to increase his or her leverage, which is the ability to buy more for less. In real estate the prospective buyer must go to a bank to acquire a mortgage. This allows the purchase of a home or piece of property for about 10 to 30 percent of its selling price.

Commodity futures trading is somewhat more complex but also closely related. Instead of buying and selling pieces of property, a company, or land, traders exchange contracts for the delivery of goods (commodities) at some point in the future. Hence the term *commodity future.* The individual who buys at a given price stands to make money if the price rises. As in the case of stocks and real estate, the object is to buy at a low price and/or to sell at a high price. Margin is also used. In this case, however, only 1 to 5 percent of the total purchase money is necessary to complete the transaction. Consequently, a much smaller amount of a buyer's money is necessary to make—or to lose—large sums. In comparison with other markets, commodity futures is the most speculative and fast-moving of all.

As you can see, all markets have several things in common. First and foremost, they involve the exchange of money for goods. Second, they can all result in a profit or a loss. And third, they all depend to a varying extent on human beings for their existence. For transactions to be completed a market must be created. And in order for this to occur the human element is necessary. The final act of buying or selling must be performed by people. Hence it is not only necessary to know the basics of market terminology and operation, but, in order to invest successfully, it is also necessary to be familiar with the workings of the human mind.

SUCCESS IN THE MARKET

Each market has its own special terminology, and to acquire a better working knowledge of each market's basic instruments, you will need to read and study intensively. But however intensive—or extensive—your knowledge of a market, of economics, or of technical systems, you will *not be guaranteed* success as a buyer and seller.

Several years ago I had the good fortune to meet a floor trader from the Chicago Mercantile Exchange who helped me understand that knowledge of fundamental factors is not necessary for success. His specialty was the futures market in Treasury bills. After discussing our individual involvements with the market, I asked his opinion of the long-term outlook on interest rates. "What's an interest rate?" he replied. "What do you mean 'what's an interest rate?' " I retorted in amazement. "I don't know what an interest rate is," he reiterated. "I know that interest rates have something to do with T-bills, but I'm not quite sure how they're related," he explained. "But if you don't know what interest rates are and how they're related to Treasury bill futures, how can you trade the market?" I asked in total disbelief. "Oh, that's easy," he quipped, "all

I need to know is that a one point move in T-bills is worth $25."

This true story tells in simple form what might take many months to teach. Here is the case of a very successful floor trader who buys and sells many times daily but who has no knowledge other than *how to buy and sell.* He is basically ignorant of the many facts that affect prices. This vacuum, in a sense, has been a friend. He can relate to the market only as he sees it without outside influences. This is not to say that one cannot be successful with a thorough knowledge of the markets and the factors that influence them. But it *does* clearly demonstrate that some other important quality, or qualities, are necessary.

You will observe that I have clearly departed from the traditional explanations of stock and commodity trading. I have chosen to place only limited emphasis on mechanics, definitions, fundamentals, explanations, and trading systems. Such information can be found in many available texts. My emphasis is almost exclusively on the internal and external processes of human behavior as they relate to the ultimate profit or loss in trading. I take for granted that you have the necessary working knowledge of trading and investing. I reiterate that for my purposes the individual seeking to improve his or her investment success need not spend hours studying the theories of economics, the details of market supply and demand, or the rules of price charting. Time, in my opinion, is best spent studying the theories and principles of human and animal psychology. It is from this understanding that market knowledge will achieve its intended purpose.

REVIEW

1. Stocks, commodity futures, and real estate all adhere to the same basic economic principles.
2. Aside from the basics of how to place orders, vocabulary, terminology, and knowledge of the risks involved, no further understanding is required.
3. It is possible for a person to profit handsomely on a consistent basis in the financial markets with only a working knowledge of the markets themselves.

4. More important than any of the above is a person's ability to know and remain in touch with herself or himself. The emotional factors that make markets are perhaps the only ones that must be known fully.
5. Those who do not have the required understanding of market functioning should acquire same prior to reading the remaining chapters.

Basics of Psychology 3

Although this discussion is not designed to function as a psychology text, several concepts must be understood before the markets themselves can be tied into the picture. What follows is merely a general discussion about the psychological functioning of animals, human and nonhuman. For a more detailed picture, any comprehensive up-to-date college text will suffice.

Throughout history there have been repeated attempts to understand the factors that make people and animals do what they do. Theories have ranged from the astrological to the medical. Explanations have varied from demonic possession to self-determination. And in every case the popular theories have been very much a reflection of the times. Peculiar behavior in some societies is totally ignored whereas in others, such as ours, it receives a great deal of attention. The complex interaction of life experiences within social structures molds an even more complex picture of human behavior. At times the factors affecting human beings appear so numerous and varied that any attempt to understand them seems futile.

During the dark ages these mysteries were no less a problem than today. In attempting to deal with the demons that supposedly came from within, human beings employed many techniques. Whether in the form of trephining (drilling a hole in one's head to let out the spirits) or bloodletting, they were doomed to failure. But as humans became more enlightened and abandoned magical cures, such practices were replaced with scientific procedures.

Through trial and error, systems and theories of human behavior were developed to explain and to treat psychiatric problems. At best, these techniques have, in most cases, been no more effective than the old black-magic cures. In fact, until recently, researchers have aimed to explain rather than predict and change human behavior.

Generally, then, the metamorphosis in understanding the human psyche has been slow and difficult. Despite dramatic technological advances in other sciences, psychology and psychiatry are still very much in their youth. This is perhaps due to the fact that humankind is most resistant to finding out the truth about itself. The facts may induce unhappiness rather than happiness. And so it is with many traders. Roadblocks, self-imposed to be sure, are constantly being thrown in our path. The enemy lies not in what surrounds us, but, in fact, we surround *it* since *it* dwells within. Fortunately there has been steady progress through the 1970s and more definitive techniques for understanding and changing behavior are available. These will be discussed later. Throughout what I say, try to focus always on the relationship between yourself and your place in the picture I sketch.

In the modern psychological world there are essentially two schools of thought, which are, in my opinion, similar to the two schools of thought in the trading world. As you know, traders generally divide themselves into either *technicians* or *fundamentalists*. Some traders, whose methods are not pure enough for either group, practice a bit of both. Since many investors can relate well to the continuum of technician versus fundamentalist, I will begin by discussing these polar outlooks among traders in the market world.

In commodity markets, the fundamentalist point of view focuses exclusively on economically related indicators. These indices are used to arrive at a picture of where prices should go. Such basics as crop size, weather conditions, supply and demand figures, export news, plantings, breeding intentions, and consumption are taken into account. The essence of this approach is to determine just where the balance of supply and demand rests and how it will affect future price. In stock markets the same approach is valid. Here economic conditions, inflation rate, corporate sales, profits, long-term and short-term debt, and so on, are carefully assessed.

All this is done to determine what the price of a given stock may be several months or years hence. The point of view arrived at depends on the availability and accuracy of information. It also depends to a certain extent on the prevalence of so-called normal conditions. Any exaggerated shift in conditions can distort the data and the outcome as well. Persons who speculate or invest in the real estate market are subject to the same limitations and potential problems when analyzing fundamentals.

The *technician,* on the other hand, makes judgments by purely mechanical and/or mathematical rules. He is not concerned with the economy, supply, demand, crop size, earnings, or weather. He is cued into particular chart formations, mathematical indicators, moving average signals, geometric formations, cyclical events, and so forth. Even those who trade the markets according to astrology are technicians of a sort because they follow very specific guidelines. Insofar as they are true to their principles, technicians do not look at anything but their data. If true to his work, a chartist, who is a technician dedicated to following specific kinds of chart patterns, will not want to spend any time either reading or discussing the fundamentals. Being a market technician has certain advantages: it permits greater objectivity; it allows for more mechanical execution of trades; and it deals with the true data, namely, prices. On the debit side, the technical approach isolates the trader from worldwide events, which can and do have serious impacts on markets. For the technician himself, this debit appears as more of an asset than a liability because it excludes from his calculations unquantifiable fundamental developments.

Ultimately, the relative success of each market orientation seems to be more a function of the individual person holding it than of the approach itself. In fact, despite the seeming objectivity of technical trading rules and of fundamental statistics, the end result is almost entirely dependent on who interprets the data. This point will be covered in considerable detail later on.

There is a third and less well-defined school of market forecasting. It consists of traders who are either too uncertain about the two major techniques or who are too insecure about being totally committed to one side to the exclusion of the other. Their eclectic approach leads them to accept input from as many sources as possible, both technical and fundamental. The rationale behind this approach is very simple. Since information from any source may be helpful, it is prudent to gather as much of it as possible. "Open all the floodgates," such traders reason, "and we're in a better position to isolate the best trades and trends." Those who favor this approach subscribe to as many publications, advisory services, and newsletters as their budgets will permit. There would be nothing wrong with this approach if the markets did indeed function according to the information that traders study. The major drawback to this type of market analysis is that very often the amount of information available is overwhelming, contradictory, and confusing. Frequently, when all indicators are in agreement, the opposite event occurs. And all too often, weak individuals are paralyzed by the sheer magnitude of information confronting them.

The final category of market analysis is not really a firm approach at all. In fact, it is a nontechnique. Those who approach the market through this nonmethod attend selectively to whatever they desire. One day they may buy for a reason that will be used as a rationale for selling the very next day. They do not justify their trading on any basis other than "gut feeling." Typically, floor traders fall into this category. Their seat-of-the-pants, dead-reckoning technique works well—but only for them. If it does not bring profits, then they are not around and liquid long enough to discuss their results. There is nothing to be said either pro or con about this nontechnique. If it succeeds, then it is good; if it fails, then it is not useful. The importance of this approach is to be found in what it can teach us about the psychology of trading. As such, much discussion will be given to this last nonmethod.

The science of price forecasting is relatively young. In fact, there is doubt whether it can indeed be called a science. Some individuals and research groups have constructed complex econometric models to assist in their prediction efforts, and they find it possible, through the use of computer technology, to forecast economic trends well in advance. This technique has also spilled over to the stock and commodity markets. In essence, it is a fundamental method that still requires interpretation. Despite recent advances the relative infancy of economic forecasting makes it clear that we have much more to learn. This same youthful awkwardness is found in the science of psychology. In fact, psychologists and psychiatrists typically align themselves along a continuum comparable to that of investors.

In any academic field there are usually many schools of thought, which ultimately divide themselves into relative positions along a continuum. The extreme points of view are found at opposite ends and variations on each theme are found between the two poles. This model can be used to represent anything from religious groupings to political affiliation. Market fundamentalists and pure technicians fall at opposite poles while other types of market analysts cluster at different points somewhere in between. And so it is with psychologists and psychiatrists. On one extreme we find the traditional Freudians while on the other reside the behaviorists.

The traditional psychologist is essentially similar to the market fundamentalist. He studies what he believes to be the underlying causes of human behavior. He is concerned with such issues as:

Why do people act the way they do?

What are the underlying causes of behavior and mental disturbance?

How can we use the life history of an individual to help him?

What motivates people to act in certain ways?

What are the sexual and unconscious processes that stimulate behavior?

These questions are very similar to those asked by the market fundamentalist. By seeking to determine the *why* of price movement and the underlying causes of market fluctuation the fundamentalist is of the same general orientation as the traditional psychologist.

The behavioral psychologist, on the other hand, studies only overt and clearly measurable behavior. He is interested in the following things:

How often does a certain behavior occur?

What are the events that maintain behavior?

What happens before and after a given behavior?

Can the behavior be changed by manipulation of environmental conditions?

How long does it take to change behavior using certain methods?

How long has the current behavior been present?

In asking these questions the behaviorist is working on an essentially technical level. He is interested in measurement, detection of specific trends, frequency counts, and the application of operational techniques. This is very similar to the specific trend detection and measurement methods employed by market technicians. Although they cannot control or change market behavior, they look for overt symptoms and not underlying causes.

TRADITIONAL PSYCHIATRY AND PSYCHOLOGY

The founders of traditional psychiatry are Josef Breuer and Sigmund Freud, two physicians who were in medical practice in Vienna at the end of the nineteenth century. During the early 1900s Freud formulated a theory of human behavior by studying early childhood experiences and various theoretical structures of the human mind. Most actions, he felt, were a result of unconscious impulses. His entire theory is complex, intricate, and difficult to explain in a limited amount of space. Freud and his followers felt that most behavior was shaped by the interaction of internal mechanisms. The dream and its symbols were used as tools in the understanding of mental processes and behavior. An elaborate list of symbolic meanings was devised by some Freudians. In so doing, it was theorized, the psychiatrist could get in touch with the true reasons for an individual's behavior. By talking with the patient and employing various techniques, among them hypnosis, the conflicts could theoretically be resolved by getting the patient to see his behavior in relation to the underlying drives and their repression. Whatever may have been troubling the patient could be "cured," given the proper use of this technique. This method was termed "psychoanalysis."

The study and development of psychoanalysis and psychiatry have taken many years and immeasurable amounts of effort. But this is not a text on the history or theory of psychology (those who wish to pursue the field will find references listed at the end of this book). My sole intent in this ultra-brief overview is to familiarize readers with the most basic concepts in order to advance to the subject at hand, which is, after all, investment.

The Freudian school of psychiatry stimulated the growth of many other theoretical concepts. The Adlerians, Jungians, and Rankians are all followers of Freud's basic concepts to an extent–each presenting a unique variation on Freud's theme. Each school has survived, and all have followers today. The most popular, however, still remain the Freudian and neo-Freudian schools. The essence of Freudian-type therapies rests in their reliance on "underlying cause." Their approach is therefore similar to the fundamentalist approach in speculation. A market goes up because supply is small and demand is large; crops are poor; weather is bad. Prices go down because crops are large; export demand is slow; earnings are poor; sales are lagging, and so on. A patient acts anxious because of an early childhood trauma; he fears the vengeful arm of authority because he is fearful of his father; he fears his father because he has guilt about his own sexual attraction toward his mother; he fears punishment from his father. As you can see, both the Freudian approach to the understanding of human beings and the fundamentalist approach to financial market study rest on underlying causes–*fundamentals.* In this respect, they are very similar. In fact, the shortcomings of each, as well as the potential advantages, are similar.

The Freudian school of thought can also be called the "medical model" of human behavior. In the same way that a physician attempts to isolate a germ or organic dysfunction as the causative agent in disease, the medically oriented therapist seeks to uncover the causes of undesirable behavior in order to "cure" the patient. This orientation is reflected in the medical training that all psychiatrists must have in order to practice. It is also seen in the medical approach to treatment of behavior disorders. Contemporary reliance on drugs and medication are outgrowths of the belief that medical treatments must reach the cause. And the cause must be internal. And if the cause is internal, then it can probably be treated or helped with medicine. Hence the large number of tranquilizers and sleep medication taken by Westerners. The term "medical model" derives from its medical focus.

BEHAVIORAL PSYCHOLOGY

On the other extreme we have the so-called behaviorists, beginning with John B. Watson, B. F. Skinner, Edward Lee Thorndike, and others. Their theories will be discussed in considerably more detail later. For now, suffice it to say that their point of view is one that deals exclusively with symptoms and not with causes per se. Whereas the medically oriented practitioner will examine such things as guilt, unconscious processes, sexual fantasies, castration fears, and defense mechanisms, the behaviorist looks only at outward behavior or symptoms, believing that the only problem we can treat is the problem we can see. We cannot empirically observe unconscious processes–but we can study behavior. And through the study of behavior, and behavior alone, we can determine what it is we want to change and how we want to go about changing it. The process of change or treatment consists of very straightforward conditioning or learning techniques after the principles of Skinner, Watson, and Pavlov. The technique is very mechanical and it has been subjected to considerable criticism by those aligned with the medical school.

The numerous variations on the behavioral theme are closely related in their basic belief. The essence of this model is very simple. It is assumed that the environment acts on or stimulates an organism. The organism then responds. Depending on the results of the organism's response, behavior becomes habitual or is terminated. If the behavior brings about desirable consequences, then its likelihood of future repetition is good. If it does not bring the desired result, then a new behavior is attempted. All of this will be considered in detail later.

The behavioral orientation is similar to the market orientation of the technician. Remember that the true technician watches for clues and symptoms of market direction. He acts upon the meaning of his signals and is totally unconcerned about the underlying

Fundamentalist		Technician
Freudian	————————	Behaviorist
Medical model		Conditioning model

Figure 1 Fundamentalist–technician continuum.

cause or causes. Figure 1 characterizes the two opposite camps. These camps have a long history of antagonism. There are both benefits and liabilities in strict adherence to one approach or the other, and yet there seem to be more disadvantages to a middle of the road position than to an alignment with either extreme.

Now, with this simplified background in the basics of each approach to speculation and psychology, let's examine some of the other relevant aspects of psychology as they relate to speculation. There are many different areas within the field of psychology. One can easily spend an eternity exploring the numerous theories and concepts. In fact, one can devote a lifetime to studying only the controversies and disagreements. So vast is this quasi-science that discussion must be limited to those topics necessary to provide a working knowledge of the material presented here. If you are already familiar with the field, or even if you have had only an introductory course in psychology, then this is really all the information you need to benefit from this book.

My concern is primarily with those concepts and theories that can be applied to successful speculation. Here is the general plan I shall follow. First, I will familiarize you with some of the general beliefs of various psychological approaches. Then I will discuss speculation within this framework and demonstrate what individuals generally do when trading and how their results can be markedly improved through the use of psychological techniques. And finally, I will present an overview of how we can best use the teachings of psychology and psychiatry to maximize our success in speculation.

THE IMPORTANCE OF TRADER PSYCHOLOGY

Why study psychology in relation to speculation? If you will remember the bit of autobiographical trading experience I shared earlier, I made a considerable sum of money despite the fact that I had no knowledge of the commodity market. The money was soon lost thanks to three important shortcomings on my part:

1. I was cocky, overconfident, unrealistic, and conceited.

2. My knowledge of the markets themselves, their price behavior, and volatility was lacking.

3. These two combined to create a losing attitude.

This is most likely the same set of failures to which most traders fall prey. There are many things that can be done to alleviate item 2: book learning, studies, classes in trading, reading, and direct experience can all help. But what about item 1? No amount of direct experience with the markets can change one's attitude toward the market. But self-knowledge can be the key to success. It's one thing to know that you're beating your head against the wall; it's a far greater achievement to know how to stop.

Psychoanalytic Theory 4

The traditionally oriented psychologist or psychiatrist attributes many behaviors to unconscious motivation. The human mind is divided into id, ego, and superego. These mechanisms are responsible for behaviors that ultimately seek expression in waking and sleeping life. A child is born with basic needs related either to the taking in of food or the letting out of wastes. These are the child's greatest needs, and the child comes to see the world in relation to body openings. The mouth and all activities associated with it become centrally important in the reduction of a need state and the production of satisfaction. The fondness for oral satisfaction is then generalized to other oral activities such as biting, licking, and tasting. The world is experienced orally. This stage of development continues during the first year of life. These are "id impulses."

The next issue of importance, particularly between parent and child, becomes sphincter control. During very early childhood little emphasis is placed on the child's eliminative habits. But as the child grows older, parents become tired of cleaning up the mess and begin to expect self-care from the child. This represents the first struggle between child and outer world. It is the first true experience between child and authority. Freud claimed that activities surrounding elimination also take on a pleasurable tone. You will note that the central theme of his theory is based on the "pleasure principle." The child acts in certain ways because they bring pleasure.

Following toilet training and the opposition which it brings from the child, interest in the rectal area declines and shifts to the genitals. From what begins as curiosity, the child develops a profound interest in these parts not only as a result of their pleasure-giving ability, but also as a means of differentiating one sex from the other. Following this period of development, the early instinct-life of the child makes a transition into what is called the "latency period." The important things to remember about the child's early development are (1) the child functions on the "pleasure" principle and (2) these experiences are not remembered later in life. This principle of "infantile amnesia" is a central feature of Freudian doctrine.

The latency period is one during which the child develops what Sigmund Freud called "defense mechanisms." This elaborate system of protective attitudes and actions serves to defend the individual from childhood memories and experiences which are either too painful to remember or too threatening to deal with. In connection with this I list a number of defense mechanisms. They will be more fully explained in our discussion of trading.

Sublimation. This term describes a process of refining childhood impulses into socially acceptable behavior. The belief of Freudians is that unacceptable childhood behaviors–thumb sucking, smearing of feces, withholding of feces, and the like–are transformed into acceptable acts in adulthood. Withholding of feces, for example, can be sublimated into stamp collecting (or any other form of collecting). This is an adaptive mechanism which can be very helpful in the markets. More on this later.

Castration Complex/Oedipal Complex. These two concepts are the cornerstones of Freudian theory. Without much discussion, suffice it to say that the child, at some point in his or her life, fears punishment by parents in the form of castration. These perceived threats may result from sexual attraction to the opposite-sexed parent. The guilt of such attraction and/or sexual fantasy is transformed into fear. Fear that a part of the body, particularly the sex organ, will be cut off is termed castration complex. There has been considerable controversy about this aspect of Freudian theory. Some theorists and social scientists claim that this experience is not common to all children. They claim, in fact, that very few children experience it. Furthermore, it is believed to be more of a cultural phenomenon than a general fact. Freudians argue that these feelings are buried deep in the unconscious mind, hence they cannot be remembered and it is impossible to prove that they do not exist. This controversy is currently unresolved, but the burden of proof rests on the Freudians.

Repression. This term applies to the "forgetting" process associated with early childhood experiences. It can, in fact, apply to any traumatic event. There is a tendency for us all to repress, or push into the unconscious, extremely painful experiences.

Suppression. The intentional repression of negative experiences is termed suppression. It is a conscious act of pushing events from memory as opposed to the unconscious nature of repression.

Regression. Under stress some individuals tend to resort to childlike behaviors. Some psychiatric patients will soil and/or urinate. Others will act silly, talk in "baby talk," or assume any number of childhood behaviors. This is called regression.

Reaction-Formation. Some individuals have an unusually strong dislike for certain situations or behaviors. Psychoanalytic theory tells us that this very strong overreaction derives from the child's having acted in a similar way. Now the adult does not remember this behavior, following the forgetting process discussed earlier. Nevertheless, this person feels very strongly about certain behaviors and tends to act the opposite way.

Intellectualization (Rationalization). In certain instances individuals resort to the "refined" defense mechanism known as intellectualization. This form of self-protection is based on what seems to be rational and intelligent reasoning. The individual believes that a particular problem can be "explained away" through the use of what appears to be logic and common sense. Someone who is a habitual smoker may reason as follows: "Not all people who die of lung cancer or heart disease smoke, and not all smokers die of lung cancer or heart disease . . . smoking is not such a bad habit after all. . . ." There are many ways in which a situation can be intellectualized. This is by far the most common defense used by speculators.

Throughout this book I refer to other defenses and coping mechanisms. The essence of Freudian theory as it relates to defenses is therapy oriented. The object of treatment is to free the individual from his or her inappropriate use of defenses through the gaining of insight. Once the conflicts that are being shielded from consciousness are "ventilated," or brought to the surface, change, the theory states, will occur and emotional difficulties will have been successfully treated. The manner in which such treatment is given varies according to the particular therapist and branch of psychoanalytic theory. Primarily, it is the role of the therapist to arouse transference in the patient. Emotions, feelings, attitudes, and conflicts which the patient originally felt about his or her father and/or mother are transferred to the therapist, who in effect acts as a substitute parent so the patient can ventilate feelings in a less threatening environment.

ID, EGO, AND SUPEREGO

Another central feature of psychoanalytic theory is a tripartite division of the mind. *Id* is the term Freud used to describe the "lowest" of the three aspects. Within id dwells all animalistic, instinctual drives, impulsiveness, childishness, and the pleasure principle. Id seeks only self-satisfaction and avoidance of pain to the total disregard of social control. *Ego* seeks to apply some control over id impulse and tempers its drive. This controlling mechanism develops during the latency period and reflects authoritarian attitudes. It is in essence an internalized parental voice. *Superego,* the most highly developed mechanism, rules over all other drives and reflects the social and self-controlling efforts of the individual. Moral and social values come from superego.

The various ways in which id, ego, and superego express themselves in conscious life is the substance of psychoanalytic study and treatment. We can learn a great deal about ourselves if we learn to recognize the source of our drives. The fear and greed so often experienced in speculation reside within id. Id impulses may get us what we want at times, but they tend to ignore the inherent dangers to self which can accompany their fulfillment. This is discussed in detail later.

DREAM INTERPRETATION

Freud believed that dreams represent a symbolic acting out of id impulses and conflicts. Frequently dreams are not understood since they are disguised by the unconscious to protect us from their real, threatening meaning. During the therapeutic process the analyst uses a patient's associations to dreams as another key in the process of gaining insight.

There are many interpretations of the dream. Neo-Freudians believe that the dream is not nearly as important as Freud had believed. Others see dreams as a problem-solving technique. In any event, the dream can tell us a great deal about how we really feel. For some individuals who are not aware of their feelings, impulses, and expectations, an understanding of their dreams can provide valuable insights. This will also be discussed in a later chapter.

These basic aspects of traditional psychoanalytic theory will certainly not qualify you to do any analysis, but this background will permit you to understand the material that follows. Those who have never been exposed to these ideas may be inspired to do some soul searching and self-evaluation. There are many detailed texts on the subject which do more justice to the topic than I can in this limited space.

It may be difficult for you to imagine how Freudian principles can be applied to the market. Before considering the basics of learning theory, I'd like to give you an example illustrating one of the key aspects of Freudian analysis. Forgetting, according to classical theory, is not merely a random event. An individual forgets because he or she does not want to remember. Recall the previous brief discussions of repression and suppression. These two mechanisms are, for the most part, totally instrumental in the forgetting process. Now take the case of a trader who "forgets" to place orders to liquidate a commodity contract in sufficient time to avoid delivery. Has this trader really forgotten? According to the traditional Freudian interpretation, no. A strong case could, in fact, be made for an unconscious desire to take delivery! Since there is no "forgetting" according to analytic theory, the act of "not remembering" is given deep symbolic significance in the therapeutic situation.

The individual who repeatedly forgets is revealing some highly significant aspects of personality, motivation, desires, and unconscious processes. I remember a trader who was constantly "misplacing" his commodity trades. He kept only mental notes of his positions. All too often he "forgot" about a trade and by the time he was reminded, a large loss had accumulated. To rectify the problem he initiated a record-keeping system (which he should have had regardless) and entered each trade as it was made. The system seemed to be going well until he "forgot" where his record book was. This soon became a habit and he realized that the new system would not work. It was suggested that he have his broker read the positions to him daily. This technique achieved immediate results, but unfortunately they were short-lived. It seems that our wayward friend found it increasingly difficult to remember his broker's telephone number!

This may sound improbable to many of you. But for the individual who is afflicted with such emotional problems the anguish is very real. And there are many people who suffer from symptoms which are considerably more destructive. How would such a problem be treated? What does the "forgetting" mean? According to psychoanalytic practice there would most likely be a different answer for each individual, dependent upon his or her history. In this case, the habitual "forgetter" was telling us quite clearly that (1) he was anxious about his trades and hence chose to forget them in order to avoid the fear and/or anxiety, (2) he was unconsciously creating a situation which would eventually bring him a large enough loss to drive him out of the markets entirely. Both results confirm an unconscious desire to fail.

This is a simple yet profound example of how one might explain seemingly innocent behavior using the traditional Freudian approach. Many behaviors that traders exhibit daily can provide useful insights. Through the use of insight the therapist can help one overcome these and even more serious problems standing in the way of financial success. The three goals of psychoanalytically oriented therapy are to confront problems, interpret their meaning, and restructure in a positive way.

REVIEW

1. Sigmund Freud is the founder of psychoanalytically oriented psychotherapy.
2. This view of human psychology attributes considerable influence to early childhood experiences and explains present-day personality in relation to such experiences.
3. The "pleasure principle" is a central feature of Freudian theory, as is psychosexual development and the development of defense mechanisms.
4. Development proceeds through various stages, and specific conflicts characterize each stage.
5. After the first few years of life, most early childhood experiences are forgotten.
6. Id, ego, and superego develop as unconscious control mechanisms.
7. The dream is assigned an important role in psychotheraphy.
8. The gaining of insight, the ventilation of conflicts and feelings, and transference are all goals in traditionally oriented therapy.
9. There has been considerable controversy regarding the lack of experimental and scientific validation of traditional analytic concepts. It is difficult to test Freud's theories in a scientific and objective manner.

Learning Theory 5

Gypsies have been reported to train bears to dance to music by a simple conditioning procedure. The bear was chained to a surface under which a fire was built to heat the stone on which the bear stood. The gypsies played music while the bear moved about to relieve the pain in his feet. The music became a conditioned stimulus. After this experience the sound of music elicited foot movements that resembled dancing.

L. M. Stolurow, in Wolman, 1973, p. 483.

BASICS OF LEARNING THEORY

The "technician" of psychology is the behaviorist. Not only does this school of psychological theory find itself at one end of the continuum, but it has also aroused considerable controversy in recent years. I will attempt to give you an unbiased working knowledge of the principles and issues, but this chapter may reflect my leaning toward the behavioral school.

Behaviorism dates back to the Russian physiologist I. P. Pavlov. His experiments on the salivary reflex of dogs are familiar, but few of us understand the ramifications of his work. In the 1920s Pavlov demonstrated that various animal responses could be conditioned to arousal by stimuli that were not originally related to the response itself. His work was deceptively simple. A dog was made to salivate in response to meat powder. The amount of saliva produced was measured. Just before the presentation of meat powder a bell or buzzer was sounded. The meat was then presented and the salivary response resulted. After a number of simultaneous buzzer and meat presentations, the meat was no longer given. The animal, however, responded, or salivated, when the buzzer was sounded. The amount of saliva was measured. If meat was totally eliminated the buzzer continued to elicit a salivary response. With each presentation of buzzer alone, the amount of saliva decreased. This decrease phase was termed "extinction." It is, in many ways, analogous to "forgetting." The process of attaching the buzzer stimulus to the salivary response through the use of meat powder was called "reflexive conditioning." It is possible to condition virtually any reflex to any secondary conditioner in animal and human.

Pavlov's work marked the start of a behavioral revolution in the psychological world. His full theory and experimental procedures are too involved to be discussed fully here. For a good look at his early work I recommend reading his classic text *Conditioned Reflexes* (1927).

During the same period of time, American psychologist E. L. Thorndike was involved in work on human and animal intelligence. Another American psychologist, John B. Watson, applied principles similar to those of Pavlov in his study of human emotion. His work was important not only for its discoveries about the human learning process, but it also represented a total departure from traditional methods. His beliefs were almost radical at the time and they flew in the face of everything considered right and proper. Watson made no sharp distinction between man and animal and he assigned no power to the unconscious and introspective tenets of traditional psychologists. In 1913 he wrote:

> Psychology as the behaviorist sees it is a purely objective experimental branch of natural science. Its theoretical goal is the prediction and control of behavior. Introspection forms no essential part of its methods, nor is the scientific value of its data dependent upon the readiness with which they lend themselves to interpretation in terms of consciousness. The behaviorist in his efforts to get a unitary scheme of animal responses recognizes no dividing line between man and brute. . . . The position is taken here that the behavior of man and the behavior of animals must be considered on the same plane; as being equally essential to a general understanding of behavior. (1913, p. 158)

The problem with other theories, Watson felt, was that they were not scientific or objective enough to be used consistently and successfully. Six years later he wrote:

> Psychology as a science of consciousness has no community of data. The reader will find no discussion of consciousness and no reference to such terms as sensation, perception, attention, image, will and the like . . . I frankly do not know what they mean nor do I believe that anyone can use them consistently. (1919, p. xii)

Watson's position is in many ways comparable to the position taken by market technicians. Whereas Watson was concerned with the use of data relative to the prediction of human and animal behavior, the market technician is concerned with the use of data in forecasting market price and trend. The market fundamentalist also uses data, but the conclusions and techniques vary considerably due to the many unknowns that are part of fundamental analysis. These unknowns are subject to interpretation and opinion in the same ways that introspection and consciousness are unknowns. The objections Watson had to the use of these concepts are similarly valid in rejecting some basics of fundamental market analysis.

In a classic experiment with Mary Cover Jones, Watson was able to clearly demonstrate the role of conditioning in human beings. Using a baby and its fear response to loud noise, Watson "conditioned" fear of a rabbit. A child was placed in the experimental setting. A loud noise was introduced. The child cried bitterly in response to the noise. A loud noise was then made while a rabbit was shown. After a number of trials or repetitions of this situation the child would also cry at independent presentation (no noise) of the rabbit. This was termed a "conditioned fear response." Watson noticed that the child would also cry in response to white furry objects resembling the rabbit. The closer the resemblance, the more certain was the fear response. This was termed *stimulus generalization.* Note that the crying response could be stimulated without noise. The child had, in effect, been taught to cry in response to a once neutral or positive object.

Watson did considerably more work on the human organism

and conditioning. He believed that any human could be conditioned, or taught virtually any repertoire of behaviors. He believed that internal or unconscious processes such as those theorized by the Freudians had little or no bearing on the understanding or explanation of human behavior. His experimental work achieved considerable credibility for his theoretical position. Whereas the Freudians were lacking hard empirical data for their methods and beliefs, Watson and other behaviorists were beginning to accumulate a wealth of experimental and objective data to support their analysis.

Contemporary behavioral theory owes its status to the work of B. F. Skinner. Using animal subjects, Skinner developed his behavioral concepts into a unified system of experimental results. His work stimulated the development of behavior therapy, a clinical treatment technique based on the principles and experimental findings of behaviorism. Tolman, Guthrie, Hull, Lewin, and Wolpe, all behaviorists, made significant contributions to the field.

Simply stated, the behavioral law of learning reads as follows: the outer environment acts on the organism, which then responds. The response results in any number of consequences. The positive or negative quality of these consequences determines the future history of the response. If the consequences are pleasurable (remember Freud's pleasure principle), then it is more likely the given response will occur again. If negative or painful, then it is likely the frequency of the given response will be decreased. The model or paradigm of behavioral learning appears in Figure 2. This very specific chain of events is considered basic to all human learning. By amplifying each of the elements it is possible to explain and experimentally validate virtually all learning situations. It is possible to teach or shape new behaviors or eliminate current behaviors by manipulation of the elements. The ramifications are immense—some would say awesome.

Skinner, in his experimental work, trained pigeons to perform a number of highly complex tasks. Using similar principles and tech-

Environment→Stimulus→Organism→Response(s)→Consequence(s)

Figure 2 The learning paradigm.

niques other behaviorists have been able to train dogs, chimps, and birds to perform highly complex tasks involving everything from assembly-line work to number sequence recognition. The limits of training are bounded only by the physical ability of the organism and the behaviorist's imagination.

During the 1950s and up to 1980 behavioral therapists have slowly but surely developed clinical treatment techniques based on Skinnerian principles. These therapies have been highly effective, and the results obtained have been lasting. It has been possible to successfully treat behavioral and "mental" disturbances previously thought incurable. Specificity of technique and reliability and speed of results have accounted for the increased popularity of behavioral techniques. Virtually all aspects of treatment rest on the simple model discussed earlier. All methodology is nothing but a variation of the basic theme. In discussing behavioral principles and trading I will refer extensively to the underlying concepts.

THE LEARNING THEORY APPROACH

The behavioral approach seems to be the most promising area of market psychology. I indicated earlier that the behavioral theorist considers learning to be the basis of most human behavior. In my experience with different areas of clinical treatment I have come to know and respect the behavioral approach. In terms of results and ability to explain human behavior, this technique is unexcelled. The entire area of speculation is so easily understood and explained using behavioral principles that it appears to be the most effective approach to take. Moreover, behavioral analysis and therapy are among the most effective, efficient, and lasting techniques known to modern psychological science. There are those who argue that it is shallow, inhumane, ineffective, and mechanistic. I will discuss these points later, after I acquaint you with its usefulness.

As you recall, the basic tenet of behavioral learning theory is the reinforcement principle. The rule that any behavior followed by a positive event tends to be repeated, is deceptive in its simplicity. There are many ramifications of this learning paradigm.

Let's plunge into some of the basic applications of this rule as it relates to speculation. Remember that I am not doing justice to Skinnerian theory in this general analysis. The field is much more complex and involved than I have indicated. Those wishing a thorough immersion should read the classic texts to which I refer throughout.

Let's put the investor into our learning model. Figure 3 presents the basic manner in which we must examine the stimulus and response consequences. Let's go through the sequence of events involved in a typical transaction. I use the word typical in the sense of "ideal," although as you know, most trading in the markets is not ideal. In fact, it is far from it. But if we know how a situation should run in its typical state, then we can appreciate the deviations and possibly change them. If trades were made rationally, on the basis of signals alone, then market indicators, which are a function of the prices, would act on the speculator, whose reading of the signal would bring about a given response. This response would take the form of a buy order, a sell order, or no order at all. Time would pass and the result would be either a profit or a loss. If the result was profitable, then the trader would be more likely to follow this signal in the future. Hence if the signal was reliable, more profits would follow. If the net result was a loss, then theoretically the same signal would lose its reinforcing ability and the response to it would be extinguished. Note this sequence of events in Figure 3. Stimulus acts on the organism, in this case the investor, the investor responds, and the consequences are either positive or negative, that is, profit or loss.

Based on this model, and assuming it's perfect, most traders should eventually get better results if the system they are following

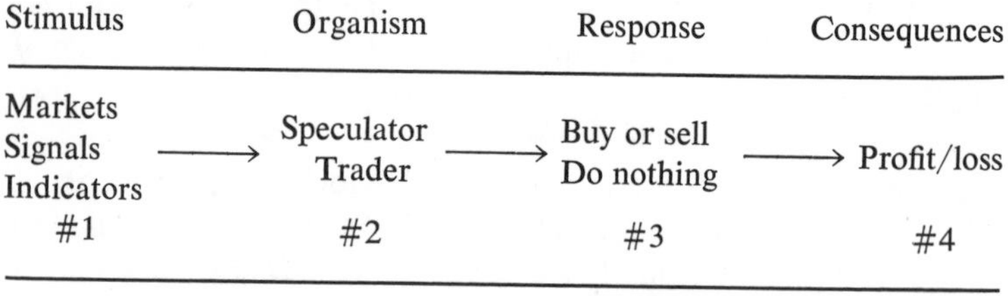

Stimulus		Organism		Response		Consequences
Markets Signals Indicators	⟶	Speculator Trader	⟶	Buy or sell Do nothing	⟶	Profit/loss
#1		#2		#3		#4

Figure 3 The investor and the learning paradigm.

has validity. In such a system experienced individuals should achieve an admirable record in terms of net results, since bad signals would be ignored as a result of their limited reinforcing ability. But alas, such a perfect state is no more of a reality than is the perfection of the market itself. Let's take a look at the many different factors that enter into the learning paradigm as conflicting and/or confounding roadblocks to perfect trading.

The first problem arises in section 1 (note that all elements in the learning paradigm, Figure 3, have been numbered). The seemingly simple task of following a signal based on market behavior is not so simple. There are perhaps as many different interpretations of signals as there are schools of market analysis. The same technical signal may result in totally different behaviors among several investors. Take the following case. A trader follows commodities on the basis of moving averages. Each time the three moving averages he monitors are moving up, or when one important average crosses the other, a signal to buy is flashed. The appropriate response would be to buy. Let us assume, however, that the trader has just finished reading the *Wall Street Journal.* The lead article discusses several bearish factors in pork bellies. The trader then turns to his chart, which clearly signals "buy bellies." He is presented with two sets of conflicting information. On the one hand, experts who wrote the article claim that prices will move lower; on the other hand, his signals say that the market will go up. What should he do? His dilemma is not unlike one experienced by all of us at some time or another.

Here are some possible outcomes. Let's assume that the trader follows his signal. This, of course, would be the best thing to do. The net result might be a profit. This has been a learning experience with positive consequences. He has not only been rewarded for following the system, but he has also been rewarded for *not* being influenced by another source of information. Whether the contradictory information came from the news media, a broker, a friend, or an advisory service, the mere fact that this trader followed his or her own system was a great achievement. Only several such positive events are necessary for the behavior to be stamped in, or learned. Unfortunately most traders never pass step one. Their very first trades often are not a result of a system but follow outside influences unrelated to the system. Their system, whether intrinsically good or bad, never has the opportunity to be tested. Hence learning is faulty from the start.

Let's assume that our trader does not follow his signal, but rather takes advice given by a report he read, a broker, or a friend. And let's assume additionally that his original signal would have been wrong and a loss would have resulted. By avoiding the negative experience of a loss the trader has been rewarded for a behavior that will not only be difficult to eliminate later but will also prevent the trading system from being tested in "real time." The probability is that this individual will act similarly in the future. Thus the system may never get tested, and, in fact, it will most likely be abandoned completely.

Let us assume a third possible outcome. The trader follows his signal and takes a loss. A negative experience resulted from following a signal. Paradoxically, the negative result will eventually have a positive effect. By repeatedly following a signal our trader will test the system in actual markets and thereby "learn" if the signal is good or not. Without consistent use of the signal there will be no learning. See Figure 4 for an analysis of the outcomes.

Of even greater importance in this situation is the concept of partial or random reinforcement. Let's assume that our trader follows some signals and not others. Let's also assume that some of the trades made by this individual are recommended by brokers, advisory services, or similar agents. Essentially this individual is on a schedule of reinforcement in which his or her behavior–selecting a trade–is not linked to any one stimulus. This con-

Trading Signal	Trader Response	Outcome	Evaluation
Valid signal from system	Follow signal	Loss	Positive learning
Valid signal from system	Follow signal	Profit	Positive learning
Signal from other source	Signal not followed	Nil	Positive learning
Signal from other source	Follow signal	Loss	Positive learning
Signal from other source	Follow signal	Profit	Faulty learning

Figure 4 Analysis of outcomes generated by response to trading signals.

founds the learning process and leaves the individual not only poorly trained but also in a state of insecurity and confusion.

The second aspect of partial reinforcement relates to the "addictive" nature of speculation and, for that matter, all forms of gambling. There is enough variability in the markets to provide most traders with partial or random rewards. This schedule will result in a strong attachment to the market, making the trading habit difficult to break. Whatever the outcome, the number of random wins will act toward the creation of a very strong bond between trader and market. You, in fact, may fit into this category, along with the thousands of others who have been maintained on a random schedule by the markets. For every one winning trade there may be ten losers. And yet the game goes on and the losses continue. Now imagine the individual who does not stick to one specific trading plan. The combined effect of partial reinforcement from the market itself and faulty learning resulting from acceptance of signals and trades from other sources can create a confused, frustrated, addicted loser.

Let me review. We have taken a look at the behavioral model of learning as it relates to the trader. We have also looked at the specific stimulus–response chain from the point of market signal to the result of a given trade. The consequences of various decisions and outcomes have been presented. The point was made that partial reinforcement can result in strong learning, productive, or loss-producing.

REVIEW

1. The principles of behavioral learning can be used to understand speculative behavior.
2. Human beings are subject to Skinnerian learning under reinforcement principles.
3. As a result of this learning process we are affected by the complex interaction of market signals (stimuli) and the many trades (responses) we can make.

4. The result of these responses–whether positive (profits) or negative (losses)–will create either a successful trader or a persistent and conditioned loser.
5. To derive the full benefit of the learning model you must avoid confounding signals.
6. Each response (trade) should be a result of the trading system. In this way it will be tested quickly and thoroughly.
7. Any response (trade) to the system that is not "pure," or exclusively part of the system, will act to confound the reinforcing action of results.
8. In some respects the study of partial reinforcement in animals can help us understand the importance of complete dedication to a trading system.

The Response Sector 6

A DISTANT LOOK AT THE RESPONSE SECTOR

Now let's take a look at what else can go wrong or right in the behavioral chain. The time elapsed between market signal and trader response usually is very brief. But the intervening process is highly complex and intricate. Looking at it piece by piece, as we are doing, should lead to some valuable conclusions.

The second phase of our behavioral chain is "response." Let's assume the trader, who is the organism in our equation, has acted on a signal. Let's also assume that his action was based strictly on his own signal and not on the advice of others. He is now set to respond. Within the intervening time lapse we can add the perceptual set dimension, another variable that will be discussed later. Figure 5 is our redrawn model. Let us further assume that the perceptual factor is not significant. In other words, the information received by the trader (signal) is received exactly as it is sent. There is no misperception of the signal. In reality this will be the case for few individuals, but perception will be considered in a later chapter.

What can the trader do once a clear-cut signal is received? One would expect a clear-cut buy or sell signal to result in a clear-cut buy or sell response. This is not the case, however. Most traders will allow any of several interfering variables to confound the response. What are the available options? There are three possible responses: buy, sell, or do nothing. Take the following example of

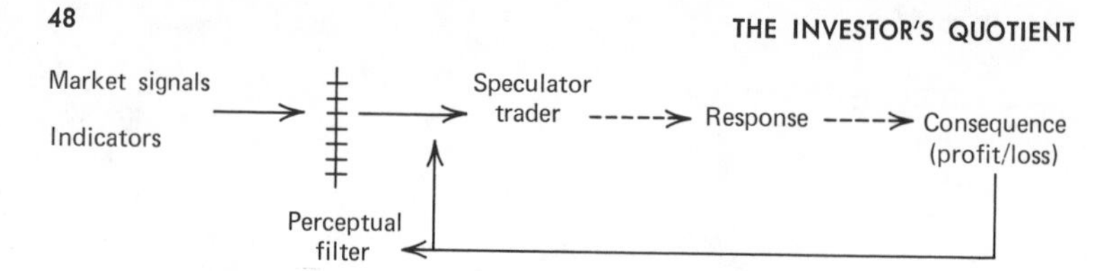

Figure 5 Trading paradigm and perceptual filter.

what can occur between the decision to buy or sell and the actual execution of the order. Our trader friend gets the signal to sell short cattle. He reads the indicator properly and calls his broker to place the order. The broker says, "Are you sure you want to sell them? The Cattle on Feed report is coming out today and you might not want to be in the market through the report." "Sounds reasonable," says the trader. And the trade is not made. The same series of events can occur as in our previous discussion. If a loss is avoided, then the trader has been rewarded for listening to something other than his or her own reading of the signals. Again, this will result in faulty learning and the outcome will be long-term negative. The most appropriate action for the serious trader to take would be strict adherence to signals and decisions regardless of input from any other source. Whether the signal indicated a buy or a sell, any deviation from it once again jeopardizes the learning process.

The decision to do nothing, regardless of a clear-cut signal, can also result in maladaptive learning. Indecision is perhaps the greatest enemy of the speculator or trader. He who hesitates is lost, particularly in the markets. There is a very specific syndrome of indecision which will be described later. It relates closely to neurotic behavior in everyday life. The advantage of making no decision at all is that no risk is taken. Hence the consequences are not negative and, in fact, may be anxiety relieving and thus reinforcing. The net result will be no real test of the system and no productive learning on the part of the trader.

Before going on I want to make certain that you understand the difference between the very first point I made concerning stimulus and the current discussion of response. In the previous situation our trader made no response to his signal as a function of competing opinions which interfered with his reading of the signal. In the current situation our trader made the appropriate analysis of his system but failed to carry it to completion. Although there is a very fine distinction between the two situations, our second trader is better off than our first, since he actually attempted to respond in the appropriate way.

In the first situation the interference came *prior* to a reading of the signal. In the second the stimulus resulted in proper intentions, but it did not result in the appropriate behavior because a competing factor appeared *after* the correct decision. Quantitatively there would be no difference for the true behaviorist. All he sees is response. Since response was lacking in both cases, they are, for all intents and purposes, similar. I, however, see a major difference between the two situations. Our first trader has much more ground to cover along the path to success. Our second trader has already arrived at the decision-making level. He has actually picked up the telephone, made the call, and placed the order. He is to be commended for what he has done. But his ultimate response was incorrect. Qualitatively his level of achievement is much more advanced and different corrective measures would be taken.

I am giving you this microscopic analysis to help you determine where you are in the behavioral sequence. If you know just where you stand, it will be possible for you to more effectively combat the problem. Some traders I have seen are so totally lost that they haven't the slightest idea of what they're doing wrong. The object of this painstakingly specific analysis is to help you identify the exact problem or problems you might have. In so doing I do not want to offend any of my readers. If you feel that what I am saying just doesn't apply to you, then skip this chapter. But if you have experienced repeated losses, and have a sneaking suspicion that there is nothing wrong with your basic market analysis, then you owe it to yourself to read on.

The first situation I presented is one in which decision making was totally avoided. Several corrective measures will be discussed in the next chapter. The second situation does not relate to a faulty decision-making process; it does, however, indicate faulty actualization of decisions. I will also discuss treatment methods regarding this problem in Chapter 7.

Each of the situations discussed can be applied to every aspect

Step	Inputs	Outputs	Effective Result
1. Maintain trading system	Data	Buy, sell, hold	Trading decision
2. Call broker	Signals	Place order(s)	Market entry or exit
3. Await new signal	Data	Buy, sell, hold	Trading decision

Figure 6 Inputs, outputs, and results of the trading process.

of the trading situation. The use of stops, placing orders to enter or exit a market, and similar devices, are all subject to the same learning model. Each individual situation should be considered as one response in a larger behavior. The entire process of trading could be broken down as seen in Figure 6. As you can see, the process involves basically three steps. Each step has its own specific result and requires a clear-cut action. It is possible to break down each individual step into its component behaviors. Step 1, for example, requires the maintenance of a trading system. Many individual behaviors enter into the use of a system, regardless of type or orientation. If you have a problem that goes back even earlier than the examples given, it will be necessary to take even more intensive corrective action, as discussed in Chapter 7.

A CLOSER LOOK AT THE RESPONSE SECTOR

Examining the behavioral aspects of any action is a relatively simple task. It is a far greater achievement to put our observations into action. Many of us have been raised and educated without exposure to behavioral concepts. We continue to believe that most external life is an expression of internal forces that are too difficult, too repressed, or too threatening to experience directly. There is much to be said for the traditional viewpoint; the acknowledgment of behavioral psychology as a viable explanation of human action does not necessarily mean that one must reject the teachings of traditionally oriented psychologists. It is possible to effectively synthesize the behavioral and the psychoanalytical.

The significance of response is no less important to the Freudian than it is to the behaviorist. Response is, after all, another term for action. And action is the only means by which we can judge the nature of underlying processes. Although it is not necessary to understand internal concepts in order to observe action, there are those whose perception of response (in themselves and others) can be assisted by an evaluation of underlying causes. Emmanuel Mounier, a French psychologist, made the following comments about action:

> The sole proof of a man lies in his deeds. They are the only irrefutable confirmation of the value of his words, and the authenticity of his thoughts. This is because we are thrown into action before we can reflect on action, compelled by urgency before we can deliberate. . . . The study of character culminates in the study of action, the nature of which dominates all other aspects. (1956, p. 122)

It follows that response, or action, is the only objective way of determining the functioning of a trader. And in order to evaluate a system we must focus exclusively on its actions and results. We must therefore be certain that the results are a true reflection of the system itself–not contaminated by influences due to a deficiency on the trader's part. The trader must respond appropriately to the system to obtain a true reading of the system's value. The trader, however, may discard a technique that has validity or continue to employ a system that has no underlying value. The final test of any trading methodology is therefore inextricably tied to the individual who is using the technique.

At this point you may be prompted to look at computer technology for the answer. But alas, the computer is no better than he who uses it. Should an individual lack self-discipline, should his response chain be defective, there will be no assistance of value from the computer. Borrowing from the psychoanalytic school, we can surmise quite accurately that a trader who has unconscious self-destructive tendencies will find a way to lose, no matter what technology he employs. Whether you adopt the behavioral or psychoanalytic interpretation, the trader is an instrumental factor in either the success or failure of a system. As I have indicated on many previous occasions, the trader is, in fact, more important than the system. It is possible for a disciplined trader (one with the appropriate responses) to profitably use virtually any system.

The value of response is therefore threefold. First and foremost, it is a key item in the real time testing of any and all trading systems. Whereas we can get a computer to test a system objectively, thoroughly, and without error (assuming correct programming), we cannot get a human being to subsequently trade the system in an objective fashion unless that individual is emotionally capable. You may ask this appropriate question: "Why not get a computer to trade the system automatically?" This is well within the realm of present technology. All one need do is acquire the necessary hardware and software–the rest is a matter of mechanics. There are several immediate drawbacks to this system. Cost is perhaps the greatest limitation. Another drawback of the computer system is that it is subject to mechanical failure. If a computer system is automatically set to make trading decisions and implement them by sending orders in the form of a wire, errors are possible. Fail-safe parameters could be built into the system to avoid such problems. The main point here, however, is that any mechanical system will be limited in its functioning by those who design and use it. If those who designed it lack discipline, then the system will reflect this liability.

The second value of response lies in its reinforcing ability. Simply stated, response will always let you know if what you did was right. Without response there can be no test. Without response there can be no result. This is why I am personally opposed to the old technique of "paper trading." There are some instructors who tell their students to trade on paper before you get your feet wet in the real market. This is supposed to let you know how well you're doing. Some also reason that people can learn how to place orders, use stops, and gain general expertise by paper trading. It is my opinion that paper trading can only teach one thing–and that's paper trading. Based on a strictly behavioral analysis of the situation, the act of paper trading (or pretend trading, as I prefer to call it) carries no risk whatsoever. Losses are not losses, profits are not profits, and errors have no consequence. Without consequence there can be no true learning. An astute instructor, using behavioral principles, will know how to generalize paper trading into real trading. But to my knowledge there are no formal courses in market study that even touch on this technique. To trade without risk or reward is to not trade. To learn how to trade by trading without risk or reward is to not learn how to trade. I will discuss how to practice trading in Chapter 8.

The third value of response is its ability to permit objective evaluation of results. Each individual, whether skilled in trading or not, must look at the record objectively. If one has taken pains to implement trading signals precisely as dictated by the system, the feedback of results is an objective test. This test, as previously indicated, will be free of most influence by the trader and his emotion.

In discussing response, I do not want to give the erroneous impression that perfection is a necessity. Human beings can only approach perfection. If we all implemented behavioral learning techniques with strict discipline, there would be no market. Markets function through the imperfect state of man. Speculation is built on the fact that individuals have different responses to similar stimuli. The thrust of what I have been telling you is directed at insight and change. Those who are not aware of their internal limitations should gain the necessary insights and then use these insights in conjunction with behavioral principles to alter their response mode in the direction of perfection.

Fortunately, the markets do not require perfection as a predeterminant of financial success. In fact, it is possible to be far from perfect and still be a winner in the markets. Were it possible to measure perfection in trading on an objective scale with computer perfection ranking a ten, and abject disorganization ranking a zero, we would find most successful traders in the seven range. Most losers would be in the five range and lower, and the tremendously successful would rank only eight or higher. This is my estimation of reality based on personal observation. If my analysis is correct, then there is only a very fine line between the response perfection of winners and losers. What I am telling you is simply that a small amount of behavioral change in your response mode can bring a very large change in trading results.

In closing this section on response I will leave you with the words of John B. Watson:

The behaviorist has been criticized for his emphasis on response. Some psychologists seem to have the notion that the behaviorist is interested only in the recording of minute muscular responses. Nothing could be further from the truth. Let me emphasize again that the behaviorist is primarily interested in the behavior of the whole man. From morning to night he watches him perform his daily round of duties . . . in other words, the response the behaviorist is interested in is the commonsense answer to the question "what is he doing and why is he doing it?" (1924, p. 15)

REVIEW

1. Response is the only thing that can lead to consequences.
2. Response and action refer to similar behaviors.
3. Response provides feedback, reality testing, and reinforcement.
4. To improve trading results, the response segment of behavior must be changed.
5. It is not necessary to be perfect to be successful.
6. Responses can be changed through the use of behavioral techniques.
7. "Paper trading" is not a good way to learn.

7 Behavioral Consequences

> The recognition of our own mistakes should not benefit us any more than the study of our successes. But there is a natural tendency in all men to avoid punishment. When you associate certain mistakes with a licking, you do not hanker for a second dose, and, of course, all stock market mistakes wound you in two tender spots—your pocketbook and your vanity. But I will tell you something curious: A stock speculator sometimes makes mistakes and knows that he is making them. And after he makes them he will ask himself why he made them; and after thinking over it cold-bloodedly a long time after the pain of punishment is over he may learn how he came to make them, and when, and at what particular point of his trade; but not why. (Lefevre, 1965, p. 117)

The words of Edwin Lefevre (Jesse Livermore) indicate clearly his awareness of behavioral consequences in speculation. It is, in fact, impossible to trade any market without cognizance of the inherent reward and punishment. Whether you call it risk (as brokerage houses do) or losses and profits, which is what it ultimately boils down to, the consequence of trading is perhaps the only observable indicator available to speculators. Eventually the market will let you know how you are doing. In the case of commodity futures the time elapsed between action and consequence is relatively brief. In stocks and other forms of speculation it may take many months before the outcome is known. But the ultimate result of any trade in any market, at any time, is a profit, a loss, or a break even. Given this cold but true fact, we can see quite plainly why the markets are best understood in behavioral terms. The "why" of behavior is relatively unimportant. There are few individuals who can benefit as much from the knowledge that comes with "why" as they can from the profits that come from "how." Lefevre recognized the importance of consequences, particularly the negative ones, but he also realized the relative unimportance of "why."

In previous chapters I indicated that the "why" of behavior is left to those psychologists who study underlying causes. The "how" of behavior is the domain of behaviorists. There are some psychologists who have integrated both the "why" and the "how." Dollard and Miller (1950), both trained in psychoanalytic techniques, applied behavioral principles to the basic Freudian concepts in an effort to explain the "how" of their existence. For our work, however, it is not necessary to delve into the synthesis of behavioral and psychoanalytic models. Much more relevant is how behavior can be changed, using the most efficient and parsimonious theoretical concepts. In many respects the most simple approach is usually the most effective. This, by the way, holds true for trading systems as well.

Reviewing briefly the behavioral learning model, you will recall that the last element in the chain is "consequence." It is consequence that determines whether a given behavior or behavioral chain will be more or less likely to occur in the future. It is impossible to overstate the power of behavioral consequences in shaping and maintaining behavior. Skinner and other behaviorists in their experimental work manipulated consequences in order to bring about, or shape, the behavior(s) they wished to develop. If a given behavior has positive consequences, it is not only likely that the behavior will be repeated, but it is also very possible that the behavior will be repeated in exactly the same fashion. In animal studies rewarded responses are frequently similar down to the most minute muscular level.

To some individuals the degree of control potentially attainable through the application of behavioral techniques is both threatening and morally unpalatable. Certainly the possibilities of behavioral engineering are practically without limit, but they can be used for either constructive or destructive purposes. Rather than devoting space to the morality of behavioral change, I will say only that in a world functioning on behavioral principles we are all instrumental in changing each other daily. We dole out social rewards and punishments, we approve of good behavior, disapprove of or punish bad behavior. The market is merely a reflection of life itself.

It is natural to assume that a profit will tend to increase a trader's use of profitable signals, whereas a loss will tend to decrease use of such signals. But this is not always the way it works. Remember that the behavioral definition of the term reinforcement (reward) considers a reinforcer to be anything that increases the frequency of a given behavior or set of behaviors. This makes it possible for an event or circumstance that is seen as negative to act as a reinforcer. For example, a classic study on classroom behavior revealed that children who were scolded by teacher for "out of seat" behavior tended to exhibit more of this behavior than children who were ignored. In other words, the "punishment" the teachers thought they were administering was actually functioning as positive reinforcement. It was possible to determine that this was happening by measuring the increase or decrease in "out of seat" behavior.

If you have ever punished children or pets only to find that they are misbehaving even more than before the punishment was started, then you know how "punishment" can act as a reward. In fact, punishment is a form of attention, and to some individuals negative attention acts as a reward. The why of such peculiarity can also be explained in behavioral terms. Suffice it to say, however, that the ultimate value of anything considered a reward must be measured in terms of its effect. If I believe that I am rewarding someone for a given behavior, and if the behavior does not increase in frequency, then I am not truly rewarding it. Another reinforcer must be found. If I believe that I am punishing a given behavior and see it increase in frequency, then indeed I am not punishing it and must look for another punishment.

I am reminded of the individual who called me one day seeking consultation on his trading. Asked to precisely define the problem, he stated, "I just can't make any money in the market. Every trade

I make turns into a loss. Every time I put in a stop it's hit. Every time I meet a margin call I get still another. And all my friends think I'm an ass."

"How do you feel when you lose?" I asked.

"Bad," he replied without hesitation.

"How bad?" I probed.

"I feel so bad that I can hardly get home from the office," was the response.

"How do you get home?" I questioned further.

"My friends drive me."

"Do you go straight home?"

"Well, not really. First we stop and have a few stiff belts at the local bar. That helps me forget about my losses. Then we have dinner at a good restaurant."

"What then?" I asked.

"Then I go home and tell my wife about how badly the market's punished me."

"And what does she do?"

"She gets hysterical. She tells me that she's going to get a divorce if I keep losing money in the market. She has tantrums and throws things at me. Then she calls her mother. And her mother gets hysterical too. Sometimes her mother comes over and throws things at me too. It's almost funny to see how upset the two of them get. It's as if *they* had earned the money I lost."

"And how do you feel when they get upset?" was my next question.

"Well, like I said, it's almost funny, if you know what I mean. I kind of enjoy watching those two shrews frothing at the mouth . . . serves them right."

"What is it about them getting upset that seems funny?"

"Well, all these years I've been working and slaving at my business while the two of them spend my money. I wish she'd honor her threat and divorce me. Then I could do anything I wanted to do. I could stay out late, not come home at all if I don't want to, go fishing when I want to, and trade the market as much as I want. If I didn't have to worry about her big mouth, then I could make money in the market. I feel good when she gets mad. I'll show her who's boss . . . who makes all the money . . . and if I want to lose it in the market, then I'll lose it in the market . . . it's my money!"

"Sounds to me like you really enjoy getting your wife upset," I observed.

"Wouldn't you enjoy it too if your wife was a nagging bitch like mine is. Wouldn't you want to get her mad and make her suffer too?" he pleaded.

"Sounds to me like you enjoy getting your wife upset more than you dread the pain of losing money in the market. In fact, it seems as if you lose in the market with the intention of getting her so upset that she'll eventually divorce you. The market is merely a tool for you. You're using it to get something that's much more important to you than either profits or losses," I noted further.

"That's the biggest bunch of bull I've ever heard," was his parting comment.

Several years later I had the good fortune to meet him at a commodity seminar. He apologized for his behavior on the telephone and told me that my original observation of his problem was correct. After going through a bankruptcy, a divorce, and several hundred thousand dollars in market losses, he was forced to stop trading. During his involuntary retirement from the market he realized the stimulus–response consequence of his behavior. He explained it to me as follows.

"The problem with my trading was not really related to my trading at all. When I first started in the market I took some losses the way all traders do. But each time I took a loss I would make a big deal about it. I complained to my friends and business partners. They felt sorry for me. And I wanted them to. Every time I took a loss, they'd try to cheer me up. I enjoyed the attention. Instead of taking the loss, forgetting about it, and moving on to the next trade, I milked it for all the attention I could get. I had a nagging feeling after a while that I might be losing on purpose. But it was hard to accept that possibility. All I know is that every time I took a loss, I got a great deal of attention. Every time I took a profit, I got no special attention. I'd tell my friends about the big profit I took and they'd say, 'That's great Chuck old boy, I knew you could do it.' And that was it. Whenever I took a profit they made no special deal about it. Possibly they were jealous. But when I was a loser it was somehow an occasion to celebrate. We'd go out and drink under the guise of 'drowning the loss.' I realize now that this was acting as a reward for losing. I should have received absolutely no attention for being a loser. We should have gone out partying when I had made a profit. The money wasn't nearly as important a reward as was the attention.

"And to make things even worse, the losses upset my family. My wife would punish me. But all the time she didn't realize that I enjoyed her being aggravated. I didn't realize it either. The consequences of my losing were serving some very important purposes in my life. Not only did they get me attention from friends, but they also irritated my wife. And that made me happy. If I had realized the connection between losses and their consequences I might have been able to change the outcome. I realize it now. Fortunately it's not too late."

I asked him how his trading was going. "Couldn't be much better," he replied proudly. "I know now that the market is much less important than me. I know that every loss is a lesson and every profit is a reward. Each time I lose I forget about it as soon as I can. I try to see if I made a mistake in reading my trading system. If I made a mistake, then I write it down and keep a record of it. I consult it often to make certain that I don't make the same mistakes repeatedly. When I take a loss it's just between me and my broker. I mention it to no one else. When I take a profit I celebrate. I spend some of the money, put some in the bank, and tell my friends about how smart I am. I pat myself on the back and enjoy all the rewards that the profit should bring."

This true story is worth more than any system, course, theory, or signal. To many it rings a personal bell. Those who cannot relate directly will recognize elements that are part of their own makeup. The essence is, to be sure, behavioral. Recalling once again my words about consequences you can see how this trader was being maintained by consequences that increased his losing behavior. Too many of us believe that the money made from trading will be sufficiently rewarding to keep us trading well. This is not the case. For those who are in touch with their goals and motivations, and for those who have few conflicts in their home life, money can serve as a great consequence. But for many traders the money gained from investing is just not enough to maintain winning behavior.

Let's look at the various consequences of market results. For each possible outcome there are only three potential consequences: reward, punishment, and break even. I will discuss each combination and its implications. Assume that a trade is made with profit as the result. Ideally the profit should be rewarding in and of itself. Since I maintain that for most traders, the profit alone will not suffice, there are several additional consequences that might assure positive reward. If you find your trading is not as profitable as it should be, examine the consequence accompanying each profit. Most likely you will find that your profits are not bringing you anything more than financial reward. Personally, that's enough for me. But for those who do not find money sufficient there are many additional rewards that should be used.

Table 1 lists positive consequences that could be added to each profit after it is taken. Remember they should *not,* under any circumstances, be used *unless* a profit has been taken. In other words, do not reward yourself *before* a trade has actuallv been completed. A completed trade is defined as one round turn in the market. This consists of a buy and a sell, or a sell and a subsequent buy. No rewards are in order for open positions, intended positions, imaginary positions, paper trades, or "I would have" trades. The best time to apply positive consequences is immedi-

Table 1 Positive Consequences of a Profitable Trade

1. Enter winning trade in ledger or record book.
2. Pat yourself on the back. Tell yourself how well you did.
3. Tell others about your trade. Seek out their verbal praise.
4. Celebrate. Have a party; treat yourself to an expensive meal.
5. Buy something. Now's the time to get that new car or tape player.
6. Immediately tell your broker to send you a check for 25 percent of the profit.
7. Put some of the profit in your savings account.
8. Solicit your broker's approval.
9. Gloat over the profit for several days.
10. Don't feel any guilt about being immodest.

ately after the profit has been taken. Table 1 is a list of possibilities. You may find some of them amusing. I know for a fact they can help.

What about a profit that results in punishment? Is it possible that taking a profit can bring negative results? This can most certainly happen. In fact, it is very common. A brief example will illustrate the point. You take a profit of several thousand dollars and feel rather proud. You tell a "friend" about the great event and he says, "You know, there's a loser for every winner in the market. Don't you feel bad about the poor slob who lost that money? You're taking his money and he might not have enough to feed his family." Another punitive statement comes from the "friend" who reminds you about taxes. "Sure you took a profit of 6000 bucks, but by the time Uncle Sam gets through with you you'll only have $2000 left–big deal." Another "friend" might say, "Well, that was sure a lucky shot, probably won't happen again." With friends like those, you don't need enemies. If you know that the profit was not a result of your trading system, then avoid any of the frills listed in Table 1. But if you're certain that the profit came from strict adherence to your system, shun any and all attempts to make you feel bad. Avoid all negative statements either by yourself or by others. If you find others who are consistently negative when you take a profit, then avoid them. Even consider terminating your relationship with them. Table 2 is a list of things to *avoid* when a profit has been taken.

Although in the minority, some individuals feel guilt or shame after taking a profit. They feel that another trader has suffered because of their personal gain. Some traders get sheepish and others feel that they must continue to "perform." There is absolutely no place for such feelings in the repertoire of successful traders. Each victory, if based on the trading system, must be fully and totally enjoyed. No attempt whatsoever should be made to minimize the gain. Avoid everyone who seeks to punish or otherwise negate your positive consequences. If such negatives are permitted to enter into the behavioral chain, they will reduce the rewarding power of financial gain and thereby decrease the overall success rate of your trading system.

Another possible outcome of trading is the "break even." There

Table 2 Negative Consequences of a Profit (avoid them at all costs)

1. Do not attribute the trade to luck.
2. Do not refuse praise from others.
3. Do not minimize the profit in any way, shape or form.
4. Do not allow others to minimize the greatness of your accomplishment.
5. Do not accept any guilt from anyone.
6. Do not feel sorry for the person who lost.
7. Do not worry about the taxes you'll have to pay.
8. Do not allow the profit to cause you anxiety about the next trade.
9. Do not feel ashamed for having been right.
10. Do not allow any negative fantasies to enter your mind.

are several ways to relate to this event. If, after you deduct commission from the profit, you break even, then you have, in reality, taken a profit. A break even trade is, in effect, a winning trade. It should be treated in the same way as a profit. Breaking even on a trade is merely an indication that your trading system is working. The consequence should therefore be a positive one. Certainly it is not possible to reap any of the financial rewards, but all others that apply to profitable trades should be taken. Any attempt to make a break even trade bring punishment should be avoided as in the previous example.

What can we say about the consequences of a loss? First and foremost, it is much more difficult to deal appropriately with losses than with profits. If you have taken a loss, then you already feel bad. How much more punishment is appropriate? Here are some guidelines regarding the appropriate consequences of losses. As in the case of a profit being ideally sufficient to maintain behavior, a loss should be sufficient to result in fewer losing trades. For most speculators this is not the case. In an earlier discussion I stressed the importance of making certain that your trading signals are entirely a result of your own indicators. Assuming that they are, and assuming further that you take a loss, you can reach either of two conclusions. First, the loss may reflect the intrinsic limitations of your system: all systems take losses. Second, the loss may be caused by your misreading, miscalculation, poor order placement, early exit, or abuse of stop loss. If your loss is a result of some limitation of your system, then you would want to deal with it in a different way than you would with the second possibility.

If you take a loss trading your signals with proper follow-through, then nothing else should be done in the way of consequences. Merely accept the loss, enter it in your record book, double check that the loss was justified by the signal, and forget about it. Too much attention to a loss will reward it. Avoid all attempts by yourself or others to soothe the losing experience. Table 3 is a list of don'ts that should follow a justifiable loss.

Above all, do not allow anyone to make your loss into something positive. You will note that item 10 mentions overeating, overdrinking, and sex. This does not mean that each loss should result in starvation or celibacy. It *does* mean that you should not respond to the loss by excess in any of these areas. There is no such thing as "drowning a loss in wine" or "eating a loss into oblivion." These behaviors will merely reward you for losing. The time to engage in satisfaction of these primary needs is after profits and *not* after losses.

How about the loss which results from an error in implementing your trading system? What should be the consequences of such

Table 3 Consequences of a Justifiable Loss

1. Accept the loss and forget about it.
2. Record it in your ledger and do not "rehash" it.
3. Do not recruit anyone's sympathy or sorrow.
4. Do not feel sorry for yourself.
5. Do not feel as if you have been punished.
6. Do not discuss the loss with anyone.
7. Do not accept ridicule or blame from your broker.
8. Do not punish or hate yourself for losing.
9. Do not blame your trading system.
10. Do not soothe your loss by going overboard on food, drink, or sex.
11. Do not allow yourself to accept any punishment from loved ones.
12. Do not alter your technique, system, or methods.
13. Do not fear making the next trade.
14. Do not respond by allowing your market studies to fall behind.

a blunder? What kinds of errors should be considered? Here are some of my thoughts. Each loss, if not justifiable, must be a lesson in proper trading. An observation from the writings of Jesse Livermore (Edwin Lefevre) is in order:

> Of course, if a man is both wise and lucky, he will not make the same mistake twice. But he will make any one of the ten thousand brothers or cousins of the original. The Mistake family is so large that there is always one of them around when you want to see what you can do in the fool-play line. (1965, p. 117)

There are indeed hundreds of things one can do wrong in the market, but only a precious few that one can do right. It is possible to blunder at any step in the behavioral chain. For every one correct behavior there may be more than a hundred possible errors. How can they be avoided? Here are some behaviorally oriented suggestions. If you have taken a loss due to error on your part, then I suggest you adhere to the points outlined in Table 3. In addition, exercise the steps listed in Table 4 each and every time you blunder. Perhaps the most important role of errors is the educational one. Any trader who makes a mistake and then forgets about it is not getting full benefit from his tuition money (loss). I recommend a specific procedure for dealing with errors that is designed to make their recurrence less likely. I consider the rectification of errors so very important that Chapter 8 is devoted entirely to its diseussion.

Table 4 Consequences of a Nonjustifiable Loss (market blunder)

1. Specify the exact error as precisely as you possibly can.
2. Record the error in a "mistake book" kept for this purpose.
3. Place the error in its appropriate category.
4. Review the error or errors to make certain that you were indeed at fault.
5. Relive the situation from start to finish (more on this in Chapter 8).
6. Recruit the help of a broker if the error is one that can be recog nized by others.
7. See if you can devise a system to signal the error before you make it.

REVIEW

1. It is more important to learn *how* to correct market errors than *why* the errors were made.
2. The profits that come with good trades and the losses that come with bad trades are not necessarily enough to change behavior.
3. To determine the reinforcing aspects of a behavior it is necessary to thoroughly observe and record its consequences.
4. Many positive and negative social consequences follow profits and losses.
5. It is important to distinguish between market errors and a justifiable loss.
6. The behavioral learning model can be used for effecting positive change as well as for the analysis of errors.

8 Using the Investor's Quotient

Whether you're a conservative investor or an active speculator you must know your strengths and weaknesses. Each individual must have the most thorough and extensive self-knowledge possible. Although one might reason that knowing one's self is a rather simple thing to do, paradoxically, it is one of the most elusive and difficult tasks any individual can assume. Our many defense mechanisms make it almost impossible for us to know ourselves thoroughly. Vanity, pride, fear, jealousy, denial, repression, and suppression are all instrumental in preventing self-awareness. There are, however, a number of techniques that can be used to acquire the necessary self-knowledge.

Most psychotherapy is designed to bring insight and self-knowledge. Although many people have pushed feelings out of awareness, they have not repressed them beyond retrieval. But if you are guilty of defensiveness, you will not find it possible to invest successfully, no matter how hard you try to follow a specific plan. If you cannot change, regardless of effort, you might want to seek professional help. The market may not be your major problem. If your life, marriage, job, and interpersonal relationships are defective, then intensive help is necessary. And in such cases the techniques and suggestions covered in this book may not suffice.

Frequently the most efficient, prompt, and economical way to evaluate your own goals and emotions is through the use of a checklist. This requires responses to a series of statements and/or questions. By answering all items honestly, you may be able to obtain a general idea of your overall strengths and weaknesses, should you not be aware of them as yet. The checklist provided here is drawn strictly from my own experiences and observations. It is not a validated or standardized test of trading readiness. Remember that my intention is only to highlight areas that may be causing problems with your trading.

INSTRUCTIONS

Respond to each question with a yes or no. Please answer all questions. Evaluation of your responses appears at the end of this chapter. Remember that total honesty is necessary if results are to be meaningful.

	YES	NO
1. I subscribe to several advisory services.	_____	_____
2. I believe that brokers should give advice to their customers. It's a broker's job to know which trades are good.	_____	_____
3. My investment strategy is planned well in advance of actual trades.	_____	_____
4. Most of my market exits are due to stops being hit.	_____	_____
5. I trade primarily for the long term.	_____	_____
6. I keep several accounts at different brokerage houses so that I can get a good idea of what the experts are thinking.	_____	_____
7. My behavior at home is intolerable when I have lost money in the market.	_____	_____
8. I like to trade for the challenge of winning.	_____	_____

	YES	NO
9. I have been a net loser in the market for over five years.	____	____
10. The market is "fixed." Only insiders make money.	____	____
11. Brokers make you lose money because they make you trade too much	____	____
12. The market is all luck.	____	____
13. I buy on good news and sell on bad news.	____	____
14. I'm primarily a bull. Most of my trades are from the long side.	____	____
15. I don't like to buy when prices are high or sell when they're too low.	____	____
16. Some of my largest profits have come from trading upside or downside breakouts.	____	____
17. The pit traders always try to "pick" your stops. That's why I never use them.	____	____
18. I tend *not* to get too frustrated by the market. A loss is a loss.	____	____
19. I often lose sleep over the market.	____	____
20. My average profit is larger than my average loss.	____	____
21. I have a set time for studying the market.	____	____
22. I set specific price objectives for all of my trades.	____	____
23. Before making a trade I try to get as many opinions from others as possible.	____	____
24. I'd make more profits if I had a better trading system.	____	____
25. I have never read the writings of		

	YES	NO
Livermore, Gann, Baruch, Pugh, or Wyckoff.	_____	_____
26. The best way to be successful in the market is to isolate yourself from others' opinions.	_____	_____
27. I never (or hardly ever) change my mind about a trade once it has been made.	_____	_____

EVALUATION

Now that you have responded to these items let's go through and examine the "best" response and my rationale.

Item 1. Most successful traders *do not* subscribe to more than a few advisory services. It is the emotionally weak investor who draws advice from too many sources. Perhaps two or three reputable advisory services are all that is required. A "yes" response to this item is *not* a positive indication. Score yourself 0 for a "yes" answer and 1 point for a "no."

Item 2. It is *not* the job of a broker to give advice. It is the job of a broker to provide good execution of orders, quick response time to an order, and correct fills. With few exceptions, those who depend on brokers for anything more than good service are net losers. Those who expect more from a broker are usually disappointed. If you truly believe that it is the job of a broker to give good advice, then you are most likely not a successful trader. If you answered "yes," then score yourself 0. If "no," then score 1.

Item 3. If you answered "yes" to this item, then add 1 point to your score. It is the mark of a successful trader to plan investing and/or trading strategy well in advance, carrying out plans to their completion. If you answered "no," then score 0.

Item 4. This is also a mark of successful trading. A disciplined trader places stops and lets them ride until his system indicates. Stops are the key to success for many traders. They tend to limit losses. Notwithstanding the time-tested value of stops, their use is a distinct mark of trading maturity. Stops need not actually be entered–but they must be used! It takes an even more disciplined trader to not enter stops, keeping them in mind and using them when the appropriate price level has been hit. If you answered "yes," then score 1; score 0 for "no."

Item 5. If you answered "yes," then add 1 point to your score. Another indicator of successful trading is "long-term orientation." Typically, those who trade for the short term (excepting pit brokers, floor traders, and professional traders who have this as their sole occupation) are net losers. The most successful individuals are those who buy and hold, or sell short and hold. If you answered "no" and if you do not trade as a profession, then score 0 for this item.

Item 6. It is also characteristic of immature traders to keep accounts at several different brokerage houses so they may obtain "good information." Typically, this results in a confused trader, inasmuch as he or she receives so much contradictory information that a profitable decision is unlikely. It is also a sign of insecurity. There is nothing wrong with having several different accounts at several different brokerage houses. It is the rationale in this case that is faulty. One ought not depend on brokers for information. Score 0 for "yes" and 1 for "no."

Item 7. This is an obvious item. Certainly if you admit that your behavior at home is intolerable when you lose, then you are aware of your shortcoming. This is symptomatic of emotional traders. I hate to punish you for your honesty, but if you answered "yes," then score yourself 0. If you answered "no," then add 1 point to your total score.

Item 8. This is not a good reason for trading. One might as well go out and climb a mountain. The only acceptable reason for trading the markets is to make profits or to hedge and to avoid losses in cash market operations. Those who trade merely for the challenge are not necessarily effective traders. They are prone to gamble, take chances, and trade for thrills. They will most likely end up net losers. If you answered "yes," then add a 0 to your score. Add 1 point for a "no" answer.

Item 9. The single best indicator of emotional ability in the market is your net performance over the past five years. Even if you have broken even you are well ahead. But if, after five years, you are still a net loser, then you are most likely in need of some psychological shaping up. Read the rest of this book carefully, and do some deep soul searching. Also add 0 to your score. If you are about even or a *small* net loser, then you may add 1 to your score. Also add 1 if you are a net winner.

Item 10. This attitude is typical among those with a losing orientation to the market. It is also common among those who have never been net winners. If you answered "yes," then you have negative attitudes that will most likely lead to further losses. Score 1 if you answered "no" and 0 if you responded "yes."

Item 11. It is foolish to state that a broker "makes" one do anything. The trader alone is responsible for his or her losses. Those who indicate that their broker "made" them do something or "not do" something are basically immature and have losing attitudes. Score 0 for a "yes" answer and 1 for a "no."

Item 12. Another losing attitude is embodied in this statement. Those who believe that the market is all "luck" do not believe in themselves as the instrument to success. Thus they will not be successful traders and have most likely not made too many profitable investments in the past. Score 0 for a "yes" and 1 for a "no."

Item 13. Unsophisticated investors and traders buy in response to good news and sell in response to bad news. Knowledgeable traders buy in anticipation of such news and sell into the actual event.

They buy on expectation and sell on realization. Those who answered "yes" to this question are revealing their "public" attitude. They are most likely net losers in the market. It takes emotional maturity to buy into bad news and sell into good news. A "yes" answer should be scored 0. For a "no" answer score 1 point.

Item 14. This is another representation of "public" attitude. It's a fact that knowledgeable and successful traders play both sides of the market. It is emotionally difficult to sell short. Those capable of doing so have the necessary qualifications for profitable trading. Whereas it is true that large sums of money are made on the long side, it is also true that the fastest money comes from short positions. If you trade from the long side exclusively or primarily, then score 0 for this item. Score a 1 for "no."

Item 15. The successful trader does not stop to think about whether prices are too high or low. If a signal is flashed, then the signal is followed. Little consideration is or should be given to price. The novice trader, or the investor who is not capable of emotionally following a buy or sell signal, will always be second guessing his system, saying things such as "prices are too high now, I'll wait for a pullback before buying." This is *not* to say that there *never* are times when prices are too high or too low. Certainly there comes a time when prices are too high to buy. This time will be so indicated by most reliable trading systems, technical or fundamental. *It is when the relative cheapness or expense of a stock or commodity is used as an excuse for not following a signal that it is destructive and indicative of poor discipline.* Score 0 for "yes" and 1 for "no."

Item 16. Trading with the trend is a hard thing to do. It is a fact, however, that trading with the trend, buying on strength and selling on weakness, buying into breakouts and selling into breakdowns is a successful technique. It requires emotional readiness. Those who can do it usually show large profits and emotional discipline as well. Score 1 if you answered "yes" and 0 if you answered "no."

Item 17. This is an excuse for not using stops. If you use this excuse, then you are most probably a net loser in the market. Score 0 for "yes" and 1 for "no."

Item 18. No investor is perfect. We all have our frustrations, successes, and failures. But for the most part, those who trade profitably tend not to get frustrated by a loss. Their usual response is to forget about the loss as soon as possible. If you dwell on a loss, brood over it for days, or let it affect you by undermining self-confidence, then you are not emotionally ready to trade. Score 0 for a "no" answer and 1 for a "yes."

Item 19. This item relates to 18. We all tend to lose sleep now and again. We do so, at times, because of the market. If, however, one loses sleep frequently over positions or trades, then one is too emotionally tied to the market, and a problem exists. This is a prime symptom of insecurity, lack of confidence, and poor skill. Score a 0 if you answered "yes" and a 1 if you answered "no."

Item 20. The size of your average loss, compared to your average profit, is an indicator of trading discipline. Those investors and traders who follow a well planned strategy tend to show smaller average losses, and fewer total losses, on a per trade basis. If you fall into the larger average loss category, then you are probably not trading in accordance with effective psychological principles. You are, perhaps, riding losses too long, contrary to your trading system. Score 0 for "yes" and 1 for "no."

Item 21. This is perhaps the single most important indicator of winning discipline. And winning discipline is possible only through emotional control. Traders and investors who are successful, year after year, have a well scheduled and planned time for studying the markets. Regardless of orientation, technician or fundamentalist, they spend a specific amount of time on the market, at regular intervals. If you answered "no" to this question, subtract 2 points from your score. If you answered "yes," then add 2 points to your score.

Item 22. It is further a mark of trading maturity to set objectives. This suggests that the individual is following a disciplined trading program. As such he or she is a mature investor, capable of sticking to a plan of action. This ability is a prerequisite to profitable trading. If you answered "yes," then add 1 point to your score; if "no," add 0.

Item 23. Those who need to assess the collective opinion of others are highly insecure individuals. Such a need is symptomatic of poor emotional readiness, and is a definite psychological handicap. In fact, it is common knowledge that the consensus of opinion is usually wrong. Only a secure trader can carry out a trade from initiation to completion without the approval or advice of others. Score 1 if you answered "no" and 0 if "yes."

Item 24. Such statements are made by investors who have not as yet realized that they alone are responsible for their profits and losses. The trading system itself is not nearly as important as what is done with it. An idiot driving an expensive automobile is still an idiot, albeit a "classy" one. If you blame your lack of profits on a trading system, then you most probably lack the necessary psychological readiness for trading. Score 0 if "yes," 1 if "no."

Item 25. The experiences of successful traders and investors have been put into writing so that we may benefit from them. An investor who wishes to improve his or her results will be seeking a better way. Undoubtedly this investor will have turned to the great masters' writings. If you have not done so, then I recommend you explore these sources of knowledge as soon as possible. Score 0 for "yes" and 1 for "no."

Item 26. The truly successful investor and trader recognizes the importance of isolation. Many of one's best decisions and trades are made in isolation. It is a sign of emotional readiness and ability to block out interfering stimulation. Score 1 for "yes" and 0 for "no."

Item 27. Firm resolve and follow-through are also characteristic of profitable trading. If you lack the ability to stay with a trade through its prescribed conclusion, then you lack a key element in the formula for profitable trading and investing. Score 0 for "no" and 1 for "yes."

RESULTS

Now add up your score. The highest possible total is 28 points.

If Your Score Was in the 21–28 Range. You are probably a very successful trader. If you scored this high *but do not* show large profits, then you may very well be using a poor trading system. I suggest you experiment with different trading methods.

Score of 15–20. You have the right idea, but still need a little polishing. You are on the way to profitable investing and trading but need to develop more discipline. Many of the exercises in this book can help. Pay particular attention to the items you answered incorrectly.

Score of 10–14. You have scored 50 percent or less. This is *not* indicative of pending success in your trading, and is a warning that you need to work on your discipline. I urge you to pay particular attention to the behavioral trading programs outlined in this book.

Score 9 or Less. Be careful! It is my belief that you are heading for losses if you have not already found them. You must begin to reeducate yourself emotionally at Step 1. I would even go so far as to suggest you stop trading until you have evaluated your specific problems and formulated a comprehensive program to deal with them.

It's one thing for me to tell you that you need help. It's a far greater thing for me to tell you exactly how to go about getting help. Certainly, the many techniques and suggestions in this book can be instrumental in the progress of change. But if you are one of those investors or traders who has been losing money for years, then it may be very difficult to take even the first step toward change. If you lack the self-discipline for profitable trading, then it is natural to assume that you lack the necessary discipline to retrain yourself. In this case I have a number of suggestions I truly believe can help. Remember that my comments are directed primarily at those who score *less than 15* on the evaluation scale. Some of the suggested methods will be helpful to all traders regardless of score.

1. **Take time away from the market.** I suggest you start by reading some of the classical texts on investing. I recommend LeFevre's *Reminiscences of a Stock Operator* as an ideal first assignment. At the end of this book you will find a list of recommended reading. You may wish to study most of these books prior to trading again. The best way to end a losing situation is to get out of the situation, at least temporarily. This is why I recommend standing aside. If you continue to beat your head against the wall, you will become immune to the pain and won't realize that you are destroying yourself and possibly your family as well.

2. **If you must continue to trade, then form a club or group.** This can help keep checks and balances on your trading. Group pressure and guidance is a very helpful asset for the wayward investor. Investment clubs are easily found or formed. The degree of discipline which the democratic process can instill is truly amazing. It often takes such clubs many days to decide on a specific buy or sell. But the process is thorough, well researched, and frequently profitable. When you have internalized some of their techniques you can reevaluate yourself and strike out on your own.

3. **Don't "paper trade"!** My specific objections to this common technique are stated elsewhere in this book. Paper trading will not, in my opinion, teach you a darned thing about the real market world. It will only give you a sense of false confidence and could very well frustrate you to the point of error.

4. **Obtain professional help from a counselor.** If you are having difficulties in other areas of your life, find a mental health professional. Problems in the home are a good indicator of emotional difficulty, as are extreme mood swings.

HOW TO RECTIFY TRADING ERRORS

All human beings, at one time or another, make mistakes. But some individuals seem to make many more errors than others. Psychologically there exists a relationship between anxiety and accuracy. Up to a given point a certain amount of pressure and/or anxiety can be beneficial. Some individuals perform very well under pressure. But beyond the point of maximum benefit, stress and anxiety can increase significantly the degree and seriousness of errors. In the market, where anxiety is high, stress typically results in loss. Whether or not the given error or errors are being made with an unconscious desire to lose, it is possible, in my opinion, to structure the trading environment in a fashion that will minimize not only their frequency but the relative intensity of each error as well. The individual who has at his or her disposal the necessary behavioral tools (as described herein) to alter error behavior, but who does not do so, may require more intensive therapeutic assistance. I do not believe, however, that this is necessary in most cases. One can, in fact, overcome many problems with the behavioral approach. Before attacking the many blunders a trader can make, I would like to acquaint you with some details about the behavioral concepts of *shaping* and *extinction.*

You will recall that the term shaping applies to the behavioral learning process. A psychologist decides to teach an animal to press a bar. The bar is connected to a switch and pressing it will cause a pellet of food to be delivered into a dish. Food reward will maintain the bar-press behavior. But animals are not born with bar-pressing skill. They must learn it—enter "shaping." In order to teach an animal the bar press, we observe its behavior very closely as it walks about. As it approaches the bar we drop a food pellet into the cage. Before too long our subject is standing close to the bar, since he has been rewarded for proximity to it. Time passes and we continue to give rewards for closeness to the bar. We now place a food pellet on the bar. As the animal touches the pellet, he accidentally applies pressure to the bar, and another pellet drops into the attached dish. After several such repetitions the animal presses the bar independently. A behavior has been shaped (taught).

We now put our subject on a schedule. We decide to reward him once for every five presses of the bar. After he is responding steadily we change the rules and reward him once for every twenty presses of the bar. After some time we increase the behavioral requirement to fifty presses, and so on. By employing such a reinforcement schedule it is possible to obtain a great deal of work or behavior from the subject. Assume that after several weeks of training we drop the reward entirely. What happens? You naturally assume that the animal will stop pressing the bar after a while. This is true. But what happens first? The animal's initial response to termination of the reward is an *increase* in response rate. It is almost as if he is trying harder. This "frustration effect," as I like to call it, is a common element in all behavior once reward has been terminated. As time passes, and food is not given, the bar press will be extinguished (forgotten). From time to time the animal may try the bar press again. But the longer reward remains absent, the increasingly rare will be the bar press. Figure 7 is a typical learning curve from acquisition to extinction.

Assume now that we put our animal on a random schedule of reward, that is, reward will be given at irregular intervals, whether time based or response based. No matter how many times the bar

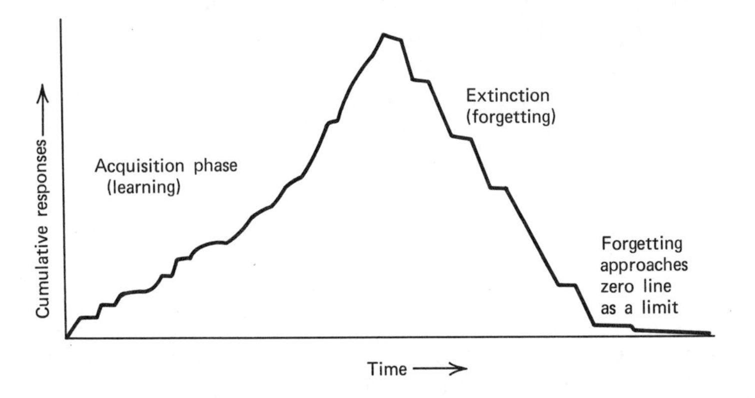

Figure 7 Typical learning curve.

is pressed, reward could come at any time. The learning curve for this behavior will be somewhat different. Although the behavior will take longer to acquire, it will ultimately be much more resistant to extinction. Some experimental animals maintained on a variety of random schedules seem to go on responding indefinitely, even after reward has been totally terminated for many months. The market, in many respects is similar to the random reinforcement schedule. Even after rewards have been absent for many months, traders go on trading. There are many parallels to gambling behavior.

After a behavior has been present for many months or many repetitions, it becomes so engrained that it is virtually impossible to avoid. It becomes a habit. Not all habits, as you know, are productive. Many individuals continue with self-destructive habits to the point of death. Smoking and drinking are just two obvious examples.

I belabor the point in order to remind you that trading the market is also a habit. It can be a productive habit or a self-destructive addiction. How can inappropriate and/or painful habits be changed? The ultimate answer is simple. Remove the positive consequences, apply negative ones, redirect the behavior to a productive end, and reward it. But that's easier said than done. In the experimental situation, where the psychologist has total control over the subject, it is a relatively mechanical task. But in human beings such change becomes difficult to implement. It is hard enough for a therapist to help the patient change. And it is even more of a challenge for the individual to change without assistance. The precise organizational scheme outlined below is presented in an effort to make change more likely when self-administered.

RECORD KEEPING

There are several tools that must be used in order to initiate the change process. The first is record keeping. I suggest all traders keep an ongoing record of trades. The record should list date, buy or sell, signal for entry, date of exit, amount of profit or loss, and, most important, reason for loss. Reason for loss should be listed by code in one of several categories. A justifiable loss–one that cannot be directly related to the trader (as discussed earlier)—should, for example, be assigned a given code letter or number. As losses occur you will become familiar with the reason(s) for their having occurred. Each trader will have his or her own set of weaknesses. Some of the typical reasons are indicated in Table 5. You may have reasons that do not fit these categories. Your list might include such things as "had hangover and couldn't read chart correctly" or "didn't show up at the office and forgot to put in stop." The reason should be specifically indicated. If and when a new behavior crops up you must also list it. Generally traders will have only two or three major classifications of mistakes with many subsidiary errors falling under the group headings.

Keep a running tally of which mistakes are most frequent. In addition, it would be a good idea to note any particular rewards or punishments that followed the error(s) and any noteworthy events that preceded them. Figure 8 shows how such a record sheet might look.

At the end of each month review your record sheet. Note any errors that seem to be very frequent. Also make note of any previous conditions that are repetitive. The thing to look for is a pattern or patterns of behavior inherent in your trading. Once isolated, these patterns will become your target behaviors. But unless you

Table 5 Typical Reasons for Market Losses Attributable to the Trader

1. Not using stops.
2. Listening to broker.
3. Not following signal to liquidate.
4. Not raising stop.
5. Getting out too soon.
6. Getting in too soon (before signal).
7. Taking a tip.
8. Making a trade due to government report (or earnings report) but no signal.
9. Anticipating a sell signal prior to stop getting hit.
10. Nonspecific fear or greed.
11. Margin call forcing liquidation before signal.

Trade	Date In	Date Out	Profit/Loss	Trading Rule	Reason for Loss–Comment
Bot–Dec 79, corn	6/17/78	6/21/78	–$ 247.50	6, 3	Stop loss hit–rules followed
Sld–Feb 79, hogs	6/23/78	8/11/78	+$1250.50	6, 5	Rules followed–no loss
Bot–100S GM	7/11/78	7/12/78	–$ 245.20	11	"Scared out" too early
Bot–Feb 79, gold	8/12/78	9/12/78	+$1450.00	12, 7	Profitable trade but got out too soon on news report
Sld–Feb 79, hogs	9/15/78	9/23/78	–$1227.60	None	Bot on rumor and took large loss one week later
Bot–200S IBM	9/26/78	9/27/78	+$ 250.00	None	Bot on bullish earnings report –broke trading rules
Sld–Jan 80 OJ	11/12/78	1/14/79	+$2560.00	3, 7, 2	Followed all rules–1st trade after reevaluation of rules
Bot–100S PRD	1/23/79	2/17/79	+$ 980.50	1, 5	Followed rules and made another good trade!!!
Sld–100S PRD	2/17/79	5/25/79	+$1160.50	1, 2, 3 5, 7	All trading rules followed to the letter–profit!!!
Sld–100S XRX	6/11/79	6/15/79	–$ 768.90	5, 4	Followed rules for entry but did not liquidate on stop
Bot–Mar 80, corn	7/01/79	9/11/79	+$ 143.50	3, 4, 5	Entry OK but did not use a stop and gave back big profit

Bot–Mar 80, oats	9/13/79	9/15/79	–$ 265.00	3, 6, 1	Followed rules but still lost –getting frustrated . . .
Bot–Mar 80, oil	9/15/79	9/17/79	–$1220.00	3, 7	No use of stop. Overtrading– very anxious–be careful!
Bot–100S LVO	9/19/79	9/23/79	–$ 550.00	None	System working but I'm not– taking break to evaluate

Trading rules:

1. Buy on penetration of 3-week high–sell on penetration of 3-week low.
2. Buy/sell penetration of 10-day moving average.
3. Buy/sell on 50 percent retracement from breakout.
4. Buy/sell on penetration of triple high or low.
5. Place stop at 75 percent once in excess of $1000 open profit.
6. Buy/sell 3-day pullback to trend change point.
7. Buy/sell on weekend rule (close on high or low of week).
8. Buy/sell on 2-day upside reversal (downside reversal).
9. Buy on penetration of contract high with open interest high.
10. Close out position after key reversal.
11. Buy/sell on new 5-week high or low.
12. Buy/sell new all-time high or low.

Figure 8 Trading record.–Hypothetical Trading Rules

have a clear idea of what you are doing incorrectly, it will not be possible to effectively change. It is therefore impossible for me to overemphasize the importance of record keeping.

Let's take a look at where we stand prior to beginning the important topic of treatment. Here is a brief synopsis of steps taken so far:

1. The behavioral learning model has been discussed with particular emphasis on the stimulus-response-consequences chain.

2. The point was made that behavior is maintained as a function of consequences. If, for example, a behavior continues we must assume that the consequences of it are rewarding even though they may *appear* to be negative.

3. By changing the consequences of behavior we can change behavior itself.

4. In order to change consequences we must analyze them as specifically as possible.

5. This can be achieved by the use of a trading record. The value of such a record is both educational and therapeutic.

6. Behavior change (treatment), according to the learning model I have presented must follow an objective, specific, and organized series of steps.

Even if you do not accept the tenets of behavioral psychology, you will most likely agree that the methodology of this approach is highly organized and objective. To accomplish the scientific technique that I believe necessary in behavior change, we must ignore some of the more subjective terms that most of us are accustomed to. This does not mean that feelings and thoughts are useless in my approach. It means, rather, that for the time being we shall not attempt to deal with any entity that is not clearly measurable, observable, and visible.

CHANGING BEHAVIOR

The next step is to begin "treatment." Perhaps just a bit of background into some of the techniques that behavioral psychologists use to implement therapeutic change would be helpful here. As you will recall, the principle of extinction refers to the unlearning or forgetting process. Depending on the type of reward schedule used in the learning process, behavior change will be either a relatively simple task or a rather lengthy one.

It is safe to assume that many counterproductive and pathological behaviors are maintained on random schedules of reinforcement. Certainly this is the case for most market behaviors. Frequently trading rules are broken, and yet a profit results. And there are times that trading rules are disregarded and a loss follows. We never know in advance if our violation of the rules will be profitable. This random type of schedule makes for behaviors which, as previously indicated, are especially resistant to change. Several procedures can be used in changing market behaviors, but before I suggest any, it is important for me to let you know the exact limitations of what can be accomplished through the written word. Since the implementation of my suggestions is not directly under my control, it is impossible to guarantee results. The absence of a therapist to supervise this program places a great burden on you, the individual, should you seek to change your habits. If you can recruit some help, you will most likely be more successful. It is, however, not possible for me to assure you of results, particularly if your market problem goes much deeper than indirect assistance can alleviate.

STOP-LOSS PROGRAM

For the purpose of our present discussion I will concentrate on market problem 1 in Table 5: Not using stops. Let's assume that the use of stops is preferable in all markets and with most trading systems. In some cases a "stop reverse" is used. This type of stop is designed to limit one's loss, and at the same time reverse the position. If, for example, one was short the market with stop reverse at a given price, then one would not only get stopped out when the price was hit, but one would also buy at the given price, thereby establishing a net long position. A stop reverse would then be entered on the new position, and so on. Many moving average systems use stop reverse orders since they want to be in the market at all times. Regardless of the type of stop used, whether it is a close only stop, stop limit, stop reverse, or otherwise, the use of stops, if indicated by a trading system, is a necessity. We can only assume that the individual who does not use stops has been maintained on a random reinforcement schedule. In other words, there were occasions which resulted in a profit even though no stop was used. Although the profit (or avoidance of loss) may have been infrequent, learning nevertheless took place and a bad habit was acquired. This, by the way, is perhaps the most common market problem. Many excuses are given for not using stops. Some are rather artful, but none is valid. The key to successful money management is and always has been limitation of losses. I will not, however, preach to you about the value of stops. I will merely assume that it is in most traders' best interest to use them or another loss-limiting technique.

How can we go about changing this problem with the assistance of behavioral techniques? You will recall the learning model given previously. Let's "plug into" it and take a close look. Figure 9 shows how the stimulus–response–consequence chain would look in our treatment approach for the use of stop loss orders.

The problem with using stops is that their use is not very rewarding. In most cases a stop will get you out with a loss, or a smaller profit than you had. This is how stops work. You can see that there is nothing positive about the use of stops, other than the avoidance of a loss. Each time a stop is hit you feel as if you have been punished. Why should you continue to use stops when all they bring is punishment. If you have a profit and use a stop, you will get stopped out at profit which is smaller than what you could have had. This also tends to be a negative experience. If you use a stop and the market hits it only to turn around, you also feel bad.

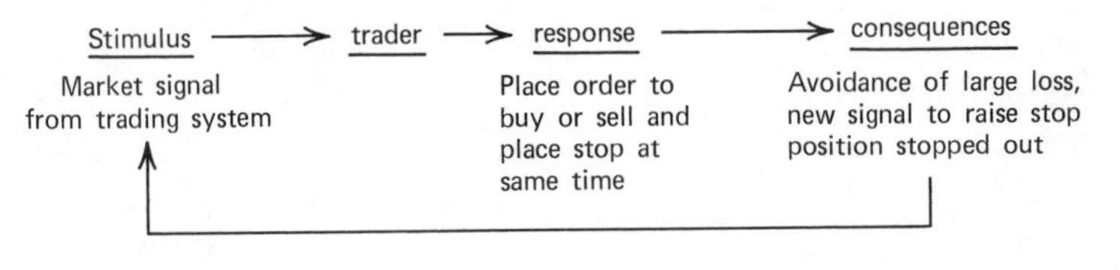

Figure 9 Stimulus-response chain and stop-loss program.

There is virtually nothing intrinsically positive about the consequences of using stops. I might tell you that you will avoid a larger loss if you use stops. But this is also a negative way of looking at things. Stops are necessary preventive measures.

This is what accounts for the hesitation that many traders experience in taking losses. Adhering strictly to behavioral principles we can see that the use of stops has virtually no immediately positive consequence. In fact, stops are like life insurance–we know we need it but hope we don't have to use it. As a result of the consistently negative experiences associated with stop loss orders, it's no wonder that many investors do not use them. In Freudian terms a loss could be compared to castration. This is not intended to be amusing. Some individuals take each loss as if a part of their body had been severed. This is why stops are so difficult to use. This is why stops are resented, hated, abused, ridiculed, and misused. What can be done? We know we need to use stops for money management purposes. How can we find some positive aspect to their use so that we can change the consequences of stops?

Step One

The first step toward changing any behavior must always be to learn an approximation of the new behavior, particularly if it is complex or if the individual is totally deficient in this area. Assume that you are an individual who never, ever uses stops. Assume also that you understand the dangers involved in not using stops. Assume further that you have had many losses and wish to change the behavior. I would not expect you to go to sleep one evening a sinner, and wake up the next morning a saint. All you need do is work on the first target behavior toward the goal. And the first behavior is to write your stops down on the record sheet, each and every time you place an order. The simple task of writing the stop will not bring you the loss or negative experience you seek to avoid. But it will help teach you to approximate the ultimate response. If you can recruit the assistance of a friend who has a similar problem, then you will be far better off. You must monitor one another's behavior. Each time you record the stop (on paper) your friend will reward you verbally. He or she will say "Good work,

I'm glad you wrote down the stop" or "Keep up the good work" or "I'm impressed with your progress." Any positive statement will do. If you are tempted to make light of this little exercise, then I suggest you "stifle yourself." You may not be functioning at this low level. You may, in fact, be using stops from time to time. If this is the case, you will want to start treatment at a later step. But for those individuals who never use stops, for those who are persistent losers, this type of help is a necessity. Remember that we are shaping behavior.

To implement this procedure you must recruit assistance from others. Not only will you find it difficult to reward yourself for recording a stop; you will be inclined to be dishonest as well. You can be more creative in selecting rewards, and you can tailor the program to suit your specific needs. As you make progress and obtain verbal rewards from those around you, you will find that your goal is getting closer. For those who cannot depend on a friend for assistance, a willing broker might be the answer. You can give him your stops, tell him to record them but not actually enter them, and you can have him keep a record of your progress. He can also reward you accordingly.

Should you be punished for not entering stops during this first phase? I do not believe that punishment will help. If you have even the slightest desire to succeed in the market, this will be sufficient motivation to carry you through the first step. If you cannot get through this step, then I suggest you stop trading. Sad but true, this one bit of advice may save you considerable grief. I am challenging your sincerity by telling you this. If you sincerely want to be successful in the market, then you will implement the program I am discussing. If you do not, then the chances you will ever come out of the profitable side are slim indeed.

Once you have achieved a perfect score in recording stops for a period of three months or twenty-five trades, whichever comes first, you are ready to start phase two. This phase consists of giving stops to your broker, but not having them actually entered. You may need to start at this step if you have no one to help you with step one. Or if you have no trouble recording stops, you should begin the "treatment" at step two.

Step Two

In order for effective behavioral change to take place one must follow an orderly sequence of steps from least to most complex. If your difficulty is very basic, then you must begin with step one. If your problem is less entrenched, you may begin at a later step. This is the manner in which behavioral change occurs. And it is also the manner in which all learning takes place. You must take each step as one small goal toward the final behavior. You must not skip any step. Should you find that you are unsuccessful at any given point, you must retrace, work back, and begin at an even more elementary level.

The second step of our stop-loss program is to begin giving stops to your broker. This step can only be started after you have reached a high level of performance on step one. Essentially the aspects of this step are no different than what was done earlier. The only change is that stop-loss orders are given to your broker in addition to being recorded by yourself and a friend. The broker should be told *not* to actually enter the orders but just to keep a record of your stops. If his or her help can be obtained, then it would be helpful for you to be verbally praised each time a stop is placed. Your broker should keep a complete list of all stops. You should keep a list as well. The object is to make stops less difficult to place by removing the negative consequences and fear associated with stops. This is achieved by not having orders actually entered.

As in step one, you should be rewarded verbally by the broker, friends, and any other individual who is working on the program with you. The goal is to achieve 100 percent stop placement rate. This should take no more than several weeks. Once this is accomplished you are ready to move on to step three, which will entail actual market entry of stops. Prior to this, however, there is another technique you may wish to use in order to attach more value to the use of stops. During the time that step two is in process, keep a record of what your market performance has been, using your current trading strategy (i.e., no use of stops or sporadic use of stops). Keep a record of what your performance would have been had you used the stops you recorded during the program. More often than not you will find your performance without stops much worse than what it would have been with stops. This is a simple exercise, but it *can* have a dramatic effect on your attitude and behavior. Once you realize the immense difference stops can make, you will be highly motivated to use them. This increase in motivation will, in turn, have a very positive effect on your overall profits.

Step Three

The purpose of any behavioral change program is to "stamp in" behavior. The repeated association of appropriate behavior and positive reinforcement is instrumental in the change process. The more frequently a behavior is rewarded, the more likely it is to occur in the future. The third phase of our stop-loss program consists of on-the-job training, as it were. This step requires the actual use of stops. We will use the same rewards as before–verbal praise by broker, friends, and others–and it wouldn't hurt to praise yourself. A record of stops will be kept, as before. Stops will be placed with the broker. The broker will enter stops accordingly. By the time you reach this phase of the program your preparation through steps one and two will have been extensive. You will find that stops are being used without fear of consequences. Be certain to continue rewards after you have started this step.

It is always best to strive for 100 percent use of stops. Anything less than 100 percent may cause you to waver from the program and will result in faulty learning. The object is, of course, for the behavior to become habitual. It has been my experience that the use of such a program for approximately three months (or 25 trades, whichever comes first) will be sufficient for the formation of a positive habit. Once you have mastered one aspect of the trading sequence you should move on to the next higher level.

Step Four

The next step is to "practice, practice, practice." I indicated earlier the importance of repeated rewards for the behavior we are attempting to change. The only way this can be achieved is through consistent and frequent use of appropriate behaviors. You will find it productive to use your skills in the correct fashion so that they may be rewarded. The same holds true for your trading system. The best way it can be tested is to use it. Once you have learned a behavior your must "use it or lose it."

REVIEW

1. To be successful at trading it is necessary to acquire positive behaviors.
2. Frequently it is also necessary to rid one's self of inappropriate and loss-producing behaviors.
3. Behavioral learning techniques such as shaping, extinction, and reinforcement are instrumental in the formation of new behaviors and the "unlearning" of old ones.
4. Reinforcement schedules can be manipulated to increase, decrease, or stamp in behaviors.
5. Effective and thorough record keeping is an asset to any program and, in fact, is a necessity in the administration of all behavior-change procedures.
6. There are at least ten general categories of market "errors."
7. Treatment, or the process of behavior change, must progress through several steps, the success of each of which is interdependent.
8. Each step in a program must be more complicated than the previous step and all behaviors must be mastered as one moves toward the ultimate goal.
9. Once learned, a behavior must be used in order to be remembered.

9 Further Details on Dealing with Trading Problems

The nonuse and misuse of stops are only two of many things a trader can do wrong. There are so very many errors that can lead to losses, it is impossible to cover even 10 percent of them thoroughly. Fortunately, most of them fit into the general categories described previously in Table 5. The teachings of behavioral psychology provide a basic format around which to structure all programs whose goal is to change counterproductive market behaviors (Table 6). By following this sequence of events, it is possible to effectively deal with any, and possibly all, market problems. In order to assist in your independent programming of changes I will go through the sequence with another common market problem, liquidating your position too soon.

When initiating a program it is always best to define the target behavior as clearly as possible. Behavioral psychologists refer to this as the "operational definition." The more concise the definition of what is targeted for change, the more successful one is likely to be. The operational definition for "liquidating a position too soon" could be stated as follows:

> *The closing out of any trade–long, short, or spread–before the specific time and/or price objective predetermined in one's trading system.*

Table 6 Format for Change

Step Number and Description	Anticipated Result
1. Keep record of behavior.	To isolate target behaviors.
2. Note conditions that precede given behavior.	To isolate stimulus or stimuli.
3. Note consequence of behavior.	To determine what is acting as the reward.
4. Define "new" behavior.	To have clear-cut goal.
5. Change stimulus events.	To help alter trader response.
6. Change consequence events.	To increase frequency of "new" behavior.
7. "Fade out" rewards.	To permit "new" behavior to take over.
8. Monitor "new" behavior.	To be certain it has been stamped in.

The next step is to go to our outline (see Table 6). Step 1 indicates that we are to keep a record of the target behavior. In other words, we are to use a record-keeping sheet like Figure 8. We are also to keep a record of how frequently this behavior occurs during a given period of time, so we may refer to it as an index of how much or how little change has taken place. We should find it possible to state, for example, that 70 percent of our trades are closed out prior to the proper time (or whatever the actual count happens to be).

Step 2 tells us to keep a record of the stimulus conditions that led to the given behavior(s). It is possible, for example, that one specific stimulus may always be the precedent condition for "closing position out too early." In my early days of trading, for example, 90 percent of my positions were closed out too early due to calls from my broker during market hours. These calls shook my confidence. It was therefore possible to change my response by changing the stimulus condition. I simply requested my broker to avoid calling me unless instructed to do so, or unless it was for the purpose of reporting back on order fills. This effectively eliminated my problem and left me free to gain positive rewards by following my system. And in turn it helped build up my self-confidence, which ultimately made it possible for me to "cope" with broker's calls. In many cases the "cure" for a given problem will be to change the stimulus event or events. Do not overlook this potentially powerful technique. All too often, however, it is not possible to isolate a specific stimulus which can be manipulated. It is therefore necessary to continue with the program.

Step 3 is "Note consequence of behavior." In this case we should find that to close out the position too early, regardless of how much profit was taken (or how little to be more accurate), tends to relieve the "anxiety" of carrying a position. The relief one feels can be rewarding. Many times one's broker will reward the liquidating act. The broker himself will not be aware that he is rewarding the act as well as being the stimulus for it. It would be well to note the verbal behavior of your broker. After you liquidate a position too early or in response to his call, he may say such things as "Let's be glad we're out of that trade" or "I'm happy you got out, the market's going to keep going down." The following are typical statements that tend to verbally reward this "jumping the gun":

"Well, that's one loss we don't have to worry about anymore."

"At least we got out with a profit."

"Better to take a small profit than any kind of a loss."

"We're lucky the trade was closed out, they'd have 'picked your stop anyway.' "

"We got out in the nick of time–the market went sharply lower right after we got out."

Along with these will be statements designed, subtly of course, to minimize the seriousness of what was done. These can take the following form:

"No harm done, if we're wrong in getting out too soon, we can always jump back in."

"The exception makes the rule."

"Not *every* trading system is *right* all the time."

"If we get out now, before the report, all we lose is one commission."

A few more words on the relief of anxiety as a reinforcer are in order. To liquidate a position too early can serve as a reward for some individuals. In some cases, such as liquidating a loss too late, the mere act of liquidating can also act as a reward. The tension of riding a profit or loss may be quite intense for some investors. By liquidating too early they are relieved of the tension, and, therefore, the mere termination of this situation will have the same result as a positive experience. They will be more likely to behave the same way in future trades. Those who ride losses to unacceptably large amounts also tend to experience the positive effects of relief. Again, the relief can serve to reward an otherwise inappropriate act. It's like the man who, when asked why he kept banging his head against the wall, replied, "because it feels so good when I stop." The investor who cannot face a loss and accept it at the right time may actually learn to take very large losses because of the intense release that comes with the final act of liquidating. In such cases it is fortunate that money will often run out quickly, thereby forcing awareness. Some behavioral psychologists, W. K. Estes in particular, have proposed the validity of termination as a reinforcing event. Hence the situations described here are highly plausible. As you can see, it is difficult to get back on the right track once a blunder has been made. This is why I stress the importance of an organized, well-planned, and methodical approach to trading and investing, first and foremost as a means of *preventing* trading errors.

Almost anyone can help stimulate premature trades: it can be friends, advisory services, floor traders, news broadcasts, in-laws, or other relatives. More often than not it is a combination of all these factors in conjunction with the trader's own insecurities. In such an event the multiplicity of inputs makes it impossible to easily change the stimulus conditions.

The next step involves a definition of the "new behavior." More often than not the new behavior (target behavior) will simply be the opposite of the behavior we are attempting to change. It is always best to operationally define the target. In this case it could be defined as follows:

> *To liquidate trades if and only if the trading system so dictates, regardless of any other information inputs to the trader.*

Step 5 involves changing the stimulus events, provided this is possible. It may not be practical to change the stimuli leading to a given behavior. But we can very often help our program along by eliminating several of the stimuli. For many years my "life-saving" rule was to avoid, at all costs, discussing, listening, or otherwise exposing myself to others' ideas or opinions about the markets. This is a very difficult thing to do. It requires one to *not* read trade journals, news reports, advisory services and brokerage house letters. It also requires one to keep one's ears "shut" as much as possible (very often the best way to do this is to keep one's mouth shut). This is an example of how I changed the stimulus of a losing behavior.

Step 6, the most important by all means, is to change the consequences. Here is where one's creativity and resourcefulness come into play. One must solicit rewards from others, from one's self, and from the market. The techniques discussed earlier all have merit and there are many variations on the theme. The key is to remember that *every time the target behavior is carried through to successful completion reward must be given immediately.*

Step 7 is to "fade out" rewards. This topic has not yet been discussed, but you can get an idea of what's involved by the very name. As time passes and the behavior we are trying to shape increases in frequency, it will be possible to cut down and eventually eliminate the rewards that are being used. Since the behavior will lead to self-satisfaction, and considerably more profit, it will become self-reinforcing.

Step 8 is to monitor the new behavior. This is not difficult since trading results will let you know how your program is working. It is best to continue recording results using the previously mentioned trading record. If there is a change in your overall behavior it will be evident from the record, if it has not become evident from your overall profits (or lack thereof).

In addition to the typical market problems already discussed there are many behaviors that must be shaped from the start since they do not tend to come of their own accord. Of these, discipline is the single most important. It is my opinion that if a behavior can be defined, it can be learned. In Chapter 10 I will discuss in detail some of the ways in which an individual can go about learning self-discipline.

The following key elements in the behavioral sequence should be followed in instituting any program directed at behavioral change. You would do well to remember them in relation to your efforts at improvement.

1. Define all behaviors as specifically as possible.

2. Keep accurate records of all stimulus events.

3. Keep accurate records of all response consequences.

4. Define target behavior as specifically as possible.

5. Rewards should be given immediately after completion of the target behavior.

6. Continue to monitor behavior after the program ends.

7. Fade out rewards when behavior has reached nearly 100 percent.

8. All behaviors are important as part of the overall trading plan.

9. Constantly be on the lookout for symptoms of change in your trading. These will most likely be reflected in increased losses.

10. Obtain as much assistance from friends, relatives, and brokers as you possibly can.

11. Do not minimize the possible benefits of controlling stimulus events.

12. Be organized in your trading. Effective organization makes it possible to keep a good record of all the necessary behaviors, their stimulus-response conditions, frequency, and improvement.

13. Approach your program in a scientific way. Look for behavioral clues, count frequency of behaviors, keep a tally of their occurrence.

14. Avoid introspective reasoning. In other words, do not try to spend too much time understanding why you do something. Take for granted that you are not doing something the proper way, design a program, implement it, and change your behavior.

REVIEW

1. In order to change an old behavior or to shape a new one it is necessary to follow a series of specific behavioral steps.
2. The required steps are outlined in detail.
3. All programs for behavioral change must be highly organized.
4. Help from others should be solicited as frequently as possible.
5. Time should not be spent wondering about "why" a behavior occurs.

10 Scheduling and Self-Discipline

In previous chapters I have referred to scheduling and its importance. The value of working from a detailed schedule is threefold:

1. A schedule will help you avoid costly errors and omissions.

2. A schedule will help you maintain a disciplined and orderly approach to trading.

3. A schedule will help you develop effective habits and attitudes.

For the learning process to achieve its fullest and most lasting results, the learner must adhere to a well-organized, specific, detailed, comprehensive, and pragmatic schedule. It is absolutely amazing how many things an organized person can accomplish. And it is equally amazing how much free time a well-organized person will have left. Last, and certainly not least, an almost immediate improvement in attitudes and, of course, profits can be derived from careful scheduling. Certainly there are many successful traders who do not use schedules and have perhaps never used them. They don't need them. They have already achieved what you are attempting to accomplish. It is therefore not wise to use these people as an example. Once you have arrived at your destination you can dispense with your schedule, for it will have been internalized. If there is only one thing this book inspires you to do, then let it be the creation of a schedule as discussed in this chapter.

WHERE TO START

To construct an effective schedule you must start by listing all the things you wish to include. Since I am talking about a schedule that focuses on your market-related activities, only these goals are included. Should you wish to construct a more comprehensive timetable covering other areas of your life, it will be a simple task once you have made your trading schedule. Some suggested schedule activities include reading market reports, preparing charts and graphs (or fundamental data), making trading decisions, updating your record of trades, reading market-related material, studying trading rules, testing and developing systems, spending time away from the market, and working on a five-year plan.

Once you have decided on what should be included, you can assign each activity, based on its frequency, a particular time slot, as in Figure 10. Those who trade the market daily will find much more time available. Many individuals are not involved on such an intensive basis. In these cases it would be preferable to work on the market daily, even if for a brief period of time. This should be done either before or after a daytime job. It is not a good idea to mix one task with another. I do not recommend studying the market while at a full-time job.

It is more effective to work for short periods of time than for longer ones. I would therefore suggest that you focus on most target behaviors daily, but briefly. It is necessary to cover some goals

Day	Time	Activity
Monday	7–8 PM	Read market reports
Tuesday	7–8 PM	Plan long-term goals
Wednesday	7–8 PM	Analyze performance results
Thursday	7–8 PM	Study trading rules
Friday	7–8 PM	Summarize weekly results
Saturday	2–3 PM	Update charts for week
Sunday	7–8 PM	Plan weekly strategy

Figure 10 Daily record.

Week of ________

Monday 7PM–9PM. Work on stop-loss program step 3. Evaluate progress made during previous week. Plan steps for current week.

Tuesday 7PM–8PM. Analyze trades of previous week to determine if all rules have been followed per trading system. Calculate profit to loss ratio.

Wednesday 8PM–9PM. Discuss progress of stop-loss program with broker to determine if any changes have been noticed. Set next target behavior.

Thursday 8PM–9PM. Review chain of behavioral consequences to make certain that adequate rewards follow the target behavior(s).

Friday 8PM–9PM. Define and operationalize next step in trading program. Determine approximate starting date. Evaluate overall progress of current goals and make changes as necessary.

Weekend. Weekend reserved for work on technical trading system and planning of trades for coming week.

Figure 11 Trading program schedule.

daily, whereas others can be worked with weekly. Figure 11 is a typical schedule for one who has a full time job, other than the market.

It is also advisable to make a new schedule sheet for each week. By doing this you can check off each activity as it is completed, which will provide you with the necessary feedback concerning your progress.

HOW MUCH TIME IS BEST?

It has been my experience that too much time spent on the market can be just as destructive as too little time. Ideally the market should not require more than an hour on a daily basis, and even this may be too much. Each trading system has its own time requirement. Ideally I recommend no more than 50 percent of your daily allocated time be spent on actual market study and analysis. The remainder should be devoted to analysis of results, self-evaluation, and such things as a five-year plan. As your schedule becomes more firm, you gain experience with it and you will become more capable of assigning each activity its proper amount of time.

If you have scheduled some of the behavior change programs outlined elsewhere in this book, then you will need to devote more time daily. It is also best to spend about twice as much time over the weekend preparing yourself for the coming week. Generally you should find that two hours over the weekend is more than enough to prepare your trading for the coming week.

FOLLOW YOUR SCHEDULE RELIGIOUSLY

If you truly want to get results, then it will be necessary to follow your schedule closely. In fact, I suggest you place your daily schedule above all else until it has become part of you. To acquire the discipline necessary for successful trading it is absolutely necessary to schedule your time appropriately. Shaping the necessary discipline your schedule requires must be the single most important thing you do each day. Without it you will most likely find it impossible to achieve the kind of trading results you may truly want.

BE FLEXIBLE BUT FIRM

The key to developing positive feelings about your schedule is an appropriate combination of flexibility and firmness. If you maintain a negative attitude toward your schedule, consider it boring or hard work, then you will not make it work. Very often flexibility in scheduling will help in the creation of positive affect toward your schedule. If portions of your daily routine are redundant, extremely boring, or otherwise nonproductive, eliminate them and replace them with free time or a more important activity. You may find it more enjoyable to make frequent daily (or weekly) routine changes. Some individuals work better when schedules change from time to time, whereas others work best on a fixed and firm schedule. You must discover which pleases you most since this will bring the best results.

PRIORITIES, NECESSITIES, FREE TIME

What should ideally be included in your schedule? To a certain extent this is an individual matter. There are, however, some very specific goals I recommend every trader and/or investor cover on a regular basis.

1. Market preparation. If you're a market technician, then you must do work on a regular basis. I prefer to do such work daily. Some investors will find that once a week is sufficient, particularly if their trading or investing decisions are not short term. If you are a fundamentalist, then you will want to study the relevant statistics or read the necessary reports frequently. Preparation is the single most important aspect of any total trading system. The most consistent and concerted effort must be applied here. Scheduling this activity should always be foremost in your mind. If you will recall my previous mention of market symptoms and negative attitudes you will remember that failure to keep up with one's market work will quickly lead to losses. You have most likely found that many big moves begin when you have fallen behind in your work. Once your attitude changes and you update the missing material you will say to yourself, "I never would have missed that move if my charts were up to date." This is precisely what your schedule will help avoid. I strongly recommend you have a set time of the day or week, and a specified length of time for such market work. Even if you choose not to set aside time for any other activity, make certain that you have a set time for your market analysis. I cannot emphasize this point to its fullest importance. Most market-related problems have an immediate and negative effect on market studies.

2. Trading decisions. Most investors make their trading decisions as they are updating their charts or doing technical work. I *do not recommend* you use this procedure. Rather, I advise you to make decisions *after* all technical and/or fundamental work has been updated. This necessitates scheduling a time slot for decision making. I recommend this separate time slot because of the importance of the decision-making process. Typically a trader's mind will be cluttered with information and data on all markets when he or she is updating work. This tends to interfere with effective and rational decision making. It is possible to be more objective when making decisions after all market studies are complete. Each market then can be viewed in its totality without competing input from your other work. Decisions should always be made in an unhurried and detached way. I have found that having a special time slot for this process makes the results more reliable.

3. Record keeping. Equally important is the record-keeping system discussed previously. You must schedule time for this. I believe that a daily review is best for active traders. I would not advise anything less than a weekly review, even for conservative investors. You must know *at all times* where your investments and performance stand. If you have skipped over the section on record keeping, please read it immediately.

4. Behavioral programs. If you have implemented any of the programs detailed in previous chapters, then allow time for their application.

5. Long range goals. Previously I mentioned the importance of having a long-term financial plan. Time should also be set aside for the formulation and specification of objectives and expectations. It helps considerably to have an established time for working on your five-year plan. When doing so it is best to put in writing your most ambitious goals, compare previous targets with actual progress, and arrive at an understanding of how promptly you are moving toward these objectives. This all takes time.

Each individual must schedule activities most suitable to his or her trading and lifestyle. For the novice investor or trader such a schedule can mean the difference between getting started on the right track or falling into a losing rut early in the game. Unless you are ready to make the necessary commitment in the form of a schedule, you are not likely to find success in the marketplace. Any attempt to profit using a disorganized, undisciplined approach is doomed to failure from the very start.

REVIEW

1. To successfully approach the markets a structured and disciplined program is necessary.
2. Several benefits can accrue from the use of a schedule.
3. Begin constructing your schedule by listing the targets or goals toward which you wish to work.
4. Schedule each activity in a specific time slot.
5. There are a number of market related goals that should be included in every schedule.

11 Trading with The Market Trend —Why It's So Difficult to Do

Experience teaches that following market trends is perhaps the single most profitable trading tool, regardless of the underlying system you are using. Stocks and commodities tend to move in long-term trends. Frequently these trends will last several years. Those who are capable of selecting investments at the start of a trend will show profits of as much as several hundred percent (if not more). Should they be fortunate enough to exit their positions at the top of the trend, or at the start of a change in trend, they will show even greater gains. Those who speculate and those who trade mainly for the short term can also benefit from knowledge and use of trends. During a given market direction, most short-term profits will be made from trading with the trend. This basic law of market behavior is underscored in the works of all market "masters" and is perhaps most simply expressed in *Reminiscences of a Stock Operator:*

> I began to realize that the big money must necessarily be in the big swing. Whatever might seem to give a big swing its initial impulse, the fact is that its continuance is not the result of manipulations by pools or artifice by financiers, but depends upon basic conditions. And no

matter who opposes it, the swing must inevitably run as far and as fast and as long as the impelling forces determine. (Lefevre, 1965, p. 88)

The value of market trend in profitable investing and trading is also recognized by fundamental and technical traders. The investor and market analyst inclined toward the use of fundamentals studies such major indicators as earnings, crop conditions, long-term debt, trends in export business, and the like, in order to determine what the long-term price move will be in response to these conditions. The technician who reads chart patterns and looks for such things as "breakouts" or "head and shoulders bottoms" does so in order to determine change in trend. Cycle analysts study economic trends and repetitive patterns in order to isolate the time frame within which trend changes might occur. Moving average systems are time based and attempt to signal trend changes. All in all, most trading systems, whether fundamentally oriented or technically based, have as their goal the isolation of specific patterns, which have profit potential. Speculators and "scalpers" who trade for the short term are also interested in determining trend. Their work is "fine tuned" and focuses on picking out trends within the shorter term. There are those individuals who trade on overreactions within the given trend. As a result they too must be aware of trend in order to know when there has been such an overreaction.

Despite all the talk about trend, despite all the moving averages, cycles, long-term patterns, signals, trend reversals, key reversals, earnings reports, and market indicators, trading with the trend is perhaps the most difficult thing for an investor to do. Were it not such a formidable task, there would be many wealthier investors and you would most likely not be reading this book. With tongue in cheek I quote Lefevre once again to illustrate how deceptively simple is the concept of trend:

Obviously the thing to do was to be bullish in a bull market and bearish in a bear market. Sounds silly, doesn't it? . . . It took me a long time to grasp that general principle firmly before I saw that to put it into practice really meant to anticipate probabilities. (1965, p. 88)

Certainly there must be a limiting factor that makes it difficult to implement trend in the profit-making formula. It is my opinion that psychological factors, in and of themselves, are the culprit. 'Tis the nature of the human beast. And even more frustrating is the fact that trends are so simple to isolate.

What is a trend? Simply stated, a trend is movement in a given direction which remains relatively fixed over an extended period of time. Figure 12*a* illustrates the relatively long-term nature of market trends in the corn market. This pattern is no less true in stocks. It is possible to isolate a given trend as I have done in Figure 12*a;* remove a portion of that trend, examine it more closely as in Figure 12*b;* study the trend within the trends, remove a portion of this trend as I have done in Figure 12*c;* study the trends, and so on, until we have moved down to the shortest trend index, tick by tick trades.

As you can well observe, the directional tendency of the market is certainly real. Price movement is *not* a directionless, up-and-down motion as typified by the oscillations of a random number generator. There are specific, lasting, directional patterns. Studying these patterns, or trends, allows an investor to buy low and sell high. The great majority of trading techniques and market analytical tools seek to accomplish one of two ends: they attempt to determine the underlying trend or they seek to determine when the trend will change. There are all types, breeds, combinations, half-breeds, indices, techniques and tools for doing this. One of the most successful investors I ever met stated bluntly, "I never use any of that garbage. All I do is look at a price chart. If the price is higher than it was four weeks ago, and if the price is higher than it was four months ago, the trend is up. I then buy stocks when there has been some bad news and prices decline due to public selling. Every now and then I buy close to the top. But there are so very few major tops and bottoms that I'm rarely wrong." And he was right!

Given the fact that determination of trend is a relatively simple task, what makes it so difficult to translate trend into profits? This is best illustrated with a chart and accompanying commentary. Figure 13 is a typical daily bar chart of the corn market. In reality it makes little difference whether we trade soybeans, IBM, or XYZ Corp. Trader reactions and responses are always the same. Most traders would rather be buyers than short sellers. I

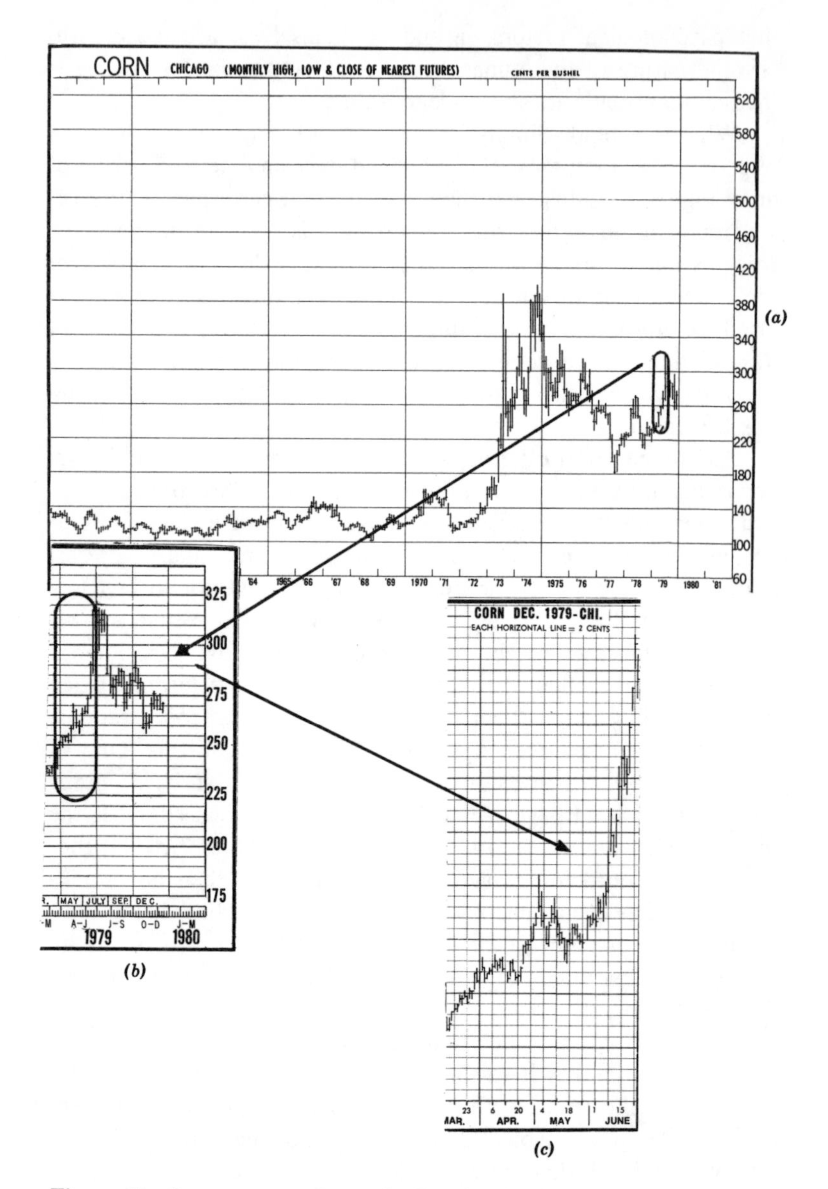

Figure 12 Long-term corn trend. (Reprinted with permission of Commodity Chart Service.)

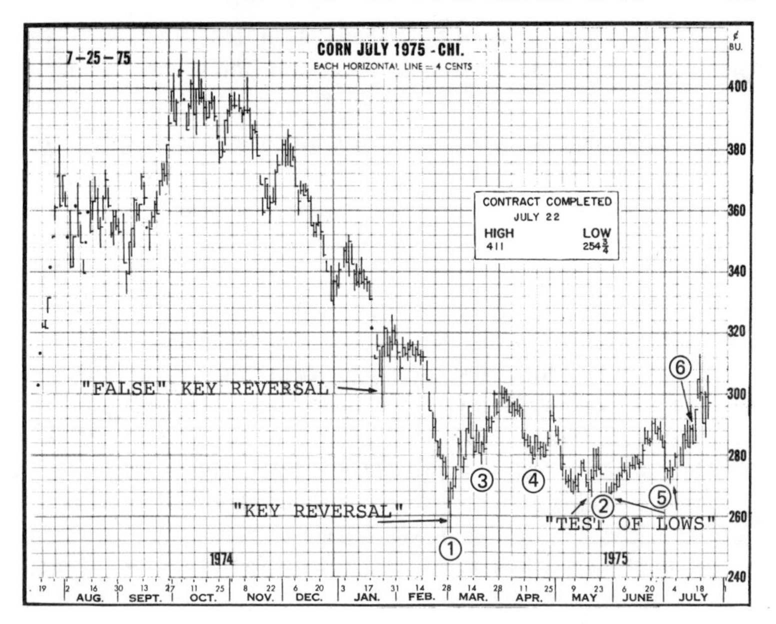

Figure 13 Daily corn futures chart. (Reprinted with permission of Commodity Chart Service.)

will discuss the reasons for this tendency in a later chapter. Let's assume that the typical investor is watching prices as they decline. He is loath to sell short, or simply afraid to do so. He waits for prices to "bottom out." Assume also that he is awaiting a specific signal. In this case he is looking for a "key reversal," a day during which prices trade outside their previous day's high and low, ending higher on the day, after a rather extended move down. It is a very specific signal seen by many traders and investors as a "key" indicator. This reversal is marked on the chart. Technically the investor or trader who is true to his or her system has no choice but to buy (you will recall the earlier discussion on the use of trading signals and systems). The big day arrives. The signal has come. Here is a list of responses most traders make to the situation:

1. "Let's wait for some more confirmation of the reversal."

2. "True, we had the reversal, but volume wasn't high enough. Let's wait."

3. "If this was indeed a true reversal in trend, then we've got plenty of time to get in because trends run for a long period of time."

4. "The decline was so severe that I'm afraid to get in. I'd rather wait a few days to make sure the trend has changed."

5. "If I get in now I might get stopped out on a 'test' of the low."

This is characteristic of investor reasoning at major market turns. They are afraid to implement their initial trend change signals since they fear a loss. They somehow believe on an unconscious level that it is possible to trade without losses. They fail to realize that losses are a necessary part of profitable trading–that mistakes are part of the game. This unrealistic attitude comes from id impulses. It is a childish fantasy which relates almost directly to the fear of castration. If Freud was indeed correct about castration anxiety and fear of loss as a response to self-assertion or parental opposition, then you can see how it might be carried unconsciously through adulthood.

Despite the fact that some very specific signals accompany major tops and bottoms, there are few traders and investors who have the emotional prerequisites to implement these signals when they arrive. Many hours are spent patiently watching and waiting, and when the big moment comes it quickly passes and no action is taken. The reasons for such behavior (or lack of behavior) are generally as follows:

1. Unrealistic fear of losses.
2. Lack of self-confidence and positive attitude.
3. Inability to act as a result of negative learning.
4. Lack of appropriate learning with trading system.
5. Acceptance of inputs from contrary sources.

Those who cannot act on major signals (and this applies to most investors) generally have some specific psychological difficulties, which also appear in other areas of their lives. The profile of such individuals is, in my opinion, as follows:

1. Very dominant father, fond of physically punishing the child.

2. Parentally created feelings of dependency that did not permit child to make his or her own decisions.

3. Punitive spouse who is verbally abusive when errors are made.

4. Lack of self-confidence due to negative childhood experiences.

Inability to act on major signals is common. And yet it is very possible to make consistent profits despite such shortcomings if one can make the necessary changes before too much damage has been done. This is, however, an equally difficult task for most of us. Let's assume that our major trend change signal was missed. In most cases the market tends to "test" the bottom or top once a signal has come. The usual responses to this test, indicated by the number 2 on our chart, are the following:

1. "Let's wait a little longer to see if we can get in cheaper."

2. "The price has come back too far and the low will probably be broken."

3. "Let's wait until it penetrates its recent high (or low) to be sure that the test was passed."

Now that the second opportunity has come and gone without action, investors use a number of defense mechanisms to protect themselves from reality. They usually rationalize or intellectualize the situation by saying, "Now that we know what the trend is we'll buy into a reaction." They wait for the reaction, which never comes, is never large enough, is never fast enough, is never good enough, or is never reliable enough. Frustration sets in and market errors increase, despite the fact that they know very clearly what the trend is, what the signals are, and what they should do.

One of the most common rationalizations is "we'll buy into a reaction within the uptrend." It's an easy thing to say, but a very difficult thing to do. We, as human beings, take pride in our emotional control. But when the situation is serious, requiring immediate and decisive action, there are hundreds of possible excuses, perhaps millions, which are used to delay action, avoid action, or otherwise sidestep the issue. It is very difficult, psychologically, to buy into a reaction since they are ordinarily quite violent, come on bad news, and are not popular trades. When the reaction we have been waiting for actually arrives it will usually look as if the trend is changing. Brokers and services will be bearish. Overall opinion will be negative, the news background will be bearish, and frequently our response will not be what it should. These outside influences can and do make it virtually impossible for the average trader to buy on weakness. And one who does is likely to become highly anxious, selling out the position prematurely. The psychological reasons for such behavior relate primarily to the factors discussed earlier.

Richard Russell, a veteran in the stock advisory business, is just one of the many market professionals who recognize the limitations of human ability at major turns in the market. In preparing for a change in the market trend he wrote the following words of advice to his market newsletter subscribers:

> So, I'm telling subscribers now to steel themselves, to prepare themselves for the possibility of a major bottom somewhere ahead as identified by this indicator . . . it's going to 'feel' very hard to buy. . . . Every fiber in your system is going to be telling you that Stocks and Wall Street are finished. At that time you are going to have to go against your emotions. But that will be the ideal time to buy. So start getting yourself ready—emotionally. (Letter #779 Dow Theory Letters)

At any given point in the market trend, there will and can be countless excuses, intellectualizations, and rationalizations for not taking action. None is valid and none brings success. Regardless of the cause for non-action, the result of such behavior rarely is profitable and more often than not is frustrating. It is, in fact, more potentially dangerous to *not* act than it is *to* act. To not act will usually bring frustration. Frustration will lead to poor judgment, lack of patience, and a concomitant increase in market blunders.

Back to our market example. Assume that the opportunity to buy was missed at points 1 and 2. Assume also that none of the small reactions (3, 4, and 5) was used to establish a position.

Now comes the next, and perhaps greatest blunder. The frustrated trader will rationalize and say to himself, "I'll wait for the next upside breakout. That way I'll be certain to buy with the trend." Comes the breakout (6) and the trader is more paralyzed by fear than ever before. "Prices are too high," he reasons. "Now that the breakout has come and I know it's real I'll wait for a pullback to the breakout area and buy in." Sometimes this works. Most of the time it does not. Again the typical investor or trader has failed miserably. By now he is very upset, lacks self-conviction, believes that he is a born loser, has a negative attitude, is frustrated, abandons what's left of his trading system, refuses to watch the market, and begins to hate himself. Ordinarily frustration will be greatest when the market is close to a bottom or in its last up leg. When prices begin to run away the public reasons that the trend has much longer to run, "throws in the towel," and buys. The actual top is usually seen within several days, very often the same day. This is why public bullish consensus is typically at its high when the market is at its top. This is why there are few bulls to be found at major bottoms. Moreover, this is why most traders ignore the top signals when they appear. At such critical times there is nothing left of self-discipline and there is no system. There is nothing but denial, hope, fear, and frustration. The losing position will frequently be held. Often it will be held until the next major bottom where frustration is again at its greatest.

And that's the usual sequence of events. If this sounds familiar to you, or if you can identify with even one or two of the blunders in this chain, then you need help. If you suffer from one or more of these symptoms, then you know the losses they bring. The sooner you change, the better off you will be. Perhaps you will not go broke before help can be obtained. It is a simple matter for me to tell you that discipline is the answer to your woes. I could tell you to go back and read the previous chapters on behavioral change. Aside from the many suggestions I have given previously, I will provide you with an additional list in the traditional orientation.

1. **Get in touch with your underlying motivation.** By this I mean plain and simple soul-searching. List the goals you have set

for yourself. Attempt to understand exactly what it is you are trying to achieve through investing. Perhaps you do not have sufficiently specific goals. If you do not know where you are going, then it will be difficult for you to get there. You must detail your direction, determine whether it is realistic, determine if it can be accomplished best through investing, and measure the commitment you feel toward that goal. In so doing it will be necessary to be as completely honest with yourself as possible. There are many who invest simply to impress others or to assert their sexuality.

2. Attempt to recall any serious conflicts with your parents. Many internalized attitudes, fears, avoidance responses, and misperceptions come from early childhood. After all, much learning takes place on both a conscious and unconscious level during these years. If you are not aware of how parental treatment may have affected you, then you do not understand enough about your underlying motivation and attitudes.

3. Determine how your marital relationship may be affecting your decision-making ability. (If you are unmarried, examine your relationship with members of the opposite sex to see if they are somehow affecting your outlook and actions.) Very often the married male investor with children will be operating under the weight of heavy responsibility, which may paralyze him. Too frequently we fear negative responses from a spouse. In many cases there is a lack of common purpose between husband and wife. Shared investment goals will be of immeasurable help in making decisions.

4. Attempt to discipline yourself by following a predetermined set of trading rules as described previously. Should you find it impossible to implement your rules, I recommend that you explore other areas of your life to determine if they are also characterized by a lack of organization and discipline.

5. Recall and relive any traumatic experiences that may be limiting your ability. Very often traumas during early childhood or elementary school days will have an unconscious effect during adult life. If and when you can remember these experiences it would be wise to "relive" them in your current nonthreatening environment. This type of reeducation, or abreaction, as it is called, frequently releases pent-up emotion which can negatively affect market performance.

6. Have a total plan of attack from initiation of investment or trade to completion. Know precisely what it is you wish to achieve, how you intend to do so, what the expected results are, what problems may be anticipated, and how long it may take.

7. Get help from others. It is frequently helpful to work with others. They can point out your shortcomings, and you can help them recognize their limitations. Many investment clubs are successful because of group input and the collective decision-making process. This can be a good place to learn the necessary discipline.

REVIEW

1. The most effective way to make profits in the market is by trading with the trend.
2. Isolating market trends is not a difficult thing to do.
3. Most traders and investors lose money despite the fact that trends and market reversals are relatively simple to spot.
4. Emotional factors are the limiting influences in trend trading. There are many reasons for not following trend signals.
5. It is possible to trade with the trend only a small portion of the time and still make fairly consistent and large profits.
6. In order to remediate lack of trend trading ability a number of suggestions can be implemented. They are designed to overcome the psychological inability to follow trends.

Advisory Services and Their Roles 12

The problem with most advisory letters lies not in their service but rather with their readership. In earlier chapters I discussed the importance of maintaining and adhering to a well-planned and thorough trading system. I cannot overemphasize the importance of such consistency. In the same way that an individual can misuse or abuse the advice of a broker, he can also inappropriately employ the advice of a market service. As the publisher of a commodity market service I am well aware of the strengths, weaknesses, assets, and liabilities that come with your subscription to a market letter. I am also uniquely aware of the many ways in which individuals attempt to pervert the recommendations of their advisors. A well-established market service that has a documented and profitable trading record can be valuable to many speculators. Experience has taught me, however, that no matter how profitable recommendations made by a service may be, there are few who truly benefit to the fullest extent. In fact, there are some individuals who actually lose money following the recommendations of a profitable advisory service. How is this possible? As you have already concluded (most likely from personal experience) the *trader* who employs (or misemploys) advice is totally responsible for the results or lack thereof.

Before detailing some common difficulties encountered by individuals in their use of advisory services, one must decide whether an advisory service should be used at all. For a majority of traders the use of an advisory service can be extremely helpful. Most speculators and investors have full-time jobs outside of the market and cannot keep up to date on their investment strategy. A service oriented to one's trading philosophy and/or technique can bring many benefits, but for the individual who is totally immersed in his or her own analytical technique, a service, other than one which provides raw data, charts, and/or fundamental information, is not necessary and can, in fact, be detrimental. To use or not use an advisory service must be an individual decision made exclusively on the basis of one's ability to keep current. Although it is not necessary to follow the market on a tick by tick basis, there are many investors and speculators who are too busy even to devote a few hours consistently over a weekend. In such cases I would recommend an advisory service.

In subscribing to any type of service, the trader must be aware of its assets, liabilities, limitations, and potential within his particular market orientation. Even though a service may have an admirable track record, not all individuals will find it possible to benefit. Once again, the inconsistent and undisciplined approach employed by many speculators is at fault. For the individual who has not mastered even the most basic aspects of self-control, an advisory service would be useless. In most cases such individuals will subscribe to as many services as they can possibly find. The result, to be sure, will be a totally confused trader who is overloaded with recommendations, conflicting opinions, and analyses. It is therefore most advisable to use a market service if and only if one has the necessary self-control to evaluate the many inputs. Only thus can benefits be derived. But opinions are not as important as the factors that will help you determine whether you should use a service. Before doing so, two types of service–informational and advisory–should be differentiated. Informational services provide charts, raw data, moving averages, and fundamental information. They do not make recommendations per se. Their main function is to provide the trader with information that can be used to make trading decisions. Advisory services, on the other hand, are concerned primarily with making recommendations on given stocks and/or commodities. Although they may also provide some informational material, their key function is to make specific trading suggestions.

There is no danger in using informational services. They can be very helpful to those who are too busy to keep their own charts, gather their own data, or keep on top of fundamental developments. The trader who employs such services will most certainly save considerable time and effort. He will not, however, benefit from the learning that comes with gathering information on his own. There is much to be said in favor of doing your own work. Close contact with the data will give you market "sense" which cannot be obtained by working with information prepared by another. In previous chapters I underscored the importance of learning. It is the learning that comes with doing one's own work that is very valuable to most traders. One should seriously evaluate these factors before subscribing. The amount of direct experience to be gained from keeping one's own market data is as important as on-the-job training in most other professions. When learning to drive an automobile, for example, classroom instruction can be beneficial up to a certain point, but only actual "hands on" training can complete the educational process. Learning to trade the market by working from charts and data supplied by an outside source is, to my way of thinking, as absurd as having someone else learn how to drive for you. Once you have learned the decision-making process you can pass the work on to someone else. If you subscribe to a chart service which is sent out weekly, you may find it difficult and time consuming to reenter your notes and drawings on each chart weekly. The work you did on your chart last week will not be on the published chart. You will therefore have to spend time rewriting your notes, redrawing trend lines, cycles, and so on. This is perhaps the most significant drawback to the use of informational services.

In summary, there is perhaps only one major objection of psychological importance that should be considered before taking an informational market service. If you have established yourself in terms of market basics and feel that you no longer require hands on experience in acquiring and implementing market information, then you may wish to subscribe. If you find, after several months' use, that the service is truly helping, then by all means continue. But if you notice that your feel for the market or overview of trends is suffering, then it would be best to do the work on your own.

The use of an advisory service—one that makes specific recommendations—is an entirely different matter. In this case a number of variables must be given lengthy and more serious consideration. Those who can successfully use such services tend to be those who have the self-discipline necessary to do so. If you are lacking in self-control, then no amount of advice from others will help. The reason behind the success of most services is their rigid approach. Typically they make recommendations, give specific objectives, stops, follow-up procedures, evaluation of risk, and liquidation orders. In other words, they adhere to a time-tested and successful method of trading. The information they provide then falls into the hands of the weak link in the chain—the trader. Before taking an advisory service you must decide whether you can follow through on their recommendations thoroughly, honestly, and for an extended period of time.

Another issue of major concern is whether the recommendations made by one's service will influence decisions that may have been made as a result of one's own research. There is an inherent danger in either reading about or soliciting others' opinions of the market. I have found that the degree of trader confusion is directly proportional to the number of advisory services an investor reads. At any given time each of ten services may have a different idea about a given stock or commodity. Some will advise holding, others buying, and still others liquidating. The total number of recommended trades may be large, much greater than the typical investor's budget will permit. Hence the average trader is faced with a very difficult decision. Typically the tendency is to make several trades from each service, or to make the trade that most agree would be best. More often than not this results in losses. Again, the culprit called consistency rears its ugly head. Any attempt to use only several of the recommendations made by a given service will not do justice to the trading system employed by that service. The result of such incomplete trading will be a dissatisfied investor who becomes frustrated. There is a tendency among investors, indeed there is a propensity among all human beings, to view only parts of a situation, excluding the whole. You must remember that performance records are based on long-term results. Typically the track records advertised by successful services have taken years to accumulate. They are based on following all recommendations precisely and to the letter. Most investors cannot muster the necessary discipline which brings such success.

In summary, then, there are two specific objections to the use of an advisory service:

1. An advisory service that makes specific recommendations must be religiously adhered to over an extended period of time for success to follow.

2. An individual investor who does his or her own research may be influenced to abandon original work in favor of a so-called expert opinion.

Generally I find that those individuals who have self-control, discipline, and an awareness of how to trade thoroughly and consistently will benefit considerably. If an individual is lacking in these qualities, he or she will not benefit from the use of a market service, no matter how well it may have done in the past. The focus, as it has been in previous chapters, is clearly on the investor, who alone is responsible for the success or failure of a market service. How can one overcome some of the associated liabilities in order to effectively use advisory information? The following list of suggestions may help:

1. Make certain that the service you employ gives specific recommendations as to buy or sell, stop losses, objectives, entry and exit prices.

2. Your service should not be of the variety that makes too many recommendations each week. It will be difficult to pick and choose. The total number of open positions should be within the constraints of your financial ability.

3. Make every trade recommended using the exact stops, objectives, and so on.

4. Do not attempt to use a service to validate or negate your own signals. Trade your own signals in a separate account. If you use a service that makes recommendations, then you must follow them rather than use them as a verification of your own work.

5. Avoid subscribing to too many services. Two or three are sufficient. The more market advice you get, the less useful it will be.

6. If you have difficulty with self-discipline, then you might be best off avoiding a market service until you have overcome your own limitations.

7. Several friends working with one advisory service can succeed if each keeps an eye on the others. Hence all the recommended trades have a higher likelihood of being followed exactly as specified.

8. Before subscribing to any type of market service you would do well to plan the precise fashion in which you will implement it. Unless there is a well-devised plan and a clear need, you would do best to avoid any input other than your own. If there is a market advisor whose word you respect, then demonstrate your respect by following his recommended trades exactly, even if you need to open a separate account to do so.

REVIEW

1. The use of advisory and informational market services is common among those investors who do not have the time to do their own market studies.
2. Such services can be either a help or a hindrance.
3. Charting-type services can save you time, but you will not benefit from the learning that comes with doing your own work.
4. Advisory services, if they are to be used, must be employed consistently, as one would apply any trading system. Lack of thorough use or the use of too many services will lead to losses.
5. Suggested guidelines for the appropriate use of a service are listed.
6. The *trader* or *investor* is the key variable in profitable use of a service.

Is This You? 13

"Here goes another losing trade!"

"I'll do my charts tomorrow."

"Let's not follow that buy signal . . . we'll only get stopped out again."

"I'm too much of a loser to make money consistently."

"I hope the market closes soon."

"My trading signals haven't been working, I think I'll just trade on gut feel."

"Let's spread up that position before it turns into another loss."

"I can't make money in the market anymore."

"I'll just close out the account now before there's nothing left."

"I must be having an unlucky streak."

"It must be time for a new trading system."

"It's that damn broker's fault . . . every time I have a good position he talks me out of it."

"I should have had my stops in like I was supposed to."

"I can't do anything right."

"Every trade I make turns into a loss as soon as I touch it."

If you have found yourself making any of these statements, or perhaps if you are saying any of them to yourself right now, then you're in the wrong place emotionally. Certainly you cannot always maintain a positive attitude, but this does not mean that your situation should be exacerbated by negative self-statements and attitudes. In order to change one's emotional status there are several steps that must be taken. The current trend in medicine and psychiatry is preventive rather than responsive. It is infinitely more effective to prevent the onset of a disease than it is to respond to the disease after it has become entrenched. The same reasoning holds true for behavioral problems.

If you develop a negative attitude, then your trading will invariably suffer. You will start to misread signals, read prices incorrectly, place orders incorrectly, and possibly make trades based on nothing but emotion. As I indicated earlier, this behavior will earn most traders nothing but losses. The ability to recognize the onset of negative attitudes is a skill all traders should develop in their efforts to practice preventive mental health. A losing streak in the markets can be made either better or worse by attitude. Let's take a look at the first step that must be taken: *recognition.*

Many symptoms will allow you to recognize the onset of a losing or negative attitude. The time to begin your surveillance of attitudes is during a period of successive losses either in the market or in your personal life. Few traders realize the fact that personal life can affect market life and vice versa. All too often we believe that if the market is going well, then all is right with the world. This is a fallacious assumption and you must abandon it entirely. Life is a total experience and influences from all areas will spill over and affect each other. If you have experienced any setback whatsoever–personal, financial, familial, educational–you are a target for negative attitude. Knowing that you are susceptible should put you on guard. The most effective way to signal the possible onset of negative attitudes is to keep a checklist. This will be covered in our review later on.

In addition, there are several behavioral correlates that can assist in the recognition process. First and foremost is a lack of willingness to keep charts, data, or other technical work up to date. You will find your market studies boring, possibly anxiety-provoking, and your level of motivation to keep current will diminish considerably. You may find yourself oversleeping in the morning, late for work, and leaving work early. You will have a "so what" attitude. These will be among the very first indicators of trouble. It is during times such as these that profitable trades will be missed. And it is during times such as these that many other traders will have similar attitudes. One day you will awaken to find that big moves have passed you by. You will look at the charts or the fundamentals and you'll say, "That was a perfect signal . . . where was I when that happened?" This will frustrate you even more, thus triggering a series of additional errors.

Another indicator of impending disaster is the negative self-statement. After the proper predisposing conditions (discussed earlier) you may begin to tell yourself and others things that clearly signal danger. Here are some examples.

> "Well, there goes another losing trade."
>
> "I can't do anything right."
>
> "There's no use even making the trade because we'll take a loss anyway."
>
> "I feel like quitting the market."

There are hundreds, perhaps thousands, of other statements that fall into the same category. They are among the key indicators of major trouble! Remember also that each individual will have his or her own response pattern. Let me tell you a few details about how I develop negative attitudes and what signals onset in my case.

It takes only four consecutive losses for the process to start. Missing a big move may be the precipitating factor. Every now and then a traffic ticket can set me off. My immediate response will be to miss my daily chart updating. Typically I will leave the office early. Another correlate is consumption of "junk food"—this is the "junk food indicator." The "junk food attack" happens on the same day that my charts are left undone. And on that same day that I leave the office early. It is not unusual for these symptoms to last several days.

The next telltale sign comes within a matter of days. I begin to talk about myself in negative terms. Losses become a part of everyday life, and I accept them as if I knew they were coming. Every stop has my name on it and I begin to talk to my brokers in a way that clearly reveals my losing frame of mind. This sequence of events may sound a bit amusing to you. But it happens to be true, and it is also very typical. I stress the point that each individual has his or her own response pattern. In many cases, the trigger is always the same. Become aware of your unique indicator! The more clearly you can define the sequence of events, the more promptly you will spot them. And speed is of the essence. You must think of it as an emotional first aid kit. Each time you fall into the pattern keep a record of what was said and done.

Not all individuals will react the same way every time. There are those who have well-developed defenses that will prevent them from recognizing the onset of trouble through the indicators mentioned above. In such cases, friends, brokers, and family members *can help*. In fact, we can always get help from others, since they tend to notice peculiarities earlier than we do. No individual should think that he or she is strong enough to make it alone. Go to those around you, particularly a spouse or loved one, and tell them to let you know when they see changes. Brokers who are in close touch with you can be extremely helpful. Remember that there is no limit to the self-deceptive ability of the human mind. This is a throwback to defense mechanisms developed in early childhood. We will avoid, repress, suppress, intellectualize, sublimate, and even fantasize problems out of consciousness. As I have told you many times (and will tell you many more times), our greatest enemy in the market is us.

Now that you have some specific information on how to recognize the onset of a destructive attitude, you must learn how it can be treated. First and foremost, the time to begin treatment is immediately if not sooner. There will be a tendency to avoid dealing with the problem even though it has been recognized. You will want to fight yourself every step of the way, and will do everything possible to make the job even more difficult than it is. This is the natural state of affairs for one who resides in a negative psychological environment. Believe me, I speak from experience both as therapist and patient. The essence of treatment is, in my opinion, brute force. There are many "romantic" things I could suggest. I could tell you to take a cold shower. Or I could say "get in touch with yourself, relax, say some prayers, free associate, be yourself," or any of the other meaningless things that we are told. But these do not work. A negative cycle feeds on itself and you must break into the chain. No matter which point you break into you must start somewhere.

What do I mean by "brute force"? Very simply, I mean that you must gather all of your effort and strength, force yourself to work on those charts, read those crop reports, make those trades, or calculate the signals. This is when you must spend the greatest amount of time working on your trading system. This is the time to respond in an opposite way from the manner in which you are inclined to act. The more you want to leave your office early, the more you must stay. The less you want to work on your charts, the more work you must do. This also applies to negative self-statements. The more inclined you feel to put yourself down, the more positive you should be. This is a very difficult thing to do. It is especially difficult the first time you do it. But it takes less and less effort each time you practice.

There are many other things you can do to help yourself. They all fall under "scheduling," which will be discussed later on. It will become clear to you after a number of such experiences that the harder you fight yourself, the more likely you are to succeed. Assuming that you are your own worst enemy, particularly when things go bad, you must learn not to trust your emotions. You must have a plan of attack available for immediate use in the event that the time comes for its implementation.

As indicated earlier, the most effective key to improvement is brute force. Another useful tool is the behavioral checklist. This method of keeping a positive mental attitude, elementary as it may sound, is extremely effective. I would recommend its use on a daily basis whether or not you are prone to develop negative attitudes. The checklist is such an important tool that an entire chapter is devoted to it.

REVIEW

1. Attitudes have a direct influence on trading results.
2. Negative attitudes can make a losing streak even worse and may, in fact, prevent effective trading by compounding the negativism.

3. Recognition of negative attitude onset is the first step toward a cure.
4. Action should be preventive in nature. This will inhibit improper mental attitude before it can start to affect trading.
5. The onset of such counterproductive attitudes can be recognized by closely observing the symptoms accompanying them.
6. Each individual has his or her own response pattern.
7. Come to know and recognize your unique pattern.
8. Treat the symptoms as soon as they occur. Do not procrastinate even one moment once you have realized the presence of onset symptoms.
9. Use the "brute force" technique to counteract negative impulses seeking to keep you from doing your market work.
10. Keep a behavioral checklist as discussed in a later chapter.
11. Obtain assistance from friends, loved ones, family and/or broker in spotting your attitudes if you cannot effectively do so on your own.

Positive Mental Attitude 14

The least frequently recognized but perhaps most effective technique for successful trading is the development of positive mental attitude (PMA). Many traders have experienced the losses that can come when they're "in a rut." This feeling is certainly not unique to investors. It is also common in athletes, executives, and politicians. For some seemingly mysterious reason or reasons, when PMA is high, everything appears to go well—profits increase, self-concept is positive, skies are blue. Conversely, when PMA is low, losses rise, more mistakes are made, and outlook for the future is poor. There are those who claim that PMA is a function of external events and not the cause of these events. But believers in self-determination, positive motivation, and PMA would clearly and totally disagree. Let's examine some of the aspects of PMA as they relate to trading and how they can improve your results.

During the Middle Ages, many peculiar behavioral cures were developed. In most cases, they were tortures designed to drive out "bad spirits." Their intent was to either force spirits out of the body or to give them an opening through which they might leave. It was reasoned that if the body was an uncomfortable place to inhabit, spirits would leave out of desperation and discomfort. If the patient survived "treatment," it often seemed to have a beneficial effect. In fact, even magical cures and spells cast by witches seemed to work well. In our age of technological and scientific sophistication we are inclined to make light of such methods. They are totally unscientific and they do not conform to the laws of physics as we know them. But the fact remains that they obtain results. By what manner do these mystical techniques obtain their cures? How does this relate to PMA? How does suggestion enter into the picture?

The essence of all magical cures is suggestion. And suggestion, albeit an age-old technique, is still not totally understood or accepted today. There are many different forms of suggestion. All can produce profound changes in behavior and attitude. Despite our seemingly advanced state of psychological knowledge, scientists still lack a thorough understanding of how suggestion and hypnotism operate. Positive mental attitude is, in a sense, what has been termed "autosuggestion." It is the individual, suggesting to himself that things will go well, that success will come, that his efforts will come to fruition, and that nothing can stand in his way. In so doing one sets the stage for success. In the early days of psychiatric treatment a popular cure based on autosuggestion was introduced by Dr. Emil Coué. The disturbed or troubled patient was to repeat to himself the following curative phrase: "Every day, in every way, I am getting better and better." Strange as it may seem to some, this technique actually achieved results. The reason behind its effectiveness rests in the power of suggestion.

It is my belief that positive mental attitude is a form of self-suggestion. But PMA is more than just a rote repetition of positive phrases; it is a way of life. The individual who practices PMA seeks out experiences that will provide the necessary rewards. Experiences that are negative are avoided, ignored, or eliminated. If we can view PMA in the context of behavioral learning, it will be much clearer. Essentially the individual who is oriented toward PMA is attempting to control both the stimulus and consequence events of his learning chain. He will not only disallow negative stimulation to enter into his life style, but he will also make certain that positive consequences follow positive experiences. Thus he will shape winning attitudes. The step-by-step process is, of course, more involved than I have indicated here.

In applying PMA we must remember that in its final state it does not function as a series of mechanical and forced steps, even though it may develop this way. It is not merely sufficient to say to one's self, "I will succeed. I am the greatest. I will have wealth and fame." A complete change of life style is necessary. Virtually every area of the individual's experience must be adapted to accommodate positive experiences. The growth of PMA will not be assured by the mere rote manifestation or assertion of will power. There must be an underlying base of positive, free imagination. There must be an internalization of positively directed will, imagination, and thought. E. Mounier comments on this concept in *The Character of Man:*

> Dr. Coué stated the rule that a forced effort of the will was always, without exception, less effective than free imagination. . . . If we wish to succeed in a difficult or dangerous action, it is often good to isolate ourselves (in this way), passively concerned with the thing to be done, rather than concentrating on it tensely: putting oneself in a state of attentive distraction. (1956, p. 154)

One can achieve the maximum benefit from will power and positive mental attitude only after they become internalized. They must become a way of life. Positive mental attitude is, in its totality, a winning way of life.

There have been many texts and courses purporting to teach positive mental attitude. Essentially, courses in PMA, self-improvement, success motivation, and dynamic salesmanship are sessions in group suggestion. Such courses, if reputable, can bring the individual investor many benefits. Unfortunately, most investors and traders are unaware of their generally negative mental attitudes. They cannot recognize the symptoms that characterize such losing self-perceptual sets. In order to change an unsatisfactory state of internal affairs it is necessary to spot the precedent conditions or symptoms of the attitude we wish to change. I recommend, a three-step process in the change from negative to positive mental attitude:

1. Recognition.
2. Initiation of change.
3. Internalization and maintenance.

A "crash course" cannot provide most traders with enough information to effect change.

RECOGNITION

Positive behavior and attitude changes rarely develop overnight. Typically they have a history of growth dating back many years. The smaller the change, the less time it has been in the formative stage. Those who are trained in the observation of human behavior can detect changes well in advance of their overt expression. And when they are recognized, a program of change can be instituted. The ability to isolate and recognize the early phases of attitude change in the investor is a highly specialized skill. It is an even more specialized achievement for one to recognize it in one's self. Many years of personal experience have resulted in my formulation of an "early warning" list. It is possible for one to exhibit any or all of the symptoms outlined in Table 7. They can occur in any order, and there are, most likely, a number of symptoms which I have not as yet discovered.

If, at any time, you begin to observe the symptoms listed in Table 7, it is an indication that all is not well. Naturally, the best time to begin the change process is the instant any one of the listed symptoms appears. Frequently we are not aware of onset and can-

Table 7 Early Symptoms of Negative Attitude

1. String of market losses.
2. Market studies not updated on schedule.
3. Unwillingness to trade the market or make investments.
4. Persistent misinterpretation of trading signals.
5. Increase in "tip" taking.
6. Increase in negative or self-critical statements.
7. Premature initiation or liquidation of positions contrary to signals.
8. Oversleeping; general physical malaise.
9. Frequent late arrival at work.
10. Feeling best described as "I can't wait until the market closes" (for those who trade daily).
11. Not wanting to know how much of a loss one is riding on an open position.
12. Loss of interest in the markets.

not observe symptoms due to the operation of repressive defense mechanisms (defined earlier). In such cases those close to us, such as family, friends, or broker, can alert us.

INITIATION OF CHANGE

In order to remediate a negative mental attitude, and subsequently develop it into a positive one, we must move on to the next step. This involves the initiation of procedures designed to change attitudes. Numerous techniques can be employed in the change process. I will outline a number of these methods below. Note that these are in relative sequential order. Certain steps should be instituted before others. The order indicated is what I recommend.

1. Any attempt to change should begin with a mechanical series of steps. Previously I mentioned "brute force" as a viable technique. I believe that you will find such methods valuable when first attempting to change a losing or negative behavior. What exactly do I mean by "brute force"? Simply, I mean persistence, effort, determination, and good old-fashioned hard work. This can be accomplished through the use of a schedule and a specific behavioral checklist, as discussed earlier. Step 1 will be covered later in greater detail.

2. Each specific symptom of negativism must be counteracted. This will require you to have a list of your precise behaviors, as well as a method of responding or treating each. The following are some examples:

a. A *string of losses,* which could easily bring with it negative attitudes, should be countered by reference to your track record. Assuming you have had a good success rate in the past, you should focus on the positive by referring to it in times of crisis. If you have a very poor or brief trading record, then do not refer to it since to do so would be a negative experience. In such cases use your hypothetical record. This is the record of results achieved by a pretest of your system.

b. *Falling behind in market work* can be best countered by use of a schedule.

c. *Negative self-statements* should be dealt with in two ways. First, find a way of signaling when you are about to make self-effacing remarks. This will help you stop such verbalizations. Second, solicit the positive comments of others.

3. Associate only with winners, positive people, and successful friends. We are not only known by the company we keep, but we also tend to behave as they do. If we allow ourselves to associate with those who have negative attitudes and experiences, then we will be weighted down by their mere presence. Since we cannot block out all incoming stimuli it is difficult to filter out the bad, allowing only the good, or productive, to enter. If we eliminate as much of the negative as we can, there will be no need to guard against it. And there will be a preponderance of positive input. Put yourself in positive situations.

4. Terminate negative relationships if you cannot repair them. Oftentimes the best way to repair a bad relationship is to end it. This is, to be sure, easier said than done. You will find, as I have, that doing so will also be helpful in other areas of your life.

5. Institute a systematic check and balance procedure for trading signals. This will help you doublecheck your work. In so doing you will remain close to your signals, thereby benefiting from the overall positive results. Review our previous discussion of scheduling if necessary.

6. Attempt to deal only with a broker who is positive. You'll be surprised how much of an effect brokers can have on your attitude (if you don't already know this). At the very minimum your broker should be neutral. It's difficult to stick to a trading plan. Negative comments from a broker don't help.

7. Set specific objectives and goals. In working toward them you will be moving in a positive direction. Keep goals in mind at all times. If goals are forgotten or overlooked negative thinking can become dominant.

8. Set ambitious objectives. Your goals should be attainable and realistic but ambitious as well. Don't allow yourself to settle for a small part of the pie. Attempt to set your goals above and beyond your ability but within reach. This will help your positive attitude by giving you a rewarding target for which to aim.

9. The "five-year plan" is a technique I use to maintain positive direction and attitude. Set yourself a month-by-month or year-by-year plan. Review your specific goals and progress monthly or semiannually. In determining your target be as specific as possible. State in precise terms how much money you plan to accumulate, where you will put it, and how you will use it to make more money. Set personal goals as well. Indicate how you plan to improve your trading, education, home life, and working relationships.

10. Keep a list of your trading rules and read them once weekly. I have found that this constant reminder will keep you on a positive track. When things appear to be heading in the negative direction you can help improve them by reading your list. This will remind you to be positive when the desire to fail is greatest. Ordinarily ten to fifteen brief trading rules are more than sufficient. These are discussed in a later chapter.

There are many other techniques and tools that will help initiate and internalize the process of change from negative to positive attitude. After you have had some experience in shaping such attitudes you will easily recognize those that work for you.

INTERNALIZATION

To maintain a consistently positive attitude toward yourself and others it is necessary to practice the foregoing procedures. Only after one has spent considerable time shaping PMA, using it, and profiting by it can it become an internal or automatic process. I therefore suggest you employ PMA in all areas of your life. Those individuals who do so tend to have successful relationships, marriages, businesses, and trading. As with most behaviors you must "use them or lose them." Organization and positive attitude work together to produce successful market results. In order to be as organized as possible the use of a schedule is highly recommended (see Chapter 10).

REVIEW

1. Positive mental attitude (PMA) can be instrumental in the success or failure of a trading system.
2. PMA is a form of self-suggestion.
3. In order to acquire positive attitudes it is necessary to follow a three-step process.
4. Recognition of negative attitudes is important. Common symptoms of negative attitudes are listed.
5. The change process must be initiated if you wish to develop PMA. There is a very specific technique for doing so.
6. Positive attitudes must be internalized. They must be used over and over again until they have become an inseparable part of the individual.
7. PMA must become a way of life in order for it to achieve its full results.

The Broker-Client Relationship 15

The relationship between client and broker can help maximize either profits or losses. More often than not, neither individual involved in this relationship is aware of the subtleties that transpire daily. Too frequently the client is likely to blame losses on the broker, and brokers tend to misread the needs of their clients. In most cases both parties, working together, can achieve results neither could accomplish alone. There are many directions the relationship can take. In the pages that follow I will attempt to achieve several results:

1. Define types of broker-client relationships.
2. Define ideal broker-client relationship.
3. Discuss ways in which improvement can be made.
4. Discuss additional aspects of broker-client interaction.

At the source of most broker-client difficulty is misunderstanding. All too often traders fail to be aware of the role, functions, limitations, assets, and liabilities of their broker. There is a tendency among traders to think of brokers as infallible, in the know, and always available. None of the foregoing is necessarily true. The insecure individual thinks of his or her broker as fully informed by virtue of physical proximity to the market. This is, to be sure, not an accurate picture at all. A broker who is close to the "action" may in fact be less accurate in trading recommendations than one who is removed from the market madness. Brokers are expected to serve a trader without error, while at the same time providing good advice, watching the market, listening to relevant news, keeping up to date on charts, and answering telephones. It is not possible to achieve such unrealistic goals.

In order to understand the relationship between broker and client let's take a look at what a broker's job should ideally consist of, and what a client's expectations and role should be. In my considered opinion every broker should be responsible for carrying out the following functions:

1. Take and execute all orders promptly and accurately.

2. Report back promptly and accurately on all order fills.

3. Keep client informed of news if client so desires.

4. Maintain and report account balances, margins, and other financial details.

5. Be available and on call each and every time client wishes to place an order.

6. Keep abreast of important changes in costs, commissions, margins, legal details, and the like, and inform client as necessary.

7. Obtain market information for client upon request.

These tasks in and of themselves are difficult to achieve, and a broker should not ideally be expected or required to do anything more. The self-reliant trader knows how valuable it is to have a broker who performs these duties thoroughly, promptly, and without error. Brokers are, however, in a peculiar position. The individuals they serve are frequently insecure, unsure of their trading, and unfamiliar with the market. Naturally they assume that the broker is in a position to know precisely what the market will do. This is perhaps the most common misunderstanding among clients. They do not realize that the broker wishes to please them by providing as much information as they feel they need. If asked to express opinions, the broker will comply.

There are many brokers who do good technical and fundamental work. Their opinions are certainly valid, and can result in profitable trades. But there are not too many brokers I have met, particularly in the commodities market, who can achieve all that is expected of them in the way of order filling while doing their market research as well.

The problem arises *not* from the advice and recommendations most brokers cannot help but give. It arises from the unwillingness of clients to follow the broker's advice to the letter, each and every time. Clients are prone to complain about brokers. As a result many brokers have become defendants in lawsuits or have been objects of censure by government agencies. All too often these actions are due *not* to any wrongdoing on the broker's part but to misunderstanding by clients and their unrealistic expectations. The broker is, after all, in the strange position of wanting his client to trade frequently, in order to generate commission. He does not want his client to "overtrade" since this not only looks bad but often "burns out" an account quickly. If there is a lack of trading, then there is a lack of commission. If there is a lack of commission, then the broker does not do well. Most brokers must maintain a delicate balance of recommendations to the client. If the broker makes recommendations to the client, then he must "hold the client's hand" as it were. In many respects the broker's job is much like the work of a supportive therapist. In recommending positions, yet in not having control over the account, he is open to considerable liability. Here is an example.

One friend to another, "My broker got me into some wheat today."

Second trader, "Think it'll work?"

"Don't know. He gets out of trades too early."

"What do you mean by 'too early'?"

"Well, sometimes he gets me out with a little bit of profit when I could have had a lot more."

"Why don't you let him get you in, and then you can get out on your own?"

"Not a bad idea, I think I'll do that from now on."

This is typical of what can happen to a broker's recommendation. In fact, this is how most good recommendations, whether from brokers, advisory services, or friends, get transformed into losing trades. As soon as an individual who is following the recommendations of his or her broker attempts to alter the trade in any way, the basics of using a trading system are violated. The results will be similar to those encountered by a trader who uses only some of the signals from his own trading system. In other words, the signals will not get an adequate or thorough test. This is where most broker-client relationships run into serious trouble. As you can see we are right back to the trader. If you will recall, I indicated much earlier that the *trader* was more important than any other aspect of the trading *situation*. Here again we see how full responsibility falls squarely on his shoulders. Another typical example of broker-client interaction will further illustrate the point:

"I think we should buy some December Cattle with a 200-point stop," says the broker to his client.

"What's the objective?" inquires the client.

"I'm looking for a 400-point profit potential. That's a two to one risk ratio," answers the broker.

"Well, OK, let's put on the trade, but let's do it now. Why wait until the price comes down? We might miss the opportunity."

"We can't do it now," explains the broker, "the price is too high and we'd expose ourselves to too much risk."

"I don't think we should wait. Let's do it now," orders the client with urgency in his voice.

"Please be patient," pleads the broker, "I don't want to jump the gun."

"Patience, shmacience," cries the customer, "what's a lousy 50 points, it's only 200 bucks!"

The broker reluctantly puts on the position. He suggests to the client that a stop loss be entered. "Stop loss," shouts the customer in surprise, "forget it! All they have to do is see my stop and they'll pick it. Don't put in a stop. You're close to the market. Just keep your eye on the trade and call me if we get near the danger point."

"That's not too good an idea," explains the broker. "I might be busy and not see the stop price get hit. And I might not be able to get in touch with you."

"Don't worry about it," the client assures him.

Time passes and the trade goes contrary to expectations. The broker calls his customer and explains the situation. After some agony the client refuses to close out the trade despite his broker's pleas. A very large loss is soon evident. But still the trade has not been closed out. The broker cannot do so without permission. The client has his head in the sand (or worse) and will not admit to the loss. The broker's hands are tied. In agony the client chides his broker, "You should have made me get out earlier!"

"But you wouldn't listen to me," explains the broker in his own defense.

"That's what you're there for," retorts his client. "You should have made me do it no matter what I said. You're just another crooked broker!"

That's how the story goes. Many is the broker who has been in similar situations almost daily. The essence here is *lack of control over the trader and all trades* but full responsibility for bad trades.

How can such a situation be rectified? The following suggestions can result in a much more productive outcome:

1. Ideally a broker should *not* be expected to fulfill any functions other than those shown earlier, unless he is the legally specified account manager.

2. If you decide to take a broker's trading advice, make certain you know his track record. Even though this cannot be verified, it will give you some indication of his accuracy.

3. If you decide to take a broker's trading suggestions, then take all of them. If you do not follow his recommendations fully, to completion of each trade, then you are not doing justice to him or to your account.

4. Never put your broker on the spot. If you vary from his recommendations, then do not hold him responsible for the result(s).

5. Never chide your broker for anything other than errors in order execution.

6. Never depend on your broker to trade for you unless you are prepared to hold him harmless from blame or responsibility.

7. Never demand advice from a broker unless you have made certain beforehand that he feels comfortable giving it.

8. Never ask a broker to rectify an error you made on your own.

9. Do not expect a broker to advise you if he has other work to do. You cannot be the only client in your broker's life.

10. Do not leave your broker "holding the bag." If he gets you into a trade, then let him get you out.

Some traders simply want their broker to be a "yes man." They put on trades, and to alleviate their own insecurity want a broker who will only agree with them. If they do not get the kind of support they want, they move on to the next broker. The value of a broker, for them, is not how well he or she executes orders, but rather how much support the broker can give. This type of "broker collector" will often have a number of accounts at different houses in order to get as much support as possible. Wherever he gets the support is where he will trade. If you are in this category, or if you are a broker who has this type of client, then I suggest caution. There is no *one* individual who can help your trade be right simply by agreeing with you. This problem must be dealt with behaviorally, according to the guidelines previously provided. If you are a broker, you can discourage such behavior by not pacifying any client.

THE BROKER-THERAPIST

Another type of broker-client relationship, similarly nonproductive and potentially hazardous, is the "broker-therapist" situation. In this case the customer expects consolation from his broker. When a trade goes bad he wants to be told that everything will turn out well. When a trade goes well, he worries that the profit will disappear and wants reassurance. His level of anxiety is very high. He calls about five times each hour to "get prices." But in reality he is calling for support and consolation. When a big loss is taken he complains bitterly and seeks advice as to how the money can be made back. All in all, this type of individual is not in need of a broker but rather in need of a therapist. We can look at the situation in Freudian terms in order to understand it better. You will recall the transference relationship between Freudian therapist and patient. This is one in which the patient looks upon the therapist as a parent substitute and seeks to resolve problems within the surrogate relationship. The therapist is seen as an authoritarian. The patient acts in compliance and defiance, and longstanding problems are worked out in this fashion. There are many correlates in the broker-client relationship. The client considers his broker as the authority. The subsequent "acting out" of problems and need for reassurance is pathological. The end result can only be losses.

THE HEADHUNTER

Some traders are "headhunters." They play the "I'll get that broker" game. These individuals seek to make others–particularly brokers–the scapegoats for losses they have had as a result of their own shortcomings. Consequently they go from broker to broker in an attempt to "get him." They look for errors, possible legal violations, or any other behaviors that will bring about conflict. This is, of course, another type of counterproductive pathology. The conflict stems from unwillingness to accept total responsibility for one's own behavior. The individual who falls into this category is in need of professional help.

BROKERS' PROBLEMS

What about brokers? Can certain types of brokers be readily identified? For the most part brokers have fewer problems than clients. The simple fact of the matter is that brokers do their work for a living. Most customers, on the other hand, do not trade for a living. If a broker has emotional problems, or if he does not do his job well, he won't be around very long. Most customers did not make the majority of their money in the market. They have other jobs and come to the market to lose their money. As such they can have many market-related problems, and as long as their money lasts, they can stay in the market. This is why I would be hard-pressed to isolate any specific type of broker in terms of behavior.

As a lot, they are much healthier emotionally than are their customers.

THE BROKER-CLIENT CONTRACT

What can we learn from this? To begin with, we must realize that for a majority of traders, the relationship with a broker can either add to or detract from net results. The broker must realize what he is up against and how to deal with it. And both individuals must realize that working together is necessary for profit and survival. I have several suggestions for broker and client that will assist in their overall productivity. Before listing these I would like to say just a few words in support of the broker-client "contract." The skills and limitations of a broker are well known to the trader who has made the market his profession, sits at a desk all day, trades his account, and/or manages others' money. He rarely relies on brokers for advice, follows his own trading for better or for worse, and is therefore not susceptible to the problems outlined in this chapter. The average trader, however, should establish a clear understanding or contract with his broker in which each party loosely outlines expectations of the other. This will help avoid many difficulties, both legal and otherwise. The contract, although not a legal document, and possibly not even a written one, would be entered into prior to the opening of an account or shortly thereafter. If, for example, a client wished no trading advice, he would so specify. If a broker wished to give no trading advice, then it would so be indicated and agreed. The agreement would be made in order to avoid any difficulties that arise from misunderstanding, unrealistic expectations, or misconceptions. I believe the following specific suggestions will benefit both customer and broker:

1. Establish a clear understanding or verbal "contract" prior to the start of trading.

2. Customers should strive to be independent of brokers' advice, using only their own trading system.

3. Brokers should avoid advice-seeking traders unless they make virtually all trades as advised, following them through to completion.

4. Brokers should avoid involvement with overly dependent traders who seek handholding and consolation rather than good brokerage.

5. Brokers should encourage their clients to trade on the clients' own signals, since this will more often than not produce a successful, lasting account.

Some readers may find it difficult to imagine the many ways in which trading losses may arise from a disturbed broker-client relationship. Certainly, the situations I have described and the behaviors I have mentioned are extreme. Remember, however, that it is the nature of emotional difficulties to be extreme and peculiar. In many cases the individual who is suffering from serious psychological shortcomings is neither aware of these problems nor willing to admit that a problem might exist. This is characterisic of the denial that accompanies emotional disorders. My purpose in outlining some of the possibilities is to inform you of what can occur if the early warning signs are ignored. Few if any behaviors have a sudden onset. They may seem to have developed overnight, yet close study of their precedent events will reveal a progression that in many cases can only be identified by a skilled professional. The essence of success in the investment game is anticipation. Trades must be made on anticipation of positive results, and losses must be limited on anticipation of more seriously negative results. The psychology of trading or investing is equally amenable to anticipation. In the broker-client relationship it is therefore necessary to practice preventive techniques. This is best done by following some of the suggestions I have outlined in this chapter. It is not necessary to implement all the recommended items. I would strongly suggest that you keep them in mind with prevention as the objective.

REVIEW

1. Broker-client relationship can be productive or destructive.
2. Relationships that are counterproductive should be avoided.

3. Behavioral techniques can be applied to the solution of problems between broker and client.
4. Various types of relationship can be defined.
5. Both broker and client should strive to be completely independent in terms of the individual functions of each. This will bring good results to both.

16 Putting It All Together — Where You Fit In

It's one thing to talk theory. It's a far greater accomplishment to obtain results. Although I have attempted to give you some real life examples of how to use psychological principles in solving investing and trading problems, there are still those who may find it impossible to implement my suggestions. How can we, without professional help, find our own way to success? Certainly the most simple, nonspecific answer is be persistent. It is difficult to reach one's goal, or overcome one's difficulty, lacking the necessary experience to do so. How might a relatively inexperienced trader gain the ability to correct his or her mistakes? My intent is to provide not a "cookbook" method to self-awareness or success but rather a checklist of guidelines that might be used in the improvement process.

Certainly by now you have realized that my bias in behavior change is primarily learning-theory oriented. I have serious doubts about the ability of traditional techniques to effect change within a brief period of time. I believe that psychoanalysis can help, but I do not believe that it can help quickly enough. Trading problems need prompt relief, as do emotional difficulties. The most effective technique I know is the behavioral method, a portion of which has been described earlier. I believe it is possible for the average trader to use behavioral principles in the overall improvement of his or her investing success. But change must proceed in an orderly fashion.

DO YOU REALLY HAVE A PROBLEM?

Many investors believe that they have market-related problems when indeed they do not. The results of your evaluation, or Investors Quotient, as I have called it (see Chapter 8), may be a good indicator. Another good indicator is your overall profit picture. I will assume that you are following an organized trading system. (If you are not, then reread my previous discussions on this matter.) Examine your profits and losses. Consider the five relevant questions asked in this chapter.

1. *When liquidating a position do you get out within 30 percent of a top or bottom, or do you generally give back more than 50 percent of your open profits?*

This is more of a technical problem than a psychological one. The answer will be found in the stop-loss or follow-up method you are using. It is often difficult to distinguish between a market or system problem and an emotional involvement. If you show overall profits from your trading and investing, then it is unlikely you have a psychological difficulty. Check your system first!

2. *Are losses taken at or near the stop-loss point?*

If the answer is "yes," then you are following your trading system and should examine it for possible shortcomings. A small adjustment in stop-loss procedure can make all the difference in the world. A net losing system can become a winner. If most of your stops are being executed quite a distance from your original market exit point, chances are that you are tampering with them. This *is* a psychological problem and should be treated according to my suggested methodology.

3. *Are your market entries based on your technical work or advisory service? Are they executed at the indicated price, too early, or too late?*

As in the case of stops, your entries should be close to the intended price. Failure of such order execution is more than just the result of "bad fills," particularly if orders are consistently being placed well outside the acceptable range. This is clearly an emotionally related problem and not the fault of your broker, friends, or advisor. Entry at the indicated price level suggests that you are following the rules. If so, any lack of profits should or could be traced back to the trading system or advisor.

4. *How do you act when you take a profit or loss? Does your behavior spill over into other areas of your life? Does your home life affect your trading?*

Some of these issues are touched on in the trader evaluation provided earlier. To answer these questions honestly it will be necessary to ask those around you for an objective evaluation of your behavior. Certainly it is normal to react in a positive or negative way to market experiences. It is, however, a warning sign to react too violently in one direction or another. If this is the case, then you are indeed suffering from a psychological or emotional difficulty.

Perhaps the most common difficulty among traders is their inability to separate system-related defects from personality-related difficulties. By failing to draw a clear-cut distinction between system failings and personal limitations the investor may assume responsibility for a loss that is not due to the investor's own inability. This will undermine his or her self-confidence, resulting in an unwillingness to use the system. There are occasions when an emotional problem will be taken to be system related. Failure to enter a stop at the appropriate time may be blamed on the system when in reality it is the fault of the trader. The single best way to overcome the potential confusion is to draw a very clear-cut line between technique and implementation. And the most effective way to accomplish this goal is by strict adherence to specified system rules. I suggest you keep a sheet which indicates *system signals* and *trader action.*

Table 8 is a sample from a fictitious trading system. Note that each and every signal generated by the trading system has a spe-

Table 8 Signal–Action

System Signals	Trader Action
1. Closing penetration of three-week high.	1. Buy next day on open at market.
2. Signal 1 above.	2. Place stop loss at 2 percent under three-week high.
3. Advance of 20 percent from signal 1.	3. Raise stop to 50 percent profit point. Use close only stop.
4. Additional advance of 10 percent from signal 3.	4. Raise stop to 78 percent profit point. Use straight stop only.
5. Advance of additional 10 percent from signal 4.	5. Raise stop by increments for every 10 percent advance. Maintain at 83 percent profit point and use straight stop.
6. Position stopped out.	6. Make no additional trades for three market days.
7. New entry signal indicated by signal 1.	7. Follow procedures 1–6.
8. Closing penetration of ten-day moving average.	8. Buy opening two days later.
9. Signal 8.	9. Place stop close only 1 percent under low of last three trading days.
10. Ten percent rise from buy price.	10. Take profit of 10 percent increase from buy price by placing open order MIT as soon as trade is put on.
11. Two successive days of downturn in ten-day MA.	11. Place stop close only at low of previous day.

cific follow-up procedure to be implemented by the trader. This is the only way in which errors of judgment versus system errors can be identified. If your trading system is not presently operationalized as indicated in the table, then I suggest you do this immediately. You may be pleasantly surprised at the results.

YOU'VE DECIDED THAT YOU HAVE A PROBLEM . . . WHAT NOW?

The severity of any emotional problem is always determined by the degree to which it limits or inhibits effective functioning in society. Clearly, an individual who is so totally psychotic that he or she cannot function will be hospitalized for treatment. The market, at times, arouses severe symptoms in investors. This is more true in the case of active traders than long-term oriented investors. The decision must be made as to how intense your difficulty really is. Several questions are in order:

1. Have you lost more money in the market than you can afford? Have you done this more than once? Are you in the habit of borrowing money to trade? Do you sacrifice some of life's necessities in order to obtain trading capital? If the answer to any of these questions is "yes," then you are a gambler and not a trader. Cruel as this may sound, I suggest you immediately stop trading and consult either a professional therapist or Gamblers Anonymous for help. This is a serious problem. It is perhaps the single most serious psychological difficulty connected with the markets. Help is needed at once!

2. Does the market cause you anxiety? Do you suffer from hypertension (high blood pressure)? Is it aggravated by your trading? Do you have other psychophysiological dysfunctions such as ulcers or colitis? Do they "flare up" when you trade? It is not uncommon for such symptoms to afflict many traders, particularly those active in the markets. Typically their symptoms are irritated by trading. This does not mean that trading should be stopped. It does, however, mean that treatment is necessary in order for the symptoms to be minimized. Those who do not get treatment for such problems may, in fact, die of the attendant complications. Psychophysiological disorders are highly responsive to treatment. Traditionally, psychotherapy and/or counseling as well as drugs are used. Excellent results can be obtained from behavioral treatment. Biofeedback, reciprocal inhibition, and counterconditioning should be investigated with an appropriate therapist.

3. Are you immobilized or incapacitated by the markets? Following a loss, do you withdraw, become reclusive, depressed, morose, and unable to work at your full-time job? If so, then you are also suffering from a serious problem. Trading, as you can see, has become more than mere "trading." It has taken on psychological importance above and beyond the mere call of the market. A loss is not merely a loss, but rather a painful emotional experience, which most likely relates back to your childhood or adolescent days. In such a case more in-depth psychotherapy is necessary. I suggest you consult a professional for assistance.

4. Do you become outraged, violent, or aggressive following a market loss? Do you "take out" your aggressions and frustrations on others either verbally or physically? Are you impossible to live with following a loss? If the answer is "yes," then you also need professional help. The market is not for you in your present condition. The best course of action is to stop trading and enter treatment with an appropriately disciplined therapist. Such reactions to market losses are also deep-rooted personality disorders and must be treated before they become even more serious.

5. Are your ups and downs closely related to market ups and downs? Is your daily life a reflection of the market? There is nothing wrong with an individual simply because the market causes him or her to act in a certain way. As long as the behaviors do not inhibit his functioning, then such people are not in need of treatment. It is only natural to be affected by events around us. It would be absurd, and even pathological, to not be happy or ecstatic when we've taken a large profit. The thing to watch carefully is the degree to which such profits and/or losses affect your overall functioning. If there is too much of a carryover, then you may be heading for trouble and should start on a program or programs to improve the situation.

MARKET PROBLEMS ARE SYMPTOMATIC OF OTHER DIFFICULTIES

The single most important thing I can tell you about market problems which are not related to your trading system is that they frequently indicate the presence of other difficulties. We do not live our lives in unrelated segments. Life and experiences are part of a larger flow of events. The teachings of most psychologists underscore the fact that we cannot separate any one human experience or failing from the totality of an individual's environment. Difficulties in one sphere of life will make their presence known in another. Problems with a spouse may interfere with trading. And problems with trading may then have a reverse effect, in turn causing marital difficulties. An anxious individual may take it upon himself to trade the market actively. His anxiety may have been the result of early childhood experiences. In turn this anxiety will result in poor trading discipline. The resultant losses will make him more anxious. In turn he will function poorly at his full-time job, or he may relate negatively to his family. An increase in anxiety will follow, and with it more losses.

This is the manner in which problems feed on each other. One aspect of life has its effect on another. The interaction of behaviors and their consequences form the total picture we call "personality." The point I am making is simple. Any market problem is more than a market problem. Any home problem is more than a home problem. Any sexual problem is more than a sexual problem. It is not unusual, for example, for men with sexual dysfunctions to compensate by extreme aggressiveness in the market. In so doing their lack of objectivity may lead to losses, hence their efforts bring only more pain.

I therefore advise you to consider your relationship with the market very seriously. Make certain that you are not using the market to achieve an end which is best achieved in other aspects of your life. Make certain that your trading decisions are not merely a reflection of difficulties in the home. If you should find that your trading is causing you considerable pain, loss, and frustration, then you must begin to look for the answer at home. Start by looking within yourself for the problem as well as the solution. Take care of yourself first—market successes will follow.

REVIEW

1. Some of the theoretical considerations previously discussed were put into a real life framework.
2. Several indicators of trading problems were mentioned.
3. Actions for beginning treatment of problems were suggested.
4. The correlation between market problems and difficulties in home life and interpersonal relationships was pointed out.

Social Psychology and the Markets 17

The net effect of a person's perceptual, behavioral, and psychosexual development is overt action as it is shaped by the interaction of these factors. The individual does not live in a vacuum. Each and every action has a reaction, which in turn influences continued behavior. Interaction with others shapes attitudes, opinions, perceptions, and ultimately behavior. The perceptual filter to which I referred earlier could, in fact, be renamed "social filter." As such it is necessary, indeed potentially profitable, to examine the social psychology of investing.

As psychology expanded its experimental base, theorists recognized the importance of studying man within his social element. Results obtained in strict laboratory settings often proved insufficient in describing the total picture. Theories frequently lacked predictive validity in true life situations. The interaction of individuals within the social structure is the raw material of social psychology. Any act that requires frequent and intensive dealings with other human beings is fair subject matter for the social psychologist. Few areas of life are immune from the effects of society. A behavior as complex as investing or trading involves the interaction of many humans. The seemingly simple act of picking up a telephone to place an order with one's broker can lead to literally hundreds of reactions, by thousands of investors. Hence an understanding of the social forces affecting our psyches can bring insights that may be valuable in the total investment picture.

A strict textbook definition of what is studied by the social psychologist might read as follows:

> The behavior of an individual in the presence of another person is at once a response and a stimulus to that other person. Because the other person (O) reacts to the behavior of an individual (S), the behavior of S is likely to be tempered by the presence of O. S may consciously or unconsciously behave so as to elicit a particular response from O. His subsequent behavior depends upon his success or failure in eliciting certain behaviors from O. (Secord and Backman, 1964, p. 1)

This brief definition of a social interaction represents only a small portion of possible variables operative in the social process. Inasmuch as the marketplace is an institution that functions on human interaction and emotion, a number of especially relevant topics should be mentioned.

INTERPERSONAL RELATIONSHIPS AND YOUR INVESTING

Like it or not we are all influenced by those around us. The most significant consequence of social interaction is that it does, on many occasions, prevent us from implementing investment decisions with the total rationality and discipline required of the successful individual. Since we are all subject to emotional ups and downs, which frequently find their origin in interpersonal relationships, it is helpful to become familiar with several aspects of relationships. Typically, difficulties that arise from an interpersonal basis operate on an unconscious or subconscious level. Before discussing this issue we would do well to understand what is meant by the term "interpersonal relationship." For the purpose of this discussion I define the term as follows:

> *Any social interaction between individuals closely related by family, marriage, or frequency of contact.*

This is by no means a firm definition. Generally speaking we must examine the role of "significant others" in our overall investment decisions. First is one's immediate family. Second we find friends and business associates. And third we must scrutinize the role of those not as closely involved, but nevertheless significant, such as brokers, advisors, and market experts. Here are some of the points to which this discussion is directed:

1. What are the specific interpersonal relationships that can affect an investor?
2. What are some of the symptoms that signal a possible negative effect?
3. How can such situations be rectified?
4. How can interpersonal relationships help you benefit?

Family relationships are perhaps the most significant and influential. These include relationships between parent and child, siblings, and husband and wife. Since almost all investors spent their formative years in a family-type situation, it is not unusual for them to be influenced by their family well beyond the actual move away from home. Psychoanalytic teachings have shown us that the guilt, anxiety, envy, fear, and identification that arise between child and parent of the same sex can have a lasting effect on adult personality. Following the processes of childhood amnesia (discussed earlier) these feelings are rarely remembered when people recall their youthful days. Nevertheless, many long-term fears originate and develop between birth and eleven years of age.

The behavioral psychologist would not agree with much of the analytic terminology but would agree that the process of learning begins as soon as a child is born (possibly sooner). As a result, many of the response styles, attitudes, fears, and opinions acquired during early childhood tend to continue into adulthood. Most individuals do not know how, when, or where they acquired many of their behavioral traits. There are, for example, many investors known as "eternal bears" or "eternal bulls." Such response sets are acquired in childhood and persist into later life. In this case (as in most) parents are the culprits.

Typically, parental attitudes are acquired by children. There is an old saying in the mental health profession that "crazy parents make crazy children." The same holds true for dyed-in-the-wool bears and bulls. For those who have been so trained in early childhood, the consequences in adult life may be disastrous. An investor may find himself constantly bullish or bearish to the point of financial ruin. He does not know where these persistent attitudes had their origin. This tends to act as an aggravating factor increasing frustration, thereby resulting in even greater losses. There are several types of parental attitudes and child-rearing methods that help shape specific investor personalities. An investor's behaviors will, in most cases, merely be a reflection of his or her overall personality. We can acquire considerable insight about an individual by observing his or her investment behavior. Likewise one can formulate a fairly accurate representation of an individual's investment behaviors by studying his personality and its development.

THE ETERNAL BEAR

The "eternal bear" often reflects negative parental attitudes. His or her parents may have been well along in years when their "bearish child" was born. Typically they have grown somewhat cold and/or cynical in their old age. Many of the romantic feelings they had as a younger couple have fallen by the wayside, left perhaps in the trials and tribulations of raising a family. They have become pragmatic, fixed in their ways, resistant to change, and generally rigid. Such attitudes are readily passed on to their child. If there are additional siblings, the effect is somewhat muted. If, however, other children have grown and moved from the home, or should there be no siblings, the consequences can be profound. Even as an infant this individual may assume "adult" attitudes. There will be a general lack of fantasy life, and a serious, down-to-earth orientation to the world. Insights can be derived by observing such a child at play. His style reflects a rigid, negativistic, and fatalistic underlying attitude. Creativity is generally lacking.

In addition, parental attitudes may be negative about virtually all new concepts, products, books, entertainments, and politicians. This readily translates into bearish market attitudes. Note that I am not passing judgment as to the relative desirability of one market position over another: both have their place in the market. I am, however, indicating that any *one* orientation, if carried to excess, is indicative of neither potential success nor mental stability. If you are an individual who is constantly bearish, or if you find yourself trading from the short side, despite losses and system signals to the contrary, you are most likely the product of such an environment. Certainly this is not the only situation that can create such attitudes. A teacher at school during adolescence, a surrogate parent, or an extremely influential relative can have the same effect. Children raised by their grandparents can develop a bearish predisposition. Infants whose parents are frequently away from home, leaving an elderly babysitter in charge, can develop an "eternal bear" personality.

Marriage may either temper or aggravate the situation. An individual who is prone to bearish attitudes may, in marrying another who is similarly inclined, develop into a "superbear." The attitudes of one's spouse tend to reinforce what the individual already believes to be true. And this may, in fact, be detrimental to the overall investment result. On the other hand, a marriage partner who is inclined either in a neutral or opposite direction may temper or dampen the attitudes and behaviors that comprise eternal bear syndrome. This may arouse anxiety and protest in the investor so afflicted. And this could, in fact, create marital discord of serious consequence.

As you can see, the extreme position taken by one who is eternally bearish can have many negative consequences, above and beyond mere market misperception and resultant losses. The investor restricted to such an extreme role has difficulties untold. Not only will his persistent market attitude lose him money, but it will also frustrate him, thereby bringing further losses. The vicious cycle of bearish attitude, loss of money, increased frustration, and poor judgment will also deteriorate the home environment.

The symptoms of such an affliction are rather ovious, and perhaps the most simple to recognize. If your trading is more than 90 percent to the bear side, over a period of several years, and if your results do not justify the continuation of such a point of view, then you are a sufferer. Most likely you alone will not see the situation as it really is. Others will tell you what is happening. You may not believe them, even though example after example is cited. Such denial is common in neurotic or preneurotic states. The more entrenched the problem, the greater resistance and denial will be. If you know such an individual, then you are aware of what I am saying.

The eternal bear is a vanishing breed. The unusually violent bull moves we've witnessed in most markets during the 1970s have all but extinguished the species. Yet there seems to be a new crop every year, and it is advisable to brush up on how they may be "cured." Here are a few suggestions:

1. Threats by family, friends and associates will not help. They may create more problems than they solve. It is best to maintain a positive attitude rather than a negative one. Why fight negativism with negativism?

2. If you are the one who suffers from this condition, then I suggest you attempt to recall the many childhood experiences that shaped the problem. By relaxing and letting your mind wander through the past, you can relive some of the key situations that influenced your attitudes and actions. This can best be achieved in a classic therapy situation.

3. Through the utilization of a behavioral training technique, as outlined in an earlier chapter, you can "unlearn" the syndrome, retraining yourself in a more realistic direction. In so doing, another's help may be necessary.

4. Discipline can be a great help as well. For those who can recruit the assistance of others I would suggest the following treatment sequence:

- **a.** Reevaluate your trading system to make certain that it's hypothetical or intended results are worthy of your efforts.
- **b.** Compare actual trading results with hypothetical results, noting any divergence.
- **c.** If there is more than 10 percent variance between the two, a change in your behavior is in order.
- **d.** Obtain the assistance of a neutral or more disciplined individual. See earlier chapters for further details.

5. Attempt to improve self-awareness. This can be accomplished through the systematic application of gestalt therapy, sensitivity groups, self-awareness courses, and the like.

THE ETERNAL BULL

The market optimist, or "eternal bull," is much happier than the eternal bear—but no more fortunate. His overall losses may be smaller, but in the long run his misery is just as intense. Typically such individuals are reared in families that preached and practiced optimism. Like Dr. Pangloss of Voltaire's *Candide* their motto, as expressed in behavior, is "all is for the best, in the best of all possible worlds." Parental behavior shapes their point of view. Failures are taken lightly. There is often no serious consequence of poor performance. In fact, parents tend to gloss over failing marks at school, looking always to the future. This may seem rather unrealistic. And it most certainly is!

The child reared in such an environment will frequently acquire similar opinions and behaviors. When he or she becomes an investor the response style which has been assumed, although a positive one, will not permit full recognition of a negative situation. This type of investor has so thoroughly adopted an eternally bullish outlook that he will not accept a loss. Rather than admit something has gone awry the typical response of such an investor will be to deny or rationalize the poor trade. Any number of excuses will be found. Certainly the market will not heed the explanation offered. And in the long run some very large losses may be taken.

There is a distinct difference between the individual who fears the short side of a market and the "eternal bull." Whereas one investor may not find short selling palatable, he can, under the proper circumstances, either sell short or close out a long position which has gone against him. The eternal bull will not only retain long positions, but he will add to them on the way down. This is distinctly different from an unwillingness to sell short. It is not necessary to trade both sides of a market. Many individuals do not comprehend the concept of selling short. As such they do not want to assume this side of a trade since they feel that their risk is virtually unlimited, whereas potential profit is very clearly defined.

As in the case of "eternal" bearishness, the undying bull will find reasons to support his position. This is a prime example of how the defense mechanism termed "intellectualization" operates. In both cases there will be a tendency to ignore fundamentals or technical patterns when their signals are not in agreement with the investor's feelings. This typifies misperception and its implications. The topic has been previously discussed.

How can one change such behaviors? Many of the suggestions given for treatment of the eternal bear are also applicable in this case. In addition I would suggest the following techniques and steps:

1. List the possible consequences of taking a loss as you perceive them.

2. Analyze each and every possible consequence, real or imagined. Determine how threatening each may actually be. Attempt to put each possible result in its proper perspective.

3. Study your parents' attitudes and opinions. You may realize that they have helped you internalize an overly positive and optimistic response set.

4. Examine the functioning of your trading system in bear markets. During major bull moves you may do very well, only to give all the profits (and more) back during downtrends. If this is the case, then your system may actually be biased to the bull side. As such it is a reflection of your bullish orientation and will not serve you well in all markets. A reevaluation and/or reformulation may be necessary.

5. If all else fails, then professional help might be necessary.

RELATIONSHIPS WITH FRIENDS

Interpersonal relationships, particularly among friends, play a significant role in determining our social perceptions and actions. Most things we do are intended not to benefit us directly but to bring social benefits. Pressures from within our families and our social circles frequently lead us to choose actions that will eventually prove contrary to our final goals. The unfortunate thing about such a situation is that it often occurs unconsciously. Since social motivation begins at a very early age, we are imbued with values and goals that derive from parental attitudes and expectations. After we have engaged in the fulfillment of these goals for so many years, the process becomes automatic. During early childhood and adolescent days we are quite conscious of what we are doing. In fact, much of the rebelliousness displayed by children is a result of their realization that what is expected of them is not what they really want to do. On the one hand, the process is a necessary one since it provides social skills required for effective functioning. On the other hand, the process has its limitations, since it teaches us to do things which we need not, in reality, do.

When a child matures, the effect of such learning and conditioning can be marked. The conflict that follows can result in emotional and behavioral disturbance. In the market such difficulties very often express themselves in the form of losses and poor discipline. Thus it is to our advantage if we acquire insight into the process by which we decide to act. Social factors are highly influential in financial situations. If a friend takes a large position in a given stock, we may feel pressured to do the same, particularly if we respect him. If a friend makes a large sum of money in the market, we may begin to feel competitive. The feelings may be translated into market action that is not consistent with good trading. We are subject to similar pressures in the home. This discussion will, however, be limited to the role of immediate friends and acquaintances, and their potential effect on your investing.

Human behavior is determined by needs. Certain psychological theories base their principles on needs and the manner in which they are fulfilled. The following discussion of relationships with friends, and their effect on the market, is based on an analysis of the needs that motivate such actions.

THE NEED TO COMPETE

As children we are taught to compete with friends and siblings. After years of experience in this area, it is only natural that, as adults, we continue to seek satisfaction of these needs. The desire to compete is a healthy and, most often, productive need. It inspires us to achieve things we might not otherwise be motivated to attempt. On the other hand, it tends to make us take chances that should not be taken. If the need to compete is intense, then we may speculate beyond the point of reason. What is it that can stimulate such speculative action? The need to be victorious is often more important vis-à-vis society than it is to us individually. Many investors are not involved in their program with the intention of making themselves happy. More often than not these needs are sufficient to make an investor ignore the basics of his or her trading program. The end result, of course, will more often than not be losses. The individual who acts irrationally in response to the competitive impulse typically is suffering from deep-seated feelings of insecurity or inadequacy. It is the need to compensate for these feelings that stimulates unwarranted action in response to achievements by others. Clearly there is an emotional aspect to the competitive need, and it is the social need that precipitates the inappropriate act.

Friends, acquaintances, and at times relatives are key persons who can arouse the competitive instinct. The need is greatest where there has been a longstanding relationship of rivalry. And when the need is greatest, the errors that follow are likely to be the most disastrous. There are several ways in which the need to compete can be channelled in a positive direction. After all, the need is a primary factor in motivation, and we would want to take advantage of the energy it stimulates. There are a number of ways in which this can be done:

1. If you know that this is one of your weak areas, spend some time thinking about exactly who is the target of your need, and precisely why you feel the need. Insights may spring from such deliberations to help you direct competitive energy in the proper direction.

2. It is better to anticipate than to respond. One way to limit the irrational aspect of competition is to be *first* rather than second. If you need to compete, make certain that *you* set the pace by taking action before your competitor does. It is much easier to be a leader than a follower.

3. Attempt to *make* the rules rather than *play* by them. There are many types of games competitors play. Don't put yourself in the position of playing another person's game. As an example, your brother-in-law, with whom you are competing, is an expert in stock options; you do not have experience with this technique. Instead of attempting to beat him at his own game, stick to what you do best. In the long run only the money that comes from trading determines who comes out on top. And this should be your primary consideration.

4. Those who can learn to ignore the need are pursuing the *best* course of action. Some of the relaxation techniques I will describe may alleviate the anxiety that often accompanies the need to compete. For example, when you receive a telephone call informing you that your chief rival has just made a killing in the market, instead of reacting with orders to your broker, use relaxation techniques.

THE NEED TO PLEASE

This is another need stemming from childhood. Since we seek to please our parents (more often than not out of fear), we will also do so in adult life. This is especially true in relation to figures of authority. The result of such actions typically detracts from profitable trading. How might such a situation arise in the marketplace? Many brokers and market advisors accept accounts from friends and relatives. If and when they begin to lose money for these people, the pressure becomes intense and incorrect decisions are made. The need to please is so intense that any disapproval is seen as threatening to internal emotional stability. The punishment that frequently accompanied failure in childhood elevates the need to perform until it is paramount, perhaps causing us to ignore other needs. Typically, the need is greatest among those who have had traumatic childhood experiences in this area. Those who were severely punished for poor school performance are prime victims. How can one successfully contend with these feelings? I have several suggestions:

1. Do not put yourself in the position of accepting accounts, making recommendations, or otherwise influencing decisions made by friends or relatives. This will immediately release you from the need to please. This is a policy I believe every investor should adhere to.

2. If you are aware of the errors in judgment that come from the need to please, then you ought to think twice before handling any investments for others, even clients.

3. Attempt to turn over the decision-making end of things to one who will follow through without concern for the "need to please" factor.

4. As always, strict discipline is necessary to avoid the pitfalls that can result from this situation.

THE NEED FOR APPROVAL

We all need approval. Whether we succeed may well be much less important than whether we have done things in a way that gains approval from others. The need for approval is not necessarily similar to the need to please. Typically, one who needs to please tends to be highly negative when it comes to self-appraisal. The individual who merely needs approval can do well on his own only up to a point. He does not need to please others, he is merely looking for a nod in the positive direction. There are many needs which, if carried to an extreme, will most definitely result in poor trading. An investor who trades only for the joy of others' approval is a sure loser. There are several ways in which this problem can be rectified:

1. Make your own approval: institute any of the programs discussed in this book.

2. Determine whose approval is important to you and for what reason. Once you have discovered who your "significant others" are, you can study your relationships with them in an effort to limit your need for their approval.

THE NEED TO BE PUNISHED

You may have laughed when reading this. Believe it or not, many individuals actually want to be punished. Just as some relationships function on approval and the need to please, other relationships function on the need for one individual to be punished. Typically, the one who punishes is operating from a need to be the punisher. In everyday circumstances there are few situations one can detect as clearly pathological in this sense. However, some relationships between friends are maintained on this masochist-sadist basis. Certainly it takes two to tango. Let me illustrate by way of a brief story.

A friend of mine was in the habit of trading without stops. As in most cases, the lack of a stop resulted in consistently poor performance. Several accounts he was trading also did poorly. These were accounts that had been opened for friends who believed in this individual's ability. After each loss, one of his so-called friends would telephone to complain. This went on for several years! In spite of the fact that loss after loss was taken, the friend kept sending money, and the money "manager" kept losing it. He made no effort to avoid the verbal punishment by either terminating the business end of this relationship or using a different trading strategy. The only logical conclusion one could reach was that this relationship was getting both parties precisely what they wanted. They were, most likely, not even aware of the situation on a conscious level.

As peculiar as this may sound to those who are not sufferers, there are many subtle ways in which the punishment factor may affect all of us. Pathology tends to build very slowly in relationships. What begins as a seemingly harmless game can end as a very serious problem. During the very slow process by which this type of learning (and many other forms of learning) occurs, one is not aware of what is happening. Any relationship that is divided along punisher-punishee lines is suspect. If you suddenly realize that most of your time is spent in being punished by a friend or mate, or if you are spending a great deal of time as the one who doles out punishment, then you are most likely engaged in this pathological situation. The end result can only be one that causes considerable pain. Typically, husbands and wives engage in such interactions. But the difficulty is by no means limited to close relationships. The relationship between broker and client can work in the same way. Take the case of a broker, or friend, who is jealous about your investment success. Each and every time you take a loss he will be pleased. He will further aggravate your pain by ridiculing you in subtle ways. You may not even be aware of what is developing. If you continue to accept the punishment, albeit subtle, then you may actually be aggravating your attitude toward the market, which, in the long run, will make things considerably worse.

The need to be punished is much more common than most of us believe. Those who are fortunate enough to realize what is going on can take steps to correct it. It is my opinion that a very specific program to detect and correct this situation can be implemented. Here is the fashion in which I would proceed:

1. *Recognize* the problem–start by taking an accounting of your relationships. If you are involved in a situation which brings you pain, and if you have been coping with the pain of punishment for more than two months, then you are most likely in need of help. If you are not aware of which relationship is causing you the difficulty, then make a written list and keep a tally of the frequency with which you experience conflict with each of the individuals. Obviously, the relationships causing the greatest number of negative conflicts are those that need to be repaired.

2. *Stop the conflict* by knowing ahead of time who is punishing you. If you do not respond to the game, then it will soon end. You can expect an initial increase in negative feedback from the person who is attempting to punish you. If you consistently fail to respond, however, you will emerge victorious.

3. *Replace the negative interaction* with positive experiences. This will quickly put the relationship back on the right track. Do it even if you must force yourself at first, since it will eventually bring the desired result.

4. *Do not substitute* another negative interaction for the one which you have just repaired. It is easy to fall into the same pattern with another person.

As you can see, there are many different directions relationships with friends can take. My best advice is to keep business and friendship separate. This will help you avoid many problems. Human relationships are extremely complex. We do things for many reasons—and more often than not we cannot explain why we have acted in a certain way. The best way to avoid the pitfalls of interpersonal relationships and their effect on investing is to stay with your program. This is just one more of the many reasons for following a disciplined trading system. The human element, as you can see, needs constant attention, close supervision, and the strictest of programs.

REVIEW

1. The role of social psychology and interpersonal relationships was examined in light of the market.
2. Several investor personality types were discussed.
3. The role of relationships with friends was mentioned as a significant factor in overall investment success.
4. There are a number of important needs whose roles can affect investment success.

18 Some Psychological Trading Rules

To those who have been in the market for many years, the time-tested and oft repeated trading rules are well known. In fact, they're so well known that few of us attend to them. Now that we have examined these maxims in the light of psychological theory, you may be more willing to use them—especially after they are restated in this chapter in a manner that makes their use very clear. In addition, I include here a number of new rules based on much of what has been covered in previous chapters. The brief description of exactly what is meant, in behavioral terms, may also help you. I have found it very useful to keep a list of these rules. I refer to them often and find that they help keep me on the right track.

1. Plan your trades specifically and in advance. Keep them available. If you are specific, organized, and act on plans, you will avoid costly errors often caused by spur of the moment decisions. A concise trading plan will help you avoid the losses that can arise from acting on the opinions of others. Regardless of the trading system you are using such a plan is necessary. In short, plan your trades and trade your plans.

2. You alone are responsible for the success or failure of your trading. You must assume total responsibility for results, good or bad. You alone are the vehicle to profits and losses. By assuming total responsibility and not blaming brokers, friends, or market letters for errors, you will realize the seriousness of trading. This will help you avoid emotional decisions. You will learn that the situation is entirely under your own control. This will make you consistent and truthful to your trading system. And consistency is the single most valuable key to success.

3. Never hope that a position will go your way; never fear that a position will not go your way. Both these attitudes lead to unrealistic expectations, emotional decisions, and negative attitudes. A position, once established, will result in whatever market action prevails. Once the trade has been made, its fate is sealed and no amount of hope or fear will make things different. W. D. Gann observed that hope and fear were two of the greatest enemies of the speculator, fostering only false perceptions. You must avoid these feelings at all costs. The more rigid you can become in your execution of trades, the more profitable will be your results.

4. Monitor your performance–feedback of results is important. One of the most important things a trader can know about his or her system is whether it is working. And the only way to know this is by keeping a thorough record of results. This will also provide the feedback necessary to reward you for good trading. At any point in time you must know how well or poorly you are doing. You must also know if poor results are caused by *your* inability or that of your trading system.

5. Attitude is your greatest asset. A good trading system is perhaps only 20 percent of the total picture. A positive attitude may very well comprise the balance of successful trading. You must constantly remain aware that the enemies of profitable investing and speculation are constantly boring from within. The only way to combat the negative effects of losses, interference from others, and poor trading signals is by the maintenance of a positive attitude regardless of how bad things may seem.

6. Cultivate effective and positive relationships. We are known by the company we keep. Moreover, we are influenced by those around us. If we surround ourselves with losers, loafers, pretenders, or depressives, we will learn no positive skills. If we associate with those who are highly motivated, who seek to achieve, who have ambitious goals, and who are willing to forge ahead regardless of obstacles, then we will acquire similar drives. Personal relationships as well as business associations should be cultivated along these general guidelines.

7. Don't take the market home with you. If you trade for a living, then you must take great care to leave the market when you leave the office. If you are only a casual investor and do not have a full-time market-related job, then you must also avoid spending too much time or thought on the markets. When things go well you may allow the market too much influence in satisfying other areas of your life. This is not advisable, since it will cause you to delay solving other problems. If the market is not going well for you, and you allow it to affect the rest of your life, this will also be destructive. The market must be seen as a means to an end. It should not become a way of life, and it should not dictate your every move. Make certain you take vacations. Take time each year to close out positions (if necessary) and "get away from it all." By being too close to the situation you may not see it for what it really is.

8. Enjoy the fruits of your labor–spend some profits, save some profits. Make it a regular practice to remove profits from the market. Spend some of them, and save some of them. You must directly experience the positive feeling of using profits to acquire some of the things you have always wanted to buy. I suggest you do this regularly, perhaps monthly. You will not be motivated to make profits if you do not experience firsthand the enjoyment that can come from spending large sums of money.

9. Avoid overconfidence–it could be your greatest enemy. There are good times in the market and there are bad times. Just as you should not allow the bad times to bring you down, you must not allow the good times to get you up too high. If you are on either of these emotional extremes, your judgment can be impaired and you will not be rational enough to realize what lies before you. You will be either too brave or too meek. The best course is to even out the peaks and valleys. Each loss should be a negative experience, but not a totally destructive defeat. Similarly, each profit should be taken in stride. Overconfidence may, in fact, be even more potentially destructive than lack of confidence, since it will make you take chances that could destroy you.

10. Your next goal should always be in sight. Once you have attained an objective make certain that your next challenge is set. A well-known commodity trader made several million dollars in the market one year. He lost it and almost went bankrupt the next year. I asked him how this could have happened. "Simple," he replied. "When you climb a mountain and you're sitting on top of the world, it gets lonely. There's no place left to go but down." If, however, you have another mountain to climb once you get to the top, you won't be tempted to go down in order to have a new challenge.

There are, to be sure, many other rules that apply. Those just discussed will not be universally useful. You may benefit immensely from a formulation of your own trading rules because you alone are the best judge of what you need. But you can only formulate your rules after you have become totally aware of your needs, assets, liabilities, skills, and goals. One of the best ways to accomplish this is through the use of a self-evaluation technique. You may be one of those rare individuals who can determine personal problems and needs by simple thought. But most likely you will need to use a specific checklist or assessment tool to evaluate your situation. The finer details of this method are discussed next.

REVIEW

1. There are a number of market psychology rules that have time-tested validity.
2. Each trader should seek to internalize these rules, referring to them as frequently as possible.
3. Ten rules are outlined, explained, and discussed.
4. Self-evaluation is introduced as a means of determining one's own trading rules.

The Perceptual Factor 19

Two investors are anxiously awaiting an earnings report on company XYZ. One is long and has bought on anticipation of a bullish report; the other is short and expects a negative result. The report is released, and even though earnings for the year are clearly lower when compared to the same period a year earlier, each investor believes that the report supports his position. "It's bearish," says the trader who is short. "Earnings are much lower than last year. If projected at this rate of decline for the balance of the year, earnings will be down over 37 percent from last year, and 63 percent from two years ago. The stock can't possibly move up."

"Not so," argues the investor who has bought. "This is a bullish report in bear's clothing. It's designed to get as many people short as possible. Although earnings are lower than last year's similar period, they're not down as much as the economy in general. With the slowdown we've seen in overall consumer spending, a 37 percent decline for the first quarter is not bad at all. In fact, the decline is less than other firms involved in the same business. Remember also that last year the company showed record sales and earnings. A small decline is healthy and not bearish at all."

"But wouldn't you rather have seen higher earnings?" inquires the bear.

"It really doesn't matter to me," responds the bullish investor in support of his position. "All I know is that the stock's going up regardless of earnings. Earnings reports are not important anyway."

"Well, they certainly were important to you last year when earnings were sharply higher," points out the bearish investor.

"That was last year! Since then I've learned all about earnings reports and how unimportant they really are. The only thing that's important is the price action of the stock. It's a waste of time to even discuss it until we see what the stock does tomorrow," replies our bullish friend.

The next day XYZ stock falls 3 points by the final bell. Certainly the investor who sold short feels that this is a victory, as well he should. The bull is still not convinced. He defends his position: "You can't really tell how a stock is going to act based on one day's worth of price behavior. The bulls are holding back and letting the bears get short before squeezing them out. I've seen this happen many times before." Within a matter of several weeks the stock is more than 15 points lower than where the buyer had put on his original position. By now he must certainly be out or, at the very minimum, demoralized. But alas, he still holds the stock. He reasons, "It's just a matter of time before the investing community realizes how bullish this stock really is. It's difficult to be the lonely bull. But I'm brave and have what it takes to weather the storm. In fact, I'm so very bullish, that the only right thing to do is to buy more of the stock. I'll average my cost down and really make a bundle when the stock turns back up."

By now, the next earnings report has come out. The eternal bull buys more of the stock and our bearish friend, who evidently has the facts on his side, stays short. And again the report is clearly bearish. Disappointed, but not ready to give up, the optimistic bull reasons that once the year has ended there will be an improvement in the situation. Even though the report appears to be bearish, it is, under the surface, quite bullish, he notes. And so continues his misinterpretation of market reality. Despite the losses and continued downmove of the stock, he holds on for the anticipated victory that does not come. And when the move finally begins, our bull will no longer be long of the stock. He will have sold out in the panic-type bottom that inevitably heralds a bull market.

What has gone wrong? How has the bullish trader been led astray? Is he suffering from delusion of grandeur? Does he feel that his mere buying of a stock signals a bull move? Where did he go wrong? What can be done about this situation? If you have ever been in a similar position, then you can fully appreciate the little scenario reported above. You may have known individuals who persist in their market attitudes regardless of fact, regardless of reason, regardless of losses, and regardless of any attempt to convince them that they are wrong. This can be the result of a perceptual problem which is very common and especially dangerous. Such misinterpretations of reality are certainly not limited to the markets. They are a part of everyday life. Each individual, as a function of life experiences, is set, or primed psychologically, to interpret a given situation in his or her own way. We are all subject to such influences. And they can be either a hindrance or a help. Clearly, in the preceding vignette, the persistently bullish perception of one investor was a hindrance to his desired goal. Let us examine the perceptual factor and see if we can learn a few things about our own misconceptions and what, if anything, can be done to reverse their negative consequences.

Consider the following situation: a woman is walking her large dog. The dog spots a cat and, in his effort to chase it, tangles his leash around his mistress' leg causing her to fall. The dog falls to his side as well and begins to bark in his frustrated effort to get loose. A male passer-by observes the situation and rushes to the woman's rescue. The dog, already in a state of uproar, begins to bark at the man who is attempting to assist the woman. Meantime, a passing male motorist spies the situation and assumes that the woman is being attacked by the man, who is actually attempting to assist her. He stops his auto, rushes out, and beings to assault the other man. Despite the pleadings of our first helper, the beating continues. A police officer happens on the scene and cannot understand precisely what has transpired. He is not certain which man is "attacking" the woman. He begins to strike both men with his club in an effort to terminate the melee. Three people and a dog have been hurt. And not a single one is guilty of wrongdoing.

Each of the three men had his own perceptual set. Certainly, in our society, it is natural to assume that a woman might be attacked in the street. It is an all too frequent event. And yet, in this case, the supposition, or perception, of the situation was incorrect. As you certainly know, reality is not what it seems to be, *but rather what we have learned to expect it to be.* If I expect a given situation to occur I will be set, or primed, to react to my expectations. And in so doing I can be fooled. There exists here a dilemma. Certainly it is important to have particular perceptions of reality. Many of them serve us well. And others do not. In due time the individual will learn what serves him well and what leads to pain. But in new situations there is no good basis for judgment. And this is where many mistakes are made. By exploring some of the underlying principles of psychological set, or perception, we should gain some understanding of the developmental process involved in the creation of faulty perception. We can then apply our findings to the market.

WHAT IS PERCEPTION?

Virtually all information that comes to our brain enters via the senses. Notwithstanding the role of so-called extrasensory or clairvoyant perceptions, which, I believe, exist, the major inputs are clearly related to overt environmental stimuli. Touch, taste, smell, sight, and hearing are the primary perceptual receptors. From the moment of conception we are constantly bombarded by a huge variety of environmental stimuli, which, combined with developmental experiences, shape our perception of the world around us. The field of psychology has long debated the relative roles of genetic and environmental factors. The net result has been a synthesis of findings, all of which have relevance to the investor and his ongoing efforts. In order to completely appreciate the differing points of view it will be helpful to review some basic findings and concepts.

Many studies have documented the existence of differential response patterns in the newborn (see Wolman, 1973, pp. 875–77 for references). Countless investigations of response and early childhood perception have documented the fact that no two infants are alike from the moment of birth or earlier. Each child, in fact, is born with a specific response pattern. Stress, for example, arouses distinctly different patterns of physiological reactions in different neonates: their tendency to experience different results from similar situations is clear immediately. Two adults may therefore respond to a similar situation in different ways. Response sets, present from the moment of birth, are with us throughout life and have a market effect on our response or perception of a similar event.

There are many other examples of how individuals differ markedly from the moment of birth. It is a known fact, for example, that children born with congenital cataracts suffer visual-perceptual problems later in life even though the cataracts are treated surgically shortly after birth. It is argued that even a short period of environmental or perceptual deprivation in early childhood can lead to serious perceptual difficulties in adult life. It has been found that there are critical periods among various organisms during which certain skills develop. Chimps whose hands are taped during childhood suffer irreversible damage to sensory and motor ability, even though bandages are removed after several months. There have been many such findings, particularly among mammals.

What it all points to is a complex interplay of genetics and environment in the development of perceptual abilities. Sensory deprivation experiments have demonstrated that dogs reared in low-stimulation environments, devoid of human contact during early childhood, appeared to seek out pain, were dull, and seemed unresponsive to normal types of learning experience. Certainly, if extrapolated to the human condition, these findings have immense implications.

The point I am making is simply this: for various reasons we all "see" or "perceive" things somewhat differently. What may appear dangerous to one individual may be enjoyable to the next. What may seem like a challenge to one man may be nothing but an exercise in dullness to another. One of the major symptoms of psychological disorders, according to Alfred Adler, relates to perception.

Adler was one of the first psychologists to break away from the teachings of Sigmund Freud. He stressed the importance of interpersonal experience and situational determinants of human behavior, dealing extensively with insecurity, feelings of inferiority, sibling rivalry, and the unity of the person. He did so in terms more easily understood and applied by the public than were Freud's theories. He was an associate of Sigmund Freud and a leader of the Vienna Psychoanalytic Society. Some Adlerian terms will further illustrate my view of perception.

Adler presented a specific set of manifestations associated with maladaptive or disturbed behavior. Among these were "perception" and "thought." Of perceptual characteristics he noted two key features associated with mental disorders:

> *Perceptual selectivity.* In the development of his "private view of the world," the neurotic does not recognize events as others do, does not respond to events which would be antithetic to his view, and selects out those parts of events that fit with his prior conceptions.
>
> *Perceptual sensitivity.* . . . He is overly ready to make certain interpretations, whether or not they are appropriate.
>
> *Thought.* Rigidity. The neurotic's thought sequences are in general more rigid and consequently less alterable than those of normal persons. (Ford and Urban, 1965, p. 341)

Let's stop for a moment and review:

1. The way we see things can develop as a function of genetic predisposition and environment.

2. Those who suffer from emotional disturbance tend to see things not as they really are.

3. Those who suffer emotional disturbances tend to interpret or perceive reality in a fashion that supports their pathology.

4. Neurotic thinking is characterized by rigidity of thought and perception, with little tendency to change.

Now let's go back to our learning model (Figure 5). Note that I have included a so-called perceptual filter in the stimulus-organism-response sequence. I will now bring the filter into play as perhaps the single most important element of the learning chain.

Assume that one's perception of a situation is faulty. Take as an example the situation related earlier in this chapter; the persistent bull has misperceived the bearishness of an earnings report. He has demonstrated his rigid thought and perception. This is certainly nothing surprising. Many individuals will defend their position with misperceived facts. They will fight to the finish for what they wish to believe, rather than for what may be real. In other words, we are all familiar with rigidity of thought, defense of an obviously losing position, and clear misinterpretation of reality formulated to defend an untenable position. These are everyday events. But as common as they may be in daily life, they have no constructive value. In fact, they tend to be destructive in the long run. In the market they are catastrophic. The fact that investors tend to misperceive reality accounts for perhaps 50 percent of their losses. That's why it is important, in my opinion, to understand the development and remediation of what I call "losing perception."

Furthermore, I consider losing perception a learned behavior that may have elements of genetic predisposition. Regardless of the genetic factor, whose existence I cannot either prove or disprove, the behavioral aspects are so overwhelmingly obvious that I believe any predisposition can be overcome by learning. Let's review how losing perception can develop in a behavioral way from early childhood. There are two very distinct ways in which such faulty perception can become habitual. Remember that we are all guilty of misperception from time to time. As long as we are not constantly misperceiving situations and relationships at critical times we will not suffer too many losses, either personal or financial. It is habitual maladaptive perception I am discussing.

Parents tend to respond to their children in a fashion predetermined by their own personalities. Let's assume that a child is experiencing anxiety in connection with a given situation. His parents could respond in one of several ways. They could tell him to ignore the anxiety, explaining logically that there is no reason for anxiety given the facts. They may then reward him verbally, or in a stronger fashion, for feeling better. After many repetitions of this stimulus–response chain the child has learned, in a sense, to ignore or reduce anxiety associated with certain stimulus events. Often the anxiety relates to school, examinations, and peer group relationships. Although the interaction is certainly more complex, this is the general way in which perceptions and responses to perception can develop and change. A child returns from school, crying and obviously upset. His parents attempt to console him. "Why are you crying?" they ask. "I'm afraid of the test," replies the youth. "Why are you afraid of the test," asks father. "Because the teacher said that all kids who fail the test will have to stay late after school every day for two weeks." "Well, now I understand why you're scared," responds the parent. "But if you're scared, then you may be so scared that you'll fail the test just because you're afraid," points out the mother. "Sometimes, if we're really afraid of something, it's hard to do that something the right way. And even though we know how to do that thing, we won't be able to do it right because we're upset," she continues. "All people have things that they're scared of, but if you ignore the scared part and study hard for the test, then you'll pass it," points out the father. Although the interchange here is quite simple, the parents have attempted to alter the child's response to a perceived threat. They will reward the child for altering his perception of the situation. Although he may still consider the test situation a threat, he will respond in a fashion which is *not affected by his perception.* Over time his perception may change in accordance with the positive consequences experienced in repetitions of the situation. The praise provided by his parents further stamps in the change in perceptual response.

Parental responses are also instrumental in shaping "losing perception." Very often they will teach a child to behave anxiously, or perceive a situation to be something other than it really is. Here is a simple example, one which was very common in the 1950s:

Child: I have a test next week.

Parent: You had better get a good grade or else!

Child: Or else what?

Parent: Or else I'll beat you black and blue.

Child: Why will you beat me?

Parent: For your own good!! Children who fail tests in school become shoemakers or street cleaners. They're poor all their lives, and live out of other people's garbage cans.

Child: Really?!

Parent: Oh, yes, that's what tests are for. Teachers give them to their students in order to find out which are smart enough to become doctors or lawyers and which will become trash collectors or bums.

Child: You mean that if I don't pass the test next week I'll become a bum?

Parent: Oh, no, you have to fail many tests to become a bum. But each time you fail one or get a bad mark in school the teacher writes it in her book. At the end of the year she sends the marks to your next teacher and so on until you're done with school. And if you get too many bad marks they kick you out of school and turn you over to a shoemaker. And you become his helper and stay poor all your life.

As foolish and contrived as this may sound, it happens to represent an attitude that was once very common among parents. By instilling fear in the child they have altered his innocent perceptual response to the situation of perceived threat. The consequences of one test have been blown out of proportion. The child is now predisposed to feel fear and anxiety. If and when the test is failed, he is punished by his parents and hence suffers double pain. After repeated exposure to such fantasies, in many situations, we have a child who develops an irrational set of perceptions. Despite the fact that he may intellectually recognize the fallacy in his thinking, the perceived threat remains. In fact, the threat may be so subtle that once our conditioned child becomes an adult, he no longer knows why he perceives certain situations in certain ways.

The role of parental attitudes in shaping, maintaining, and reshaping perceptions is significant. In most cases the perceptions we carry through adulthood are reflections of what has been taught in the home. This is why we are so unaware of their presence and this is why they are so difficult to change. Parents typically teach their children to either feel too much pain, too little pain, ignore too much, or attend to too many stimuli. Very little time is spent teaching a child "middle of the road" perceptions. In summary, then, parents can teach a child to (*a*) ignore possibly negative perceptions, (*b*) attend to and amplify the negative perceptions of a situation, or (*c*) shape new perceptions of a given situation or situations. Through the learning process such perceptions will become translated into adult behavior. Through the process of generalization they will be applied to other situations.

Now let's apply such a shaped perception to the market. Take the case of our friend, the eternal bull. He has made a given purchase in company XYZ stock in expectation of a move up. The key word here is *expectation.* His expectation fails to materialize. He does not perceive the situation for what it really is—a loss. No doubt, his failure to interpret the loss for what it really is relates to his losing perception. It is fairly safe to assume that this investor's perception is at fault. More likely than not his inability to realize, or perceive, the bearish news as bearish in fact is due to perceptual problems which developed during childhood. This faulty judgment, or misinterpretation of reality, is possibly reflected in other areas of his life. Those observing the situation are inclined to say that the investor is merely hanging on to his stock, fully aware of the fact that he is wrong, but refusing to admit to the defeat. It is true that some investors fall into this category. But there are perhaps just as many who are *not* aware of the fact that their perception is at fault.

Frequently such difficulties are part of a more pervasive syndrome. It is typical of neurotics to act in such ways either as a means of adapting the world to fit their personal reality or as a defensive technique. In either case, the role played by learning is instrumental. If you recall the behavioral learning model you can see that the more frequently rewards are given, the more permanent behavior will become. You might then ask why perception does not change as a result of the losses that follow misperception. Simply, the misperception does *not always* result in a loss. There are times when, perchance, a profit results. Thus the investor is maintained on a random schedule of reinforcement for his maladaptive perception. And this, as you remember, is one of reward schedules that help create strong habits.

The upshot of what I have told you is simply that misperception, which can be learned, is maintained on a very effective reinforcement schedule. It is a difficult quality to change and accounts for considerable losses. There are, moreover, many different facets of misperception as it relates to the market. Not only can one misperceive earnings reports and their meaning, but potential risk, underlying value of a stock or commodity, technical trading signals, brokerage house opinion, and many other important factors can be misperceived. Any information, which comes to us through sensory channels, is a potential victim of misperceived meaning.

Another aspect of faulty perception is what B. F. Skinner has called "conditioned seeing." His discussion of the subject is a clear statement of how the behaviorist explains and interprets the nature of perception and its tendency to develop behaviorally. Since this concept is central to investment psychology, I quote from Skinner's *Science and Human Behavior:*

> A man may see or hear "stimuli which are not present" on the pattern of the conditioned reflex: he may see *X*, not only when *X* is present, but when any stimulus which has frequently accompanied *X* is present. The dinner bell not only makes our mouth water, it makes us see food. . . . In more general terms, conditioned seeing explains why one tends to see the world according to one's previous history. Certain properties of the world are responded to so commonly that "laws of perception" have been drawn up to describe the behavior thus conditioned . . . we generally see completed circles, squares and other figures." (1953, pp. 266–267)

You will recall my earlier discussion of Pavlov and his canine salivators. Note that the experimental animals were conditioned to respond to a bell as they did to meat powder because the bell and meat powder had been paired. In effect, the animal learned to respond to one situation *as if* it were another. Although it is not scientifically acceptable to generalize from dog to human, I will take a bit of license in this case. It seems as if the animal is salivating on *expectation* of meat powder because of its previous pairing with the bell. Let's take a big step from dog to investor. (Actually, the analogy may not be as far-fetched as you may think. The term "dogs and cats" has long been applied to certain types of stocks; why not apply it to investors as well?) Based on this extrapolation, it may be possible for paired presentation of two stimuli to acquire equal response strength. In other words, it could very well be that "a stimulus function has been assumed by a different stimulus"

(Skinner, 1953, p. 266). Frequently we see investors buy or sell stocks for what appear to be absurd reasons. These reasons may, in fact, be stimuli which were originally related to profit making stimuli.

Such behaviors fall more appropriately into what Skinner has termed "operant seeing." In this respect I would also include the Skinnerian term "superstitious behavior." If, for example, an investor calls his broker, places an order to buy, and a profit results, the precise behaviors that led to the profitable call may be repeated in their exact fashion at a later point in time. If the investor placed the call from a red telephone, for example, he may begin to "superstitiously" associate the red telephone with profits. If, perchance, several profitable trades are made using the red phone, there will most likely develop a superstitious attachment to red telephones as a sign of profits. Thus the trader may perceive the red phone as somehow magically related to investing profits. He will be prone to generalize this response or affinity to red. It is amazing how quickly such behaviors, or perceptions, can generalize into all sorts of peculiar manifestations. Red may become the investor's favorite, or "lucky," color. He may become enamored of stocks containing "red" in their name. His investments may be made in obscure stocks. His list of holdings (fictitious, of course) might include "Red's Drive-In's" or "Red Devil Manufacturing," and even "F. *R. Ed*wards Co." Preposterous? Not really. Take a good look at your own habits and you may find examples of what I just described.

How about another example? You call your broker and he reports that there are rumors of Soviet wheat buying. "What do we do?" you inquire. "Let's buy some wheat quickly before the news hits the floor!" he shouts. "OK, buy it but get out as soon as we have a few cents profit," you respond. The wheat is bought. Within several moments after your purchase the rumor hits and wheat moves up sharply. Observing your instructions the broker liquidates the position. Within a matter of minutes you've made several thousand dollars. What could be more reinforcing? You have responded to a rumor and the result has been a large profit. Under the surface there are several other possibilities that may lead to superstitious behavior, or as I call it, inappropriate perceptions of reality:

1. If repeated in the future at a given time of the day, you may unconsciously begin to perceive a *given time of the day* as best for trading. Time of day has become conditioned as a positive event by association with profits.

2. Should you trade profitably once again, while calling from the same location, you may begin to view the *location* as a key variable in the profit picture.

3. *Activity prior to profitable trade,* regardless of what it may have been, can acquire superstitious or misperceived attachment to the profit.

There are many other examples of how investors perceive certain situations as predictive of profits or losses. When groups of investors or traders all respond to the same stimulus in the same way, then their collective response will, in effect, result in an affirmation of the perceived stimulus as instrumental in the change process. Such self-fulfilling prophecies are typical in the marketplace. If many individuals believe that a certain trading signal will be profitable, then it will, in fact, become profitable. Although the profit may last only briefly, the majority of investors will persist in their response. The ultimate winners will be those who anticipate the response, buy early (or sell), and close out their position while the majority is pushing prices in the desired direction. Certainly you have seen this happen on many occasions. The threat of a war may drive stock prices sharply lower, since a majority of traders view this as bearish. They perceive war as a threat to the market, and their collective response has been generalized. Even the rumor or threat of war is reason to respond. And, as in most cases, the perception is proven incorrect, a loss results, and those who were quick enough to act in advance of the rumor profit handsomely.

Perceptions and misperceptions are not limited exclusively to the interpretation of outer environment stimuli. Traders are also subject to misperception of internal stimuli. They believe, for example, that certain visceral feelings or physiological responses are lucky. "I feel like this is my lucky day," one is inclined to say. "I don't know why, but I feel as if I'll make it big today." This feeling is, in most cases, a conditioned perception to profits previously made when similar feelings were present. The paired association of the two has resulted in a secondary conditioning of the internal feeling or its perception.

A great deal more can be said both in favor of and in opposition to my behavioral view of learned perception. So long as the facts can be demonstrated in the marketplace my analysis should be considered plausible. What can be done to rectify faulty perception? How can the investor go about discovering defective perceptual traits in his or her market studies? How can we capitalize on the misperceptions of others? I believe the answers to these questions lie in adherence to a predetermined and systematic investment scheme. The best defense against faulty perception is a strong offense in investment strategy. The best way to avoid losses due to poor perceptual development is by making your trading plans in a structured fashion and carrying them out accordingly. This will help minimize the possibly negative effect of extraneous inputs. By not allowing them to enter into the investment scheme we eliminate their negative consequences.

REVIEW

1. All individuals react to reality in different ways.
2. A combination of genetic predispositions and environmental forces results in different responses by different investors.
3. There is strong evidence that perception can be a learned behavior.
4. B. F. Skinner discussed "conditioned and operant seeing" as examples of learned perceptions.
5. Perception and misperception are important to the investor since they can limit or enhance overall profitable trading.
6. The best way to avoid the development and negative consequences of losing perception is by adherence to a strict trading plan as described elsewhere in this book.

20 Subliminal Perception — Response Without Awareness

It is difficult, if not impossible, to thoroughly understand and specify the internal processes of intellectual activity. The stimulus must necessarily undergo a number of intrapsychic, or unconscious, transformations prior to its expression as response. Psychologists have, for many years, attempted to discover the intervening variables from moment of recognition to moment of expression. They have been interested primarily in attempting to help rectify some of the dysfunctions to which the human mind is subject. Their attempts have been inspired by a need to help relieve the suffering of those who exhibit disturbed or deranged thought processes. The ultimate goal of many psychologists is to harness the immense power of the human brain.

As mentioned earlier, there are essentially two schools of thought in the modern psychological world. At one extreme the so-called classical psychologist theorizes about internal processes, using experimental methods, observation, and hypotheses to determine the validity of theories. The humanistic psychologist, on the other hand, favors a less authoritarian approach but is still concerned about the "stuff" or "matter" of human thought and consciousness. And at the other end of the continuum we find the behavioral psychologist. In its purest from the behaviorist's attitude can best be expressed as follows:

> *The process by which behavior occurs is not nearly as important as the inputs which result in behavior. We must think of the human organism as a series of inputs and outputs. By studying what goes in, and comparing it to what is produced at the output terminal (behavior), we can formulate a series of "laws," which, if correct, will permit us to predict and control. Hence it is unnecessary to dwell on the intermediate step. Since we cannot actually "see" what goes on inside the human mind, it is much more productive to avoid dealing with it. This is not to underemphasize or minimize the uniqueness or humanness of each individual. It is, however, necessary to maintain a purely scientific, pragmatic, and empirical point-of-view, even in the analysis of human thought and behavior.*

I believe there are many lessons that can be learned from an evaluation of the underlying processes of behavior. Although we may not find it possible to change our behavior purely as a function of insight, the ideas that may be stimulated in the process of discovery can lead to the initiation of change. By discovering that we may be acting in a nonproductive or self-destructive way, we can be motivated to change.

As discussed in the preceding chapter, perceptual factors tend to act as the intermediary between pure stimulus and response. More often than not we are totally unaware of the internal processes that lead us to the decision-making response. Any light that can be shed on the intermediate steps can help us rectify trading errors.

Perhaps the most baffling phenomenon to investors is their tendency to become irrational at crucial times. The history of stocks and commodities is rich with examples of public panics at major bottoms and buying hysteria at major tops. The Cuban missile panic, the Kennedy assassination panic, the many Vietnam war "peace rumors," and the very frequent prime interest rate reactions are among them. In fact, there are numerous technical market indicators whose underlying rationale rests on human emotional response to given economic and political factors. We are well aware of the fact that any one development does not shape the course of market events. Typically the precipitating event will be last in a long progression. War does not break out without warning, nor does peace come overnight. News, as many successful investors and traders have pointed out, tends to be the enemy of most traders since they know not how to use it.

The importance of news as it relates to the market is not the news per se, but rather the manner in which news is interpreted. In other words, the investing community responds to news once it has perceived it in a given fashion. What should, in many cases, be bullish news turns out to have a bearish effect. What most investors have awaited for many months turns out to be very disappointing. Perceptions of what is bullish and what is bearish change from day to day, from moment to moment, and from trade to trade. The human element, as I have indicated previously, stands as the intervening variable between stimulus and response. Economic fact must inevitably pass through the perceptual filter called the human brain. And people will act on what has been perceived, whether the interpretation is or is not correct. Ultimately economic law will take hold, but it is all too often a long, hard journey from fact to reality. It is the time spent between economic fact and market realization of truth that accounts for more than 90 percent of all price activity. Were it not for the fact that people must act on their perceptions of situations, price response would be virtually immediate and almost always correct. There is no great discovery in what I have told you. There is no mystical truth in the fact that human weakness rests at the base of most stock, commodity, and real estate price moves.

MARKET INDICATORS

There are several market indicators whose intent, whether actual or implied, is to capitalize on the human condition. In other words, it is possible to quantify human reaction by examining some key price patterns, most of which are well known to the investing community. Let's examine just a few of these indicators.

The Climax Top—The Climax Bottom

As prices continue their trend in a given direction they tend to pick up momentum. As more and more news stimulates the price move, there is a concomitant acceleration in price (up or down). It is generally believed that the first portion of any price move, called *accumulation,* occurs as a result of professional buying. The public begins buying next, and as prices begin their greatest acceleration up or down, the public is making its greatest play, whether buying or selling. Finally, at the top or bottom, the professional community is, for the most part, out of its positions since it has slowly but surely distributed them to the public.

The public *perceives* nothing but confirmation from the news, no matter what its actual import may be. Prices shoot up or down dramatically (depending on whether the trend has been up or down), and there is no end in sight. In a bullish market climate most news is interpreted as bullish. When bearish news comes it is *seen* as an opportunity to buy on the decline. When bullish news comes, it is seen as a confirmation of the trend. And on the day of reckoning, in a bull market, for example, the typical "buying climax" will come after the following scenario:

1. Very bullish news—possibly the most bullish in months.
2. Record high trading volume for the past few months or years.
3. Record high prices for the past few months or years.
4. Highly bullish public opinion.

The configuration of prices for this time period is also quite specific. Figure 14 shows several of these patterns. Note that prices move higher for a lengthy period of time. For several days in a row they close rather strong. And then on a given day they make a new high for the move and close lower than the previous day's low on very high trading volume. This is a classic "buying climax" and is created entirely by emotional overreaction of the public. Thereafter there are several attempts to recover. They typically fail and the market changes trend. The high turnover of volume and the reversal in price on the climax top day results almost ex-

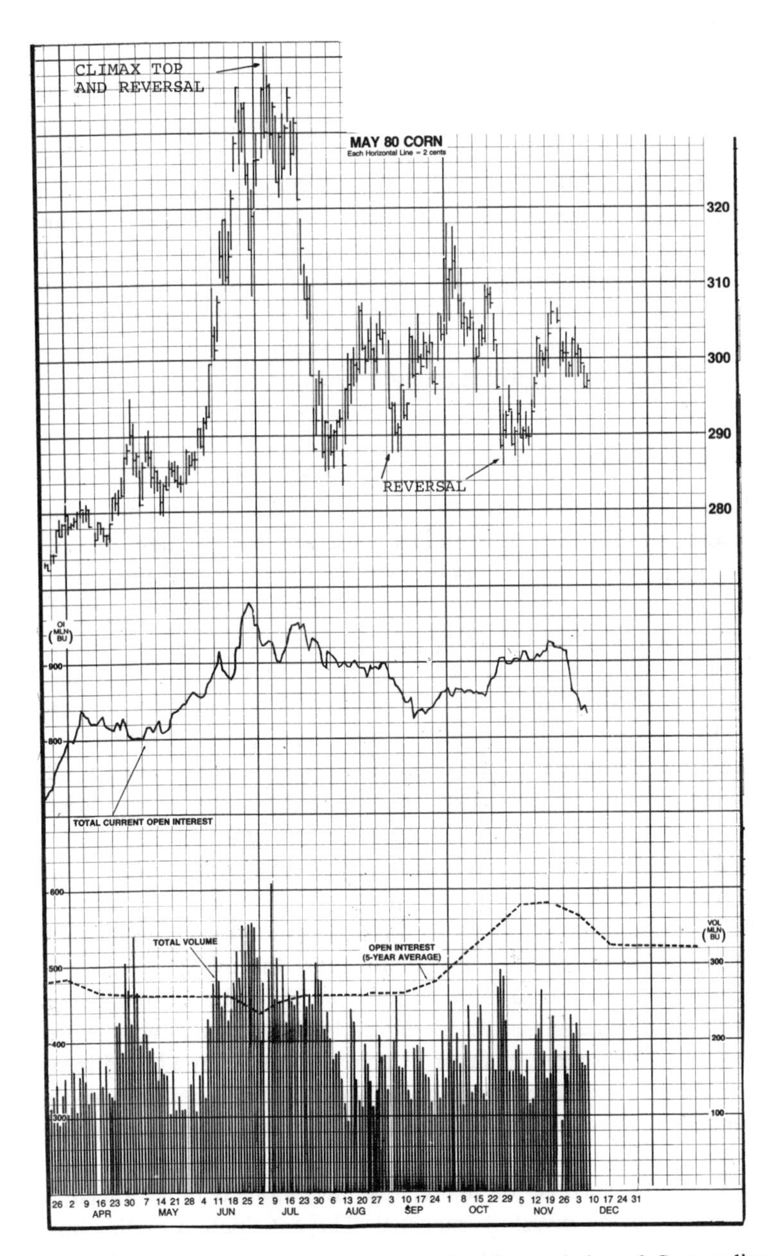

Figure 14 Typical bull market. (Reprinted with permission of Commodity Chart Service.)

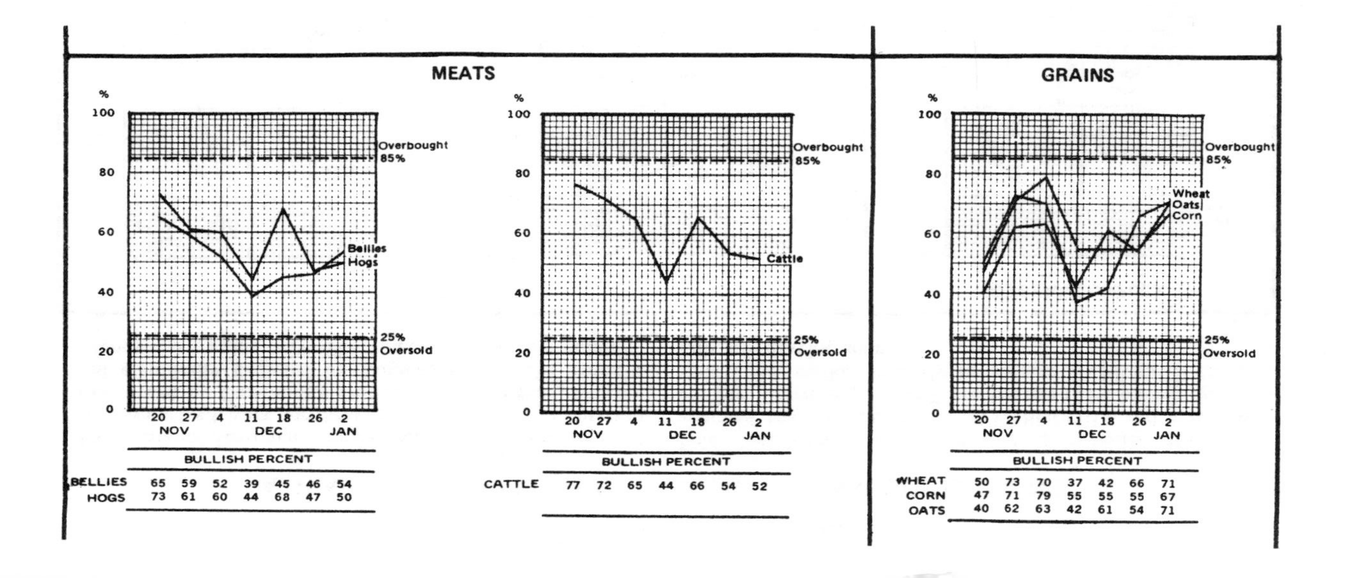

	20 NOV	27	4 DEC	11	18	26	2 JAN
BELLIES	65	59	52	39	45	46	54
HOGS	73	61	60	44	68	47	50

	20 NOV	27	4 DEC	11	18	26	2 JAN
CATTLE	77	72	65	44	66	54	52

	20 NOV	27	4 DEC	11	18	26	2 JAN
WHEAT	50	73	70	37	42	66	71
CORN	47	71	79	55	55	55	67
OATS	40	62	63	42	61	54	71

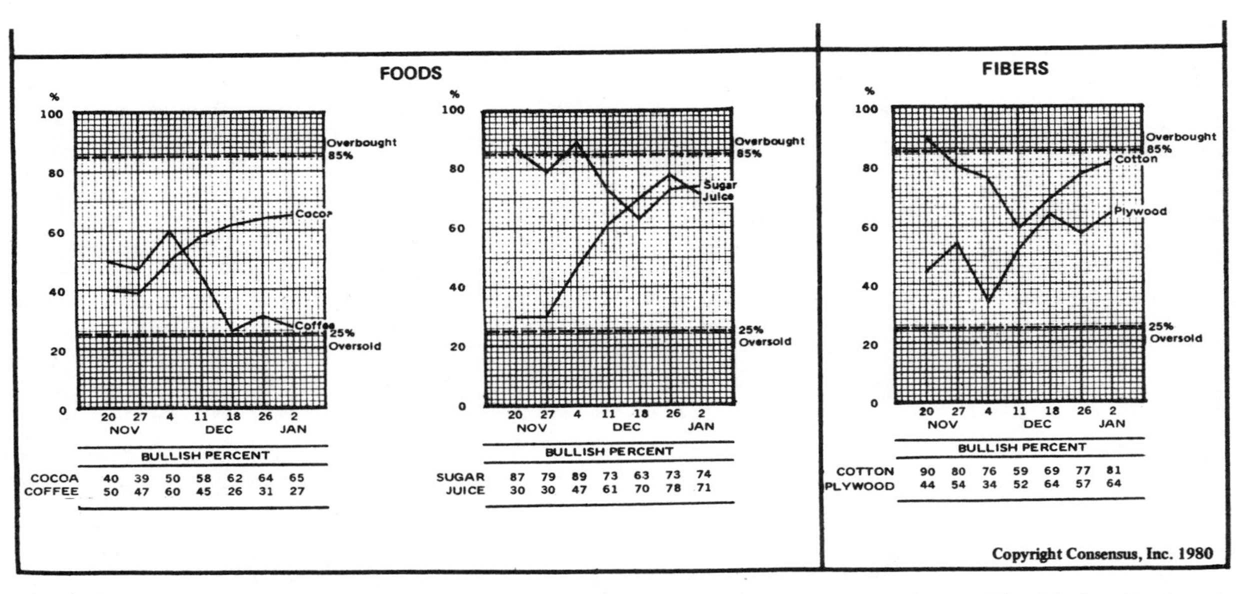

Figure 15 Market Sentiment Index—a graphic illustration of bullish consensus of opinions. The Market Sentiment Index reflects the opinions of professional advisors and brokers market letters as observed and recorded by Commodity Outlook, Inc., Portland, Oregon, and graphically depicted by Consensus, Inc. The Index is intended as a guide only. The "theory of contrary opinion" holds that when 85 percent of these analysts are bullish, it can be assumed that the market is *overbought* and a turn is coming. Conversely, if 75 percent are bearish (25 percent bullish on the Index) the market is likely to become *oversold* and a rally will develop soon. (Reprinted with permission of Consensus 30 W Pershing Rd Kansas City M0 64108.)

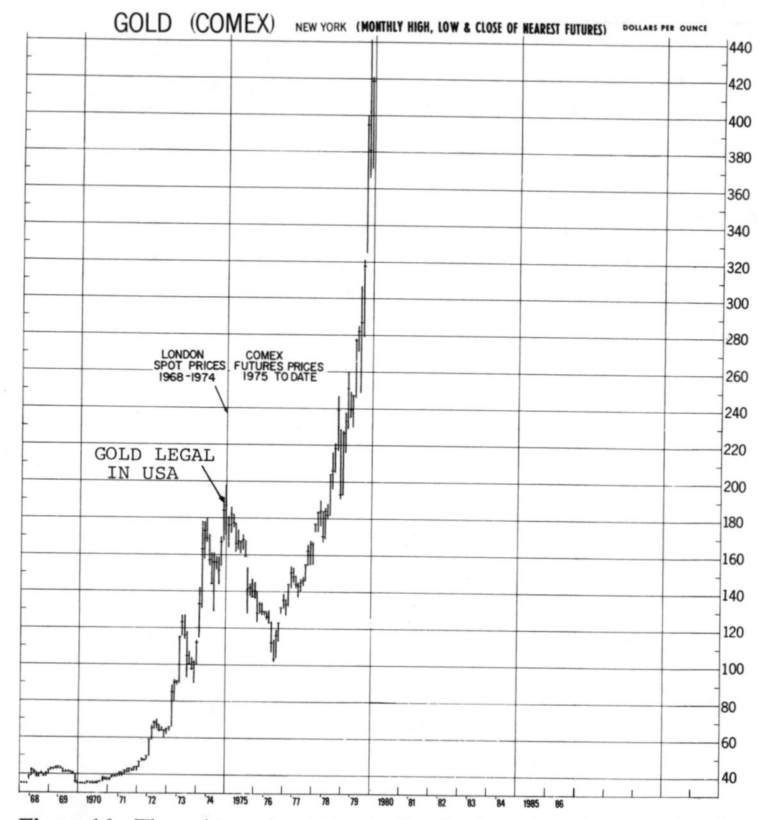

Figure 16 The gold market following legalization of gold ownership. (Reprinted with permission of Commodity Chart Service.)

who expected the move to bring higher prices. Investor perception of the facts was incorrect.

This scenario has been played out on many occasions, in many markets, for many years. It is a market truth that buying on realization of a given fact is not sound market strategy. In other words, things in the market often are not what they appear to be. Why is this so? What is it that causes most investors to act irrationally, or to misperceive reality? Is it possible to respond to a given perception without actually realizing what is stimulating us to act? Enter "subliminal perception." I urge you to pay especially close attention to what I am about to say. It is perhaps the single most important psychological fact covered in this book. It may very well be responsible for many market losses.

SUBLIMINAL STIMULATION

During the 1950s Vance Packard published his classic work *The Hidden Persuaders* (1957). The essence of this detailed examination of the advertising world was to make Americans aware of the fact that their buying habits were being manipulated with the help of some very subtle psychological techniques. Considerable concern was expressed about the ethics of using such methods as "subthreshold effects" and hypnosis.

> *The London Sunday Times* front-paged a report in mid-1956 that certain United States advertisers were experimenting with "subthreshold effects" in seeking to insinuate sales messages to people past their conscious guard. It cited the case of a cinema in New Jersey that it said was flashing ice-cream ads onto the screen during regular showings of film. These flashes of message were split-second, too short for people in the audience to recognize them consciously but still long enough to be absorbed unconsciously.
>
> A result, it reported, was a clear and otherwise unaccountable boost in ice-cream sales. "Subthreshold effects, both in vision and sound, have been known for some years to experimental psychologists," the paper explained. It speculated that political indoctrination might be possible without the subject being conscious of any influence being brought to bear on him. (Packard, 1957)

The relevance of this assertion, if accurate, is certainly in accord with our major topic. Is it possible for investors to be influenced by subliminal, or subthreshold stimulation? Is there any basis in psychological fact to this possibility? I believe that the experimental evidence supports a general conclusion in this direction. Here are some of the facts. For the purpose of this discussion I will use the terms "subliminal," "subthreshold," and "responding without awareness" interchangeably. The use of a more specific definition and the discussion of perceptual defense factors would further complicate the issue, but those interested in the overall topic can find considerable material in the current psychological literature.

Several physiological indicators are used by psychologists to determine whether human subjects have received or responded to a stimulus. The most common is Galvanic Skin Response, or GSR, an electrical measure that provides a reading of skin conductivity. It is known that changes in emotional state stimulate changes in GSR reading. GSR is one of the primary components of the lie detector or polygraph test. If a human subject is exposed to a given visual or auditory stimulus that arouses an emotional response, there will be a corresponding change in GSR reading. A number of studies (i.e., McCleary and Lazarus, 1949; Goldberg and Fiss, 1959; Wiener and Schiller, 1960; Eriksen, 1958, 1960) using GSR and verbal reports substantiate the existence of subthreshold perceptions. In other words, subjects who receive visual and/or auditory inputs that are below their level of hearing or visually presented too quickly to permit complete reading do, in fact, tend to retain some information. Secord and Backman conclude, "Experiments have suggested that, although a person does not consciously perceive a stimulus, he may nevertheless be able to respond as if he had perceived it. This is the phenomenon of subliminal perception" (1964, p. 47).

Considerably more research on the topic was carried out in the 1960s. In a detailed summary, Pötzl (1960) reported on a study cited by Freud regarding the effects of visual stimulation on dream content. Apparently, visual exposure to landscape scenes shown at the speed of 0.01 second influenced subjects dreams. The scenes often recurred as part of dream content. These findings were later confirmed by other researchers. The existence of such effects tends to lend support to many of Freud's theoretical concepts. Lest we jump to any unwarranted conclusions, let me say also that many studies refute these findings. Although the effects of subliminal stimulation are well documented, it is not known precisely how, if, or when they stimulate behavior. There are many theories about the exact interaction between such stimulation and its ultimate translation into action.

Let us assume, for a moment, that responding without awareness is indeed a reality. Certainly the body of evidence, in my opinion, tends to support this as a warranted conclusion. Studies on prejudice, discrimination, attitude and opinion change, and suggestion tend to validate my opinion. What are the implications for the investment community? Certainly they are many and significant. First, the concept of subliminal response helps explain many of the seemingly unmotivated actions taken by investors in their decision-making process. In addition, it helps us understand the immense influence opinions and attitudes, particularly of those regarded as respectworthy or expert have on our ultimate trading decisions.

In a previous chapter I mentioned the potential harm of too much information input. Advisory services and brokerage house newsletters were specifically mentioned. If an investor places himself in the position of reading the given opinions, then he may very well be influenced to act on the information, even though he is not aware of the role it has on his behavior. Note that in this case the information is certainly within the visual threshold of the reader, but it may stimulate him to action after it has been forgotten. It is therefore even more likely that unwanted influences on trader behavior will result. The same holds true for auditory inputs. Listening to the opinions of others can, and most likely does, have an unwanted competitive effect on the independent investment response of the individual. This is the basis of my suggestion that you isolate yourself from all outside opinion, both verbal and written. Many additional factors which come to us daily in a subliminal fashion and can have similar influences.

A host of social and sociopsychological variables also mediate and either accentuate or attenuate the magnitude of a given response. These concepts fall more within the field of social psychology and are covered briefly in the next chapter.

EXTRASENSORY PERCEPTION

A final and much more elusive concept in this area is that of ESP, extrasensory perception. The psychological literature is becoming increasingly keyed to ESP research. A number of colleges and universities have recognized the study of ESP as an accepted field of specialization. At this time there are insufficient hard scientific data to substantiate ESP as a viable entity. We have all, at some time or another, experienced extrasensory perception. It is believed that many successful traders who act on "gut feel" are, in effect, being motivated by extrasensory or, at the very minimum, subliminal inputs. An experience recounted in *Reminiscences of a Stock Operator* is relevant as an example of how ESP tends to affect some traders:

I stared at the last price on the board until I couldn't see any figures or any board or anything else, for that matter. All I knew was that I wanted to sell Union Pacific and I couldn't find out why I wanted to.

I must have looked queer, for my friend, who was standing alongside me, suddenly nudged me and asked, "Hey, what's the matter?"

"I don't know," I answered.

"Going to sleep?" he said.

"No," I said. "I am not going to sleep. What I am going to do is to sell that stock." I had always made money following my hunches.

I walked over to a table where there were some blank order pads. My friend followed me. I wrote out an order to sell a thousand Union Pacific at the market and handed it to the manager. He was smiling when I wrote it and when he took it. But when he read the order he stopped smiling and looked at me.

"Is this right?" he asked me. But I just looked at him and he rushed it over to the operator.

"What are you doing?" asked my friend.

"I'm selling it!" I told him.

"Selling what?" he yelled at me. If he was a bull how could I be a bear? Something was wrong.

"A thousand UP," I said.

"Why?" he asked me in great excitement.

I shook my head, meaning I had no reason. . . .

He knew it was my habit to know why I traded. I had sold a thousand shares of Union Pacific. I must have a very good reason to sell that much stock in the face of the strong market.

"I don't know," I repeated. "I just feel that something is going to happen."

"What's going to happen?"

"I don't know. I can't give you any reason. All I know is that I want to sell that stock. And I'm going to let 'em have another thousand." . . .

"I don't know why I want to sell it. I only know I do want to," I said. "I want to, like everything." The urge was so strong that I sold another thousand. . . .

I have told some of these stories to friends, and some of them tell me it isn't a hunch but the subconscious mind, which is the creative mind, at work. That is the mind which makes artists do things without their knowing how they came to do them. Perhaps with me it was the cumulative effect of a lot of little things individually insignificant but collectively powerful. Possibly my friend's unintelligent bullishness aroused a spirit of contradiction and I picked on UP because it had been touted so much. I can't tell you what the cause or motive for hunches may be. All I know is that I went out of the Atlantic City branch office of Harding Brothers short three thousand Union Pacific in a rising market, and I wasn't worried a bit. . . .

The next day we got the news of the San Francisco earthquake. It was an awful disaster. . . . On the following day, when fuller reports came in, the market began to slide off . . . I doubled up and sold five thousand shares . . . I pushed my luck for all it was worth. I doubled up again and sold ten thousand shares more. . . .

Well, the next day I cleaned up. I made two hundred and fifty thousand dollars. It was my biggest winnings up to that time. It was all made in a few days. . . . (Le Fevre, 1965, pp. 69–74)

Much more remains to be learned about subliminal and extrasensory processes. Certainly several conclusions are warranted based on the limited amount of data we have available at this time. They are stated in the review that follows.

REVIEW

1. The process that mediates stimulus and response is difficult to specify clearly.

2. It is possible to state some parameters of the perceptual filter that stands between pure stimulus and resulting response.
3. The role of subliminal response is examined and experimental data are cited in its support.
4. The role of "response without awareness" is further examined in relation to the investor decision-making process.
5. Various "technical market indicators" are examined as they relate to investor perception. Specific examples are given.
6. Galvanic skin response (GSR) is introduced as a measure of response strength.
7. The role of limited informational input as a potential benefit to the investor is reexamined.
8. Several conclusions are reached in relation to the subliminal perception concept:
   a. It *is* possible for a trader to act without being aware of the reason for his action.
   b. Typically such actions are irrational and produce losses.
   c. The opinions of others, whether verbal or written, can and do have a subliminal and suggestive effect on the investor and may cause him to act without awareness.
   d. The more limited such information input can be, the more successful may be one's overall investment strategy.
9. The role of extrasensory perception is examined through an example.

Stress 21

All individuals react differently to extreme pressure and stress. Whereas some will develop peculiar behavioral mannerisms such as tics, others will turn the pressure inward, developing psychophysiological symptoms instead. Regardless of its ultimate expression, stress is a key factor in the investment picture. In varying degrees all traders, speculators, and investors are subject to the consequences of such tensions. Inasmuch as we are all potential victims of stress, it behooves us to understand how stress develops, how it expresses itself in behavior and physiology, and, above all, what we can do to effectively minimize its consequences. It has been repeatedly demonstrated that anxiety and stress tend to cause performance to deteriorate. It is certainly true that an individual in a high state of arousal will respond more rapidly to most situations. It is the relative quality of response that suffers. Overreaction and ineffective response are typical symptoms of stress. In the marketplace this can and often does lead to unwarranted losses, inappropriate decisions, and poor discipline. Moreover, the long-term physiological sequelae of continued or intensive stress are particularly significant. To the investor who has substantial funds placed in the market, ongoing effects of stress and anxiety can be cumulative. In the long run all the financial gains of trading and/or investing may be overshadowed by the deterioration in personal health.

Fortunately, there has been a growing interest in stress and its correlates. Psychologists, particularly H. Selye, have studied virtually every aspect of tension and stress in animal and man. Selye's findings support the conclusion that stress and tension have a systemic effect on human and animal physiology. A few of the physical consequences include increases in various hormone levels; increases in blood pressure; increase in heart rate and pulse; increased gastric acid production; increased symptoms such as headache, muscle aches, back of neck pain, backaches, tiredness, insomnia; mood swings of increased intensity and frequency; increased aggression and frustration; and sexual dysfunctions. In addition, there is a host of more specific effects that are part and parcel of stress.

One can also identify a number of psychiatric disturbances correlated with stress. Some researchers claim to have discovered a close connection between certain psychotic disturbances and increases in particular hormone levels due to stress. Typically, industrialized societies show increases in psychophysiological disorders such as gastric and peptic ulcers, ulcerative colitis, high blood pressure, and migraine headaches. Considerable psychological research has been done in this area, and there are many highly effective techniques for preventing tension build-up and treating it once it has occurred. The purpose of this chapter is to delineate the possible side-effects of stress on the investor and on investment success.

EFFECTS OF STRESS ON TRADING DECISIONS

In previous chapters I characterized the successful investment process as one based on specificity, structure, sound methodology, rationality, and organization. The most profitable programs are those that remove, or minimize, negative human elements from the decision-making process. We have all, at one time or another, experienced the poor decisions that result from impulsive or anxiety-provoked actions. This so called "fight–flight" response is reserved primarily for situations that are life-threatening. The state of arousal resulting from such a case is a natural mechanism for self-defense and preservation. It is used successfully in all forms of animal life. Humans, however, have been blessed with higher mental capabilities that do not necessitate the use of survival responses in many cases. The application of calm and well-reasoned logic can, in most situations, yield far greater results than the panic response.

To deal intelligently with stress it is necessary to be aware of one's tendency in the overreactive direction. Psychologically the best technique for stimulating awareness is the use of a signaling mechanism. In other words, the ability to prevent overreaction depends on the ability to realize that this response is welling up and seeking expression. The mechanism that acts as a signal is different for each individual. The oft quoted maxim "count to ten" represents one such method. In counting to ten before responding, it is believed that the individual who has become aroused to a temperamental or aggressive response will retain his composure, thereby signaling his intellect that he is about to explode. It is hoped that the higher processes of logic and control will have sufficient time to short-circuit the fight–flight response. As overused as it may seem, there is time-tested value in this technique. To those who see themselves as more suave and sophisticated, the "count to ten" method may not suffice. The same underlying concept applies to the many methods we use daily without being aware of what we are doing. Such behavioral responses as drumming one's fingers, tapping one's foot and doodling on a pad of paper are all attempts to deal with tension. When we are anxious or tense, and understand that an impulsive response may not be the best thing, we resort to our internal mechanisms or coping styles for assistance.

The impulsive, or tension-provoked, response in investing should be treated in a similar fashion. Take the following situation as an example. An investor has just purchased a large block of stock. His broker telephones several minutes after the purchase and reports that the company has just announced a termination of its dividend. The stock begins to fall. Naturally, one's response might be the typical fight–flight reaction. If responding in flight, the investor would exit the stock immediately. This, of course, would be a violation of trading rules and will most likely lead to losses and regrets. In exercising the fight response, the investor would become angry, his blood pressure or ulcers might act up, and he may actually fight back by buying more of the stock. Ultimately, the act of buying more might prove beneficial. But in any event it was also a violation of the inherent trading system since the purchase was not planned. By using a signal to cue his possible overreaction the investor would be saved from emotional response. His signal might very well be a warning from the broker. "Be careful not to overreact," the broker could say. In fact, the intelligent investor could incorporate such a technique into his trading system. He might decide, for example, that he will not attend to any news, bullish or bearish, that might be released during the same day or week of his stock purchase. This would act as a preventive measure to overreaction caused by anxiety and stress.

The same basic response occurs in virtually all unexpected or otherwise unplanned situations. The net result of action taken in response to anxiety, perceived threat, stress, and/or tension is not only costly, but it also takes its physical toll. Frustration typically leads to aggression. Aggression leads to action and overreaction. Reaction and overreaction lead to losses, conflict, and more anxiety. As such it is necessary to break into the vicious cycle. Whereas it is a beneficial decision to avoid panic- and anxiety-inspired responses, it does not help heal the possible physical damage that can result. A number of the previously discussed treatment methods are effective in limiting losses due to anxiety and stress. It is much better, however, to prevent the emotional response in order to limit the chances of financial ruin. The ideal situation is to limit the potential physical and psychological damage that accompanies stress.

TECHNIQUES FOR COPING WITH STRESS

The best defense is a strong offense. And the best way to cope with stress is to prevent it before it requires treatment. This is, to be sure, not always possible. Assuming that many investors, and in particular active traders (speculators), are already in stressful situations, I will begin by outlining some common methods that are useful in coping with tension. I will also evaluate their potential value.

Ventilation of Feelings

This technique was popularized by Sigmund Freud. Its intended use in the psychoanalytic situation was simply that indicated by its name. By talking about the stressful, or anxiety-producing, situation the patient would "ventilate" or clear his unconscious mind of the tension and pain the situation had caused. The old adage "don't keep the feelings inside you or they'll eat you from within" is, in effect, true. By employing this method Freud was able to help many patients experience almost immediate relief.

There are many ways in which feelings can be ventilated. One form of ventilation is "abreaction." During World War II and the Korean War many soldiers experienced mental breakdowns as a result of their continued tension in combat situations. It was found that although the tension did, in fact, help them remain alert, some men could not cope indefinitely. Gradually their behavior deteriorated, they became withdrawn, often exhibiting psychotic or prepsychotic symptoms. A technique using hypnosis was employed in treating those who "cracked" under the pressure. Frequently the mental breakdown would follow a precipitating event such as seeing a friend killed in action, being trapped in an ambush, or sustaining an injury. The patient was hypnotized and then asked to recall and relive the precipitating event. In so doing, all of the accompanying anguish, tension, fear, and stress were ventilated in a safe environment. Following treatment the patient would often make an almost miraculous recovery. The key to this technique is ventilation of feelings.

Implications for the investor are obvious. In ventilating feelings many of the internalized pressures and tensions will be relieved. Before pressures can build up to the boiling point, they can be released in a socially acceptable way. This will lead to fewer losses, less physical damage, and less interpersonal conflict. What are the ways in which an average investor can ventilate feelings? There are several.

Free Association. I prefer to call this technique "talking to one's self." I recommend doing just that each and every day after the market has closed. This is advised for the very active trader. Rather than go to the nearest drinking establishment and attempt to relieve tension with alcohol, take some time to sit down in a quiet room by yourself and talk about the day's events. Pay particular attention to those that caused the greatest amount of anxiety, pain, frustration, or aggravation. If you wish, the talking could be done into a recorder. At a later time you can replay the tape. This could be of value in tracking your progress. For those who are less active in the market I would suggest a once weekly session. This method, by the way, can be used to relieve all types of stress, not just market-induced pressure.

Daily Diary. Albeit simple, keeping a daily diary is another method that will accomplish about the same result as free association. Simply jot down the ideas and tensions rather than talking about them. In both cases it is best to let ideas come to you freely. Too much structure will be inhibiting.

Physical Exercise. In addition to having healthful fringe benefits, all forms of exercise tend to be tension releasing. The recent increase in jogging, racquetball, tennis, and handball is simply an expression of the popular move to tension-relieving exercises. Any exercise–swimming, walking, roller-skating–has potential value. The rationale for physical exercise is well founded. During the course of exercise many of the harmful hormones that build up due to stress are released. Once out of the body their effects cannot be expressed in physiological disorders.

Techniques for Relaxation

There are many methods that help promote relaxation. Among these are such disciplines as yoga, transcendental meditation, self-hypnosis, biofeedback, Jacobson's muscle relaxation, and reciprocal inhibition. For the most part they all seek to accomplish the same end–the relaxation of tense muscles throughout the body. Information on all of them can be found in most bookstores. In particular I recommend Jacobson's systematic muscle relaxation method as helpful, especially for those who suffer from high blood pressure. Recent advances in biofeedback have made this the preferred method for controlling high blood pressure, and it should also be investigated by those who are sufferers. In fact, it is my belief that by 1990 there will be biofeedback techniques to cope with many diseases and psychiatric conditions.

Diet, Schedule, and Sleep

Since I am not an expert in nutrition I will not spend much time on this topic. I can only cite from personal experience and observation that these factors are also critical in relieving and inhibiting stress. I have found, for example, that a diet high in red meat increases my level of stress. This makes sense, since many of the animal hormones found in meat increase heart rate. It is a known fact, for example, that those who maintain vegetarian diets have significantly lower pulse rate and blood pressures than those who do not. Furthermore, the effects of alcohol do not, in my opinion, help release tension. Since alcohol is primarily a depressant, it may act to lock stress deep within the unconscious.

There are many physical consequences associated with the effects of nicotine and caffeine. Both can increase stress. Coffee, in particular, contains enough caffeine to stimulate neurotic anxiety in most individuals. Given the amount of coffee that most individuals consume, increases in physical tension can be dramatic. Diet is therefore another factor that can act to either increase or decrease the amount of stress acting on an individual. The more closely involved you are with the market, the more important your diet may be.

Schedule and sleep are also contributing factors. If one's day is planned without any consideration or time for adequate rest, then tension and stress will be magnified. Those in executive positions are especially prone to develop symptoms, and should pay particular attention to their schedule. It has been clearly demonstrated in psychological research that those in executive or decision-making positions are prone to ulcers and high blood pressure as a result of the stress associated with their work.

Last and certainly not least is sleep. I cannot tell you how important it is to give the body and mind sufficient sleep. Drug-induced sleep has been shown ineffective in providing the proper type of rest. Sleep must allow the unconscious mind to ventilate as it rests the body. During the sleep state dreams are stimulated by the conflicts that have been locked inside. Considerable research has shown very clearly that dreams are tension-relieving mechanisms. Many neo-Freudian psychiatrists believe that dreams are actually problem-solving mechanisms. Subjects deprived of dreams in a laboratory situation developed personality defects, hallucinatory experiences, extreme tiredness, and poor judgment. All this, despite the fact that sleep was sufficient. Dreams are necessary, and normally induced sleep is what helps stimulate dreams.

Working Conditions

All too often we do not realize the importance of our working conditions. For the active trader who sits behind a desk watching prices all day, working conditions are very important in keeping stress at a minimum. The chair and desk you sit at, the lighting, temperature and humidity, wallpaper and paint—all can either limit or intensify the effects of stress. The ringing of telephone bells, the shouting of orders, and the flashing of prices and news are all important considerations. You might want to keep noise at a minimum, comfort at a maximum, and lighting at a high level. Telephone bells might be replaced with chimes, or the loudness may be switched to a lower level.

It is also important to change the working environment from time to time. The so-called Hawthorne effect has clearly demonstrated the importance of environment on work production. Although not specifically related to stress it has been shown that a change in such things as room color, lighting, temperature, and humidity can increase the level of production.

Vacations

My last bit of advice regarding stress relates to "time away from the market." There are those who trade daily and hence build up considerable pressures. Brokers, pit traders, stock specialists, and account managers are all subject to intense degrees of stress. In order to help relieve some of the pressure, it is suggested that time be spent away from the market. The rationale is simple and need not be explained in any further detail.

SOME FINAL WORDS ABOUT PREVENTING STRESS

The suggestions I have made may not be applicable to all investors. Yet they are, in certain ways, important for all individuals, man or woman, active trader or sometime investor. Stress arises from many varying sources. Fortunately, contemporary mental health professionals have recognized the role of stress in behavioral disorders. They have also isolated the types of stressful conditions that can have physical consequences. But their greatest achievements have been in the area of prevention. I suggest you carefully consider the techniques I have discussed. A little time spent in formulating a tension-release program may well prove the best investment you have ever made.

There are many variations on the themes mentioned here. Your physician, book store, or library can refer you to numerous courses, training schools, and books. Never underemphasize the value of a well-planned stress-release program. In fact, you may want to make it your greatest priority.

REVIEW

1. The role of stress is significant in the overall investment plan.
2. Serious and continued stress can have physiological correlates.
3. Stress can also lead to many inappropriate market actions thereby increasing losses.
4. There are many symptoms of stress. Several major ones are mentioned.
5. Relaxation techniques for coping with pressure and stress are discussed, and effective alternatives to tension release are mentioned.

22 Oft Asked Questions

During the course of my frequent lectures on the commodity markets and investor psychology, many listeners ask the same questions. The question-and-answer section that follows is designed to assist with any unclear items. Should you have any remaining questions about what I have covered in previous chapters, you will most likely find the answers here.

WHAT'S THE "BEST" WAY TO COPE WITH LOSSES?

Although it is always necessary to take losses when investing or trading, this does not make a loss any more palatable to accept. It is nevertheless a mark of a successful trader to take losses just as soon as the trading system he or she is using so indicates. Any response which is either premature or tardy will lead to uncalled for consequences. Many investors refuse to take losses. The reasons for this inability or unwillingness have been discussed in previous chapters. Very often the fear of taking a loss arises from the pain one anticipates will come as a function of the loss. Whatever the reason, inability to take a loss when and as required is a psychological problem. There are, however, some investors who can take losses promptly, but who have difficulty in dealing with the pain, rejection, shame, and other negative feelings that accompany such losses. There are a number of ways in which one can cope with losses more successfully. Here are just a few suggestions:

1. Make certain that you have set your total loss limit. In other words, when you start your investment program make note of exactly how much you can afford to lose. Assume, for example, that you set a $10,000 total loss limit on your investment program. By setting the limit before initiating any trades you will know how bad things can get. Each loss will not seem like part of an endless series. As a consequence you will find a loss much less threatening.

2. You may wish to incorporate the various suggestions which I made in the section on treatment of trading problems. For example, rewards might be given for taking a loss on time. This will help you cope, since you are being rewarded for making the correct decision at the proper time.

3. Practice some of the relaxation techniques discussed in Chapter 21. It is a good idea to "relive" each loss in a nonthreatening environment. By placing the body in a relaxed state the loss will be more readily acceptable and tension will be relieved. This is the same principle that is employed in behavioral therapy and systematic relaxation. My best recommendation is to practice relaxation after each and every loss. Frequently, such a program will virtually eliminate the pain of taking losses within a brief period after it has been initiated.

HOW CAN AN INVESTOR COPE WITH NONSPECIFIC FEARS ABOUT THE MARKET?

Essentially the method described in answer to the previous question is advised. Where diffuse anxiety or tension exists it is best to use relaxation techniques several times each day. Keep a record of *when* and in response to *what* your anxiety occurs. Perhaps the best information you can have is *when* the problems begin. After keeping such a record for about a week, begin a program of systematic relaxation shortly before the expected "anxious time." Only several minutes of deep relaxation are necessary. Perhaps four or five ten-minute sessions each day will be enough to provide the necessary relief. There are some investors who exhibit symptoms that can be treated only by a professional therapist. If you have attempted some of the methods described in this book (and in others), but still find either that you are unable to relax or that your functioning is affected to a serious degree, then I suggest you consult a psychiatrist or psychologist. You can obtain help by getting a referral from your family physician, a local chapter of the American Psychological Association, or the American Medical Association. Bear in mind that fears which totally prevent your effective functioning are most likely a reflection of more deep-seated problems which have nothing to do with the market. Typically, an individual who is well adjusted and has no serious conflicts in his or her home life will not exhibit more than occasional anxiety in the market.

IS THERE AN EFFECTIVE WAY TO DEAL WITH GREED?

Many investors would be successful were it not for the forces of greed. Although many positions are correctly entered at the appropriate time, they are often kept too long once they show profits. Objectives are ignored, and the basics of rational trading fall by the wayside. There are many investors who would otherwise be successful. The problem here is one of poor discipline. As in most cases, inability to take profits once an objective has been hit is purely a function of poor organization and lack of discipline. I therefore recommend some of the methods outlined earlier. Objectives, once determined, should not be altered other than by dictate of the trading system. It may be helpful to obtain assistance from a second party when it comes to taking profits at stated or predetermined objectives. As in most cases, the key to avoiding greed's effects is organization, discipline, and trading by objective.

HOW CAN I FIND A BROKER WHO WILL BEST SUIT MY NEEDS?

This is a topic on which I could spend several weeks. Certainly there are many brokers who are quite capable at their work. And there are many brokers who are excellent market analysts as well. The difficulty for most investors lies in selecting a broker who will be compatible with the investor's personality and needs and who will not–either directly or indirectly–interfere with the investor's plan. There are several ways in which the process of selection can be approached. First and foremost, I recommend that you get to know your broker, or potential broker, prior to dealing with him or her. Make certain that you both understand what is expected of the relationship. Each party has needs, rights, and expectations. Some brokers want to be called frequently, whereas others do not wish to be disturbed after an order has been placed (unless it is for the purpose of changing the order). Some brokers will help insecure traders, whereas others want no part of the insecurity. Some brokers enjoy making recommendations to their clients, whereas others do not wish to assume the responsibility of doing so. Here are several guidelines which I believe should be followed by all investors in selecting a broker:

1. If you plan to use a broker's recommendations in your trading, make certain that you follow all of his or her recommendations. Trading on the advice of a broker is in no way different from following a trading system. If you do not intend to follow through exactly as specified, then do not insult your broker by secondguessing him.

2. Make a list of precisely what you expect of a broker. When you go looking for the right person make certain that your requirements are met.

3. Your expectations should be specific. Don't just expect a broker to get you "good information"; rather, indicate what you mean by "good information."

4. Let the broker know what you expect. Show him or her your list of requirements and see if they meet with approval.

5. It is also important to make a list of what the broker expects of you. In so doing you will not fall prey to the many pathological relationships which can occur in broker-client interactions.

6. Do not burden your broker with emotional problems. You are most likely not his only client and he does not have time to counsel you. Should you seek his assistance in a particular program as described earlier in this book, make certain that it does not infringe on his time and ability. A broker should not be depended on for consolation, support, or confidence building.

7. I would suggest that you look for a broker who has the following qualities and skills:

a. Ability and willingness to promptly execute orders correctly and without hesitation.

b. Willingness to avoid making recommendations either in agreement with or in opposition to your opinions of trades.

c. Ability to secure technical and/or fundamental market information as required by client.

d. Good record of work attendance and being on time for work. When a broker is needed he must be there!

The most certain way to determine how a broker-client relationship will work is the test of time. If you find that a broker is not making things less difficult for you, then look for a new broker. Always make certain that *you* are not to blame. My greatest successes have been with brokers who do not talk unless asked to do so. By letting a broker do his job as best he can you will also derive the maximum benefit.

It is not possible for me to overstate the important role a broker plays in the total investment picture. There are many investors who blame brokers for getting them into positions or getting them out of positions. For many years the broker has been a scapegoat of the undisciplined investor. It is time we stopped blaming brokers for our own lack of discipline. Therefore, I suggest a reappraisal of your current relationship with your broker, or thorough evaluation of a pending relationship. Don't be too quick to affix blame that might, in reality, be yours.

WHICH MARKETS SHOULD I TRADE?

Not every market is suited to the temperament of every investor. Some individuals had best stick to stocks where others might do better in commodity futures. Certainly the decision of which markets should be traded is one that must be based on three distinct factors: experience, temperament, and financial ability. Even though experience and financial ability may be present, temperament may not be sufficient. For the beginner I would advise no trading in the commodity futures market. It takes time to acquire the necessary skill and emotional strength to trade in this area. There is a tendency for small traders to take on positions in obscure, low-priced stocks and lightly traded issues. This is not, in my opinion, an advisable approach. If you are a small trader and you think small, then you will remain small. This does not mean that you should assume a position above and beyond your financial ability. You can, however, put on trades in the stocks or commodities you wish, so long as the amount of shares or contracts *is* within your limit. When a signal is triggered by your trading system you should take the signal. You need not, however, "plunge" into the trade with an unacceptable large position. Although many errors have been made in the overly bold direction, more have been made by those who were too weak.

At this time, it is also reasonable to discuss how many markets should be traded. If you are a full-time trader and do not have other responsibilities, then there is no problem in establishing several positions at one time. If, however, you are not totally committed to the market, then you had best assume only a limited number of trades. The best index for determining how much is too much is by the degree of concern or anxiety you feel when the market does not move in your direction. If you become extremely anxious, then you have instituted too many positions. In the long run, only experience will be the guide. Start slowly, trade carefully, and do not overtrade on limited funds.

WOULD IT BE ADVISABLE TO HAVE SEVERAL INDIVIDUALS PARTICIPATE IN THE DECISION-MAKING PROCESS?

Trading "by committee," as it is called, is not, in my opinion, a valid or effective procedure for most traders. Where a specific trading system exists it may be useful to have several inputs regarding the signals themselves. But if the system is effective and clear-cut, then there will be no need for interpretation or judgment of any kind. Thus it is not necessary to have more than one or two individuals decide on a given trade. Generally, there will be too much disagreement if more people are involved in the ultimate decision. The democratic process may work well when it comes to long-term fundamental researching of stocks and commodities, but it may not yield good results where fast decisions are required.

Moreover, the various personalities involved may clash. The entire process can easily become a power struggle that will cloud objective features of the system. Investment clubs usually have a number of members who put forward their points of view. This process will work if those who participate are mature enough to stick to the facts and avoid the personalities. All too often this is not possible. I have long believed, based both on personal experience and observation of successful traders' methods, that one must trade one's own line, make one's own decisions, and accept all the glory or grief alone. There is much to be said in favor of the "loser" when it comes to investment. I have indicated how and why too much information can be a dangerous thing in the market. And so it is with too many "cooks" in the decision-making process.

IS LONG-TERM INVESTMENT BETTER THAN SHORT-TERM TRADING AND SPECULATION?

This depends on the individual. Historically, the greatest amounts of money are made in riding large moves. But it is not always possible to do so. For one reason or another many investors feel that they should enter and exit a market many times, in order to protect what they have. They are afraid their profit will disappear. This is a type of insecurity that generally reflects poor discipline and technique. There are many investors who trade only for the short term. They somehow need the satisfaction that comes with immediate gratification of needs. This stems from psychological factors and may cause many losses. The best course for each individual is the one that causes the least anxiety. Since stress, tension, anxiety, and panic can lead to more than the necessary number of losses, any act that increases these tendencies is not advised. For well over 90 percent of the investment community, long-term trades are the only ones to consider. By long term I mean specifically trades that are kept for a minimum of several months. It is not always possible to keep a trade for this length of time, particularly if your loss point is hit. The trades held for brief periods of time will most frequently be losers, whereas those held for longer time spans will be winners. This is typical of most successful systems. There are few traders who can "scalp" or day trade the market with any consistent degree of success. Those who consistently do so profitably are pit traders or specialists on the exchange floor. When you attempt to compete with these people, you are working at a disadvantage which will almost always cause you considerable grief.

Clearly, long-term investment is favored over short-term speculation. Even trades that are carried for several weeks are preferable to those held for shorter time spans. I recommend that 90 percent of all investors carry long-term positions. Speculation should be reserved for those who make it their life's work.

HOW DOES ONE KNOW WHEN TO SEEK HELP FROM A MENTAL HEALTH PROFESSIONAL?

There are many individuals walking the streets who feel they need psychiatric treatment. And there are many individuals walking the streets who need treatment but are not receiving it. How does one know when, why, and where to seek help? Are there signs and symptoms that a mental health professional should be consulted? The best single indicator of necessary treatment is the ability to function. If a behavior disorder is so intense that it affects functioning, then it is high time help was sought. It is, for example, relatively normal to suffer some periods of mental depression; it is, however, a very serious problem to be so depressed you cannot leave for work in the morning. This, of course, occurs very late in the history of the behavior disorder, and there is no longer any choice about treatment. Hospitalization may be necessary. Early in the course of a disorder there are many warning signs. Any increase in symptoms over an extended period of time is perhaps the first clue. Dependence on alcohol or drugs is another symptom of impending trouble. The things to watch for are primarily an increase in symptoms, an intensification of symptoms, and/or the development of new symptoms.

What precisely do I mean by "symptoms"? Typically, symptoms include intense anxiety, depression, mental confusion, forgetting, sleeplessness, delusions and/or hallucinations, use of drugs or alcohol, intense irritability, high blood pressure unrelated to a medical condition, attacks of colitis and/or ulcer pain, tics, stuttering, feelings of depersonalization (i.e., not knowing who you are or where you are), inappropriate laughter. There are many other associated symptoms reflecting even more serious mental conditions. My advice would be not to delay if you notice any problems cropping up. An ounce of prevention goes a long way when it comes to mental health. Do not attempt to be your own therapist. Consult a professional if you find that your functioning is being hampered. Some of the simple methods described earlier are intended for the treatment of trading problems that are not indicative of more serious difficulty.

WHERE DO YOU FIND PROFESSIONAL HELP IF YOU HAVE DECIDED YOU NEED IT?

Assuming that you or a friend requires treatment, where do you start to get the help best suited to your needs? Assuming you have not waited too long, I would suggest a consultation with your family physician. He or she may decide to help you through the bad time with some medication. Although I cannot dispute this authority, I would not recommend drugs for more than a brief period of intense crisis (see next question). In most cases your family physician will make referral to a mental health professional. Either a psychiatrist or psychologist will be recommended. If you are at a loss as to where you might turn, contact any local chapter of the various mental health treatment organizations. They will help you get the right kind of help. In this respect I would also suggest you not "shop around" for the least costly therapist. Regardless of price I advise you seek help from an individual who is respected and capable.

HOW DO DRUGS AFFECT PERSONALITY AND INVESTING?

The 1970s have witnessed a sharp increase in drug use among individuals of all ages and backgrounds. Whereas the most common drug at one time may have been alcohol, this is slowly changing. Other drugs have taken its place. No matter what the drug, its effect on personality will be negative. There has also been an increase in prescription drugs, such as mood elevators, tranquilizers, and diet medication. These also tend to have a negative effect on performance in all areas. Benefits may be far outweighed by the side-effects, and I suggest you never mix drugs with investing.

ISN'T THE MARKET JUST ANOTHER FORM OF GAMBLING?

Depending on the manner in which it is used, the market may be a tool of either the investor or the gambler. If used in a predetermined, applied, consistent, and well-researched fashion, the market will protect the investor from inflation, help money grow at an above-average rate, and provide retirement security. It is neither the goal nor the ability of gambling to provide these. Motivation is at the heart of this issue. The investor who allows long-term objectives to become obscured can easily become a gambler. The incessant need to trade is one symptom of gambling in the marketplace. Losses that mount and are not cut short tend to cause more caution in the serious investor. But in the gambler they inspire more chance taking, less rational behavior, borrowing, and an almost frenzied attachment to the trend of prices. Savings are taken from the bank, home furnishings may be sold, and money may even be stolen to support a gambling habit. If things become this bad, then the investor has become a gambler and professional help is necessary.

SHOULD I MANAGE MY OWN MONEY OR SHOULD A PROFESSIONAL DO IT FOR ME?

There are many individuals who refuse to admit that they cannot "make it in the market." They continue to take loss after loss and will not allow one who may know better to manage their money. The only real difference between most individual investors and professional money managers is that the money manager does this work as his livelihood. His approach tends to be more organized, concise, objective, and professional. More often than not he can do a better job than the investor. Certainly there are financial managers who will lose more money than any investor can lose on his own. This is why the decision to employ a manager is so very important. Not only is it necessary to know the manager's "track record," but it is also necessary to know the person who is doing the managing.

There are those investors who wish to "backseat drive." Although they do not want to accept the responsibility and effort that come with investment planning, they do want to supervise the money manager. They frequently call the manager and question the moves which were made. This, of course, angers most professionals, and this is not a suggested form of behavior. There are, therefore, several questions that should be asked before you decide to have another manage your money for you:

1. Am I capable of emotionally accepting the fact that another is in control of my money? Will I be grief stricken if it is lost? Will I be ego-deflated if money is made?

2. Can I give the money manager the "breathing room" necessary for him to do his job?

3. Am I satisfied that I cannot do the job on my own?

4. Will my tension and stress be relieved by having another manage my funds?

I suggest you evaluate these questions before making the decision.

ARE THERE ANY PERSONAL QUALITIES THAT DIFFERENTIATE LOSERS FROM WINNERS?

This is another question which could take an entire book to answer. I believe that there are many specific qualities of the market winner. To name but a few:

1. **Discipline and organization.** Decisions are made from a base of secure attitude, organized investment objectives, and disciplined application of trading rules.

2. **Persistence.** The winner must be willing to try and try until he succeeds. One of the best traders I ever met refused to accept failure in any aspect of his life. If there was something he could not do, he would learn how. When his trading system failed he would go "back to the drawing board" and start over.

3. **Positive attitude.** This is an important quality. The willingness to say that you *will* be successful is important and has been discussed in a previous chapter.

4. **Independence.** There is a tendency for successful traders to ignore the advice and opinions of others. Their own work is regarded as best, and they implement decisions that have come from their own trading system. Even if information is gathered from other sources, it is recombined in a unique way and implemented with confidence.

5. **Self-confidence.** This is a combination of positive attitude and persistence. The belief that you *can* do what has to be done is a mark of self-confidence.

6. **Contrary thinking.** Quite often the successful investor is moving contrary to the crowd. When the trend is strong in one direction or another, he is moving with it. At major changes in trend he is one of the first to change course, no matter what others may say or do.

7. **Isolation.** Many successful investors tend to isolate themselves from the public world. Although some are eccentric and peculiar in their mannerisms, this is not a necessary requisite to success. There are many information inputs which cloud thinking and pervert judgment. These are systematically excluded from the repertoires of successful traders.

8. **Well-rounded personal life.** Many investors are so tuned into the market that their personal lives suffer. Eventually their trading will suffer as well. Those who live well-rounded lives–socially, interpersonally, physically, and professionally–are among the most frequent and lasting market winners.

I have outlined some of the most important qualities. Certainly there are many more. The readings which are recommended elsewhere in this book can help you learn about the more subtle characteristics.

CAN MY HOME LIFE REALLY AFFECT MY MARKET PERFORMANCE?

Just as your home life can affect your job and interpersonal relationships, it can also affect your investing and trading. If you have experienced trauma, intense personal loss, or serious quarrel in the home, you will find your ability to make decisions of all kinds affected. The best thing at such times is to back away from the market, making as few decisions as necessary. If the home situation is an ongoing aggravating factor, then your overall performance will decline even further. As such I suggest that good trading begins in the home. Solve whatever the crisis may be *before* you begin a serious program of trading.

In the same way, trading problems can affect home life. Take the necessary care to leave your problems in the office. It is important to make the separation as soon as possible, particularly if you trade the market for a living.

CAN "SELF-IMPROVEMENT" COURSES HELP?

Yes. They can be of immense help if you are serious about what has been taught. There are many individuals who tour the country giving self-improvement seminars. Only a few are worthwhile. Without mentioning names, I suggest you carefully look into the background of each such course. Only those that are well established and have a record of longevity should be considered. As with most skills, you must use them or lose them. If you intend to spend your hard-earned money on a trading course in self-confidence, self-discipline, and positive mental attitude, do not enter the class with the misperception that all the work will be done for you. Much effort is required during and especially after.

IS IT HELPFUL TO ATTEND TRADING OR INVESTING SEMINARS?

I have led many market seminars over the past few years. In most cases the individuals who attend these meetings are sincere, interested, and well intentioned. However, they are often ignorant of the best way in which to use the information that has been presented. Instead of taking notes, listening intently, asking good questions, of making cogent comments, they busily record my comments and safely tuck the tape in a back drawer when they get home. If you spend the time and money to be at one of the many expensive market seminars, make certain you get your money's worth. How to do this? I have a number of suggestions:

1. Take notes, ask questions, make comments, and participate actively.

2. Get plenty of rest the night before and make certain that you follow the speaker at all times. If you get confused, ask questions.

3. Attempt to know something about the subject matter *before* entering the meeting.

4. Have a list of prepared questions. If they are relevant but not answered, then ask them.

5. Don't be intimidated or shy. Ask as many questions as necessary. If you have a question, chances are many others have the same question as well.

6. Find out where you can acquire a transcript of the talk.

7. Obtain an address where you can write if still confused or unclear about some issues.

8. Attempt to integrate the material with what you already know or do.

9. Test the material before using it in the market. Just because a person speaks on a given subject does not mean that he or she is always right.

10. Obtain written material from the library to supplement your learning.

11. Be suspicious about those "sure fire," "get rich quick," "ultimate trading system" seminars. Generally they are expensive, hard to implement, and even harder to disprove. You will most likely be disappointed.

WHAT'S THE "BEST" TRADING SYSTEM FOR ME?

Another question frequently asked is "what type of trading system is best?" Previously I indicated that no single system contains all of the answers necessary for success. Perhaps no one method can give any investor all of the required self-control and discipline that leads to profitable investing and speculation. There are certain types of individuals who are naturally attracted to particular trading methods. Engineers, for example, tend toward mathematical and technical trading systems. Academicians and economists naturally are inclined in the fundamental direction. A majority of novice traders are enchanted with technical systems, which are less time consuming and easier to grasp than fundamental types of methods.

Regardless of the system employed, results are almost always a function of the user. This I have indicated many times, and you, most likely, have observed it to be true. It is one thing to have a good trading method; it is yet another to use it appropriately. As a result, the "best" trading system for you is the one that helps you maintain the greatest amount of discipline. Some techniques easily lend themselves to such regularity; there are others that leave too much room for interpretation and judgment. I advise you to utilize a particular system based on your level of self-discipline and confidence. If you have a history of poor adherence to trading rules, then a very rigid system is what you need. If you have mastered the basics of trading discipline, then practically any system will work for you.

Finally, the last few years have seen a marked increase in the number of trading systems offered for public sale. This has been true primarily in the commodity futures market. Typically, these techniques are sold at very high prices. The buyer agrees to keep the system secret. The seller often guarantees the system to be effective and offers a refund if this is not the case. Many books have made similar offers and claims. All appeal to a very basic lust and greed within the human psyche. Effectively written advertisements for such systems can draw an exceptionally large response within a matter of days. More often than not the buyers are sorely disappointed. This does not reflect upon the value of the system they have purchased. A large majority of the losses taken following such systems is due exclusively to trader error, emotion, poor judgment, lack of discipline, and disorganization. The system itself is never fully given the opportunity to function as advertised. Guarantees made by promoters of the systems often offer a complete refund, if it can be shown that the system did not work over a period of, for example, one year. Certainly there can be no refund given for a system that has not been implemented as required. This is not a defense of such system sales. I do not believe that anyone who has an infallible system will sell it, if indeed there exists such a beast. There are many techniques I use in the market which I do not intend to reveal to anyone, at any price. Although I have my doubts about the systems offered to the public, I have more doubts about the public that buys them.

SHOULD I SUBSCRIBE TO AN ADVISORY SERVICE? IF SO, WHICH ONE(S)?

This decision is similar to those previously discussed in the sec-

relating to services have been discussed in a previous section. Here are several additional guidelines that should be considered in subscribing to a service.

1. Does the service make specific recommendations, and do they fit into your financial limits? If too many trades are recommended, you may not find it financially possible to follow all of them. As a result, you will not be trading according to a total system.

2. Is there follow-through on each recommendation? Is every recommended position updated until closed out? If this is not done, then you may not wish to subscribe.

3. Do you really want to have the input of a service that may interfere with your own system, or one that may dissuade you from making trades based on your own work? It might be best to try your own hand at investing before allowing input from other sources.

4. Before subscribing to any service, make certain you understand why you want to subscribe, what you believe you can get from the service that you cannot do for yourself, and what factors will be used in deciding that you are actually obtaining the desired results.

5. How widely read is the service? Frequently there are disadvantages in following the recommendations of a service which is too widely distributed. You may be entering orders along with thousands of other investors. This will, more often than not, result in relatively poor order fills.

There are many advisory services, both in stocks and commodity futures, that do an excellent job of market analysis and recommendations. The majority are run by honest, hard-working, and dedicated advisors. Typically, their performance records are above average, and they help many investors who would otherwise not have the time to study every market opportunity. They cannot, however, help those who are unwilling or incapable of disciplining themselves. This point has been made many times before, and does not bear further explanation. If you intend to subscribe to an advisory service make certain you use it! Even if you find a service which has a poor record and do the opposite of what it says, make certain you are consistent in your approach and actions. There is more to be said for consistency than there is for all of the sophisticated technical work I have ever seen.

IS IT POSSIBLE TO BECOME OVERCONFIDENT?

Absolutely! Any emotional extreme is an unwelcome quality. Just as lack of self-confidence can lead to errors, so can overconfidence.

After making a number of highly successful investments there is a tendency for many individuals to become complacent, cocky, conceited, and careless. When profits come in quickly and one's trading system is working well, there is a natural human inclination toward feelings of infallibility. As a result, judgment is often impaired and decisions are made based strictly on "gut feelings." This, as you know, is not a sign of good trading and will, more often than not, result in losses. I have personally known several investors who made large amounts of money in a brief period of time, only to give it all back after falling prey to overconfidence and its accompanying evils.

It is always best to observe the "golden mean" in your investments. Nothing should be carried to excess in either direction. When you begin spending too much time on either extreme, this is an indication that something has gone wrong. The most effective action that can—and *should*—be taken at this time is to return to basics with even more self-discipline than before. You must act firmly and intensely to correct an overreaction. Another indicator that you may be in an overconfident state is your willingness to put on too many positions. The list of "symptoms" provided below can help you recognize the problem early in its development.

Symptoms of Overconfidence

1. Willingness to take larger than normal risks.

2. Accumulation of a much larger than average position in one market.

3. Accumulation of more than the usual number of positions in different markets.

4. General decline in adherence to trading rules.

5. Disregard of indications contrary to your present positions.

6. Willingness to ride losses longer than usual.

7. An increase in the "let's take a chance" type of attitude that accompanies rapid growth in profits.

8. Unwillingness to take profits as previously determined objectives.

9. A general euphoria and an accompanying belief that the best is yet to come.

Many individuals have specific syndromes of overconfidence. You are advised to study your attitudes and behaviors for a more thorough understanding of how you act when you feel overconfident. As with many other behaviors, friends and loved ones can alert you to the fact that something is wrong.

MY RESULTS IN THE MARKET AFFECT MY HOME BEHAVIOR; HOW DO I MAKE THE SEPARATION?

There are many individuals who take their work home with them. When they have had a good day at the office, all's well at home. But when they've had a bad day, those around them become the object of their work-related frustration. This is very common in the market as well. For the investor or trader who is very active in the market this is an even greater problem. It is very normal to experience such a "spillover" of emotion, and many things can be done to prevent its ruining your home life. Many investors and active traders resort to liquor. This is not the answer. Although it may provide temporary relief, it simply masks symptoms and does not permit proper ventilation of feelings. In addition, there are physical side-effects which make their presence known before too long. I recommend, instead, a series of steps that should be taken *before* entering the home. If this is not possible, then I would take the necessary action as soon as possible after arriving home. First and foremost, I suggest you employ any or all of the relaxation techniques described in Chapter 21. These will help ventilate the locked in feelings. The resulting release of stress will decrease the possibility of your striking out at the nearest human being. Second, I advise you to think through the actions of each day in light of your trading system. Discover exactly what went wrong. You must pinpoint the cause for whatever the problem may have been. If it was due to poor execution of trading rules, then accept the error, enter it appropriately in your trading record or diary, and make a commitment to rectify the error in future dealings. Third, make yourself aware of the fact that you have had a difficult day. Be cognizant that you are frustrated, anxious, and/or irritable. This will act as a signal to your self-control mechanisms. Fourth, let your family know that you have had a difficult day. Warn them that you may be on edge. This will help them keep out of your way. Fifth, take the opportunity to relax when you get home. A hot bath, a slow and leisurely meal, or soft music may be in order. Sixth, get to sleep early. Let the naturally healing process of sleep relieve the tension and frustration. Your dreams may be troubled but they will help release much of the pent-up pressure.

The importance of preventing the market from influencing your home life is obvious. But in addition to the domestic difficulties that can result, there can be a reverse effect. Once problems in the home have started they will in turn affect your trading. This will add to the stress, and more difficulty will be precipitated in the home. This is why it is important to break into the progression of events as soon as possible. It is very common for emotional problems to feed on each other. The best way to prevent the consequences of such a situation is to take preventive measures promptly.

HOW CAN THE SMALL INVESTOR TAKE ADVANTAGE OF MARKET PSYCHOLOGY?

There are two distinct ways in which the small investor can use market psychology to his or her advantage. First and of greatest importance, investors should know themselves. Their objectives and expectations must be clearly stated. As things change and goals are attained, new objectives should be formulated. The guidelines presented in previous chapters are designed to help you in this process. In addition, there are many books available which help improve insight. The second way in which an average investor can take advantage of market psychology is by understanding the psychological functioning of other investors. The meaning of such things as panics, climax tops and bottoms, contrary opinion, and news should be clearly understood. The lessons of history are many, and history tends to repeat itself in the markets time and time again. Each investor must take some independent action to learn the necessary market indicators. Although it is becoming increasingly difficult for many investors to profit through traditional types of securities, there are still many opportunities.

HOW CAN I OVERCOME DEPRESSION WHICH SETS IN AFTER SEVERAL LOSING TRADES?

Depression is perhaps one of the most difficult symptoms to overcome. There are some theories that severe depression may have its basis in biochemical factors. As a result, intensive treatment is required to eliminate the effects of serious depression. From time to time all individuals are subject to the effects of sadness, remorse, and depression. The best treatment I know is preventive rather than curative. In order to prevent depression from setting in it is vital to maintain as disciplined and organized a program as possible.

Depression has a way of keeping you from acting on matters of importance. It is a way of saying that you will not take any action at all, since all actions lead to failure. For those who fall deep into the pit of depression, the inability to act is almost a relief. If they are permitted to remain in the depths of inactivity, their depression will become increasingly resistant to change. This is why some societies treat depression with immediate action. The best thing one can do is to keep working, keep trying, and keep studying the market.

In some cases there are specific physical causes for depressive states. I would suggest that a physician be consulted promptly when such symptoms arise. He or she will determine if there is any systemic cause for your feelings. Many individuals cannot distinguish between physical feelings of tiredness and clinical depression. Consultation with a physician can help rule out any organic cause.

HOW DO I KNOW IF DISORGANIZATION IS MY MAJOR MARKET PROBLEMS?

Many problems can be minimized, if not totally eliminated by making some very minor changes in your approach to investing. Most important of these is organization. Have you ever missed a market move because your charts were not up to date? Have you ever failed to liquidate a position because you did not know you still had it? Have you ever looked for some market data which, although important, were misplaced in a pile of papers on your desk? These are all symptoms of underlying disorganization—all of which will contribute to market losses. I believe that most of the poor investors would become much more successful if they had the wherewithal to become organized. I recommend the following remediative steps:

1. Take stock of your current situation. Being totally honest with yourself can you say that you have not suffered losses as a result of disorganization?

2. Ask yourself the following questions:

a. Is my market work and related material all accessible within a matter of seconds, or is it scattered throughout the house (office)?

b. Do things disappear? Are charts or statistics you worked on several days ago stashed into a drawer or folder never to be seen again?

c. Are your trades planned daily, weekly, or monthly? Do you have a set time for your studies. Is your market work done on a regular basis? Do you have a specific time for entering orders?

d. Do you feel organized? Do you feel as if you have a good grasp on the market long term, intermediate term, and short term? Do you have a long-range plan on paper—or is it formulated piecemeal?

The answers to these questions will help you realize the degree to which you are organized. Most likely you will be unpleasantly surprised with the answer. If so, I have several suggestions:

1. Read the earlier section on scheduling.

2. Keep a daily log of what you do with your time. Write down all activities, time started, time completed, and things accomplished. You will rapidly discover where your time is going and how much time is spent in compensating for disorganization.

3. Set up a program which is highly precise, specific, and organized. Implement it for a given period of time and see how it affects profits. A positive result will most certainly let you know if disorganization has been standing in your way.

23 Sexual Aspects of the Market

Let's briefly review some of the previous material on psychosexual development. Sigmund Freud placed considerable emphasis on sexual conflicts and feelings in the understanding of personality and its dysfunctions. In fact, his theory is so heavily weighted in this area that it is termed the "psychosexual theory of development." According to the tenets of this school, sexual feelings begin at birth and pass through several changes as the child grows to adulthood. The details of Freud's theory are available in many publications, particularly his own writings. The essence of what psychosexual theory teaches is that sexual feelings, experiences, anxieties, and fears have a profound effect on us in later life. Many of the conflicts between child and parent are sexual. Many of the issues regarding authority, punishment, control, and achievement are closely related to sexual development. Following "childhood amnesia," a concept that was mentioned earlier, many of the sexual conflicts and feelings are locked away deep within the unconscious mind. Accordingly, they tend to influence our behavior without our being aware of their effect.

As mentioned earlier, the theory presented by Freud has been disputed by others throughout the years. On the one hand, there is little experimental evidence to support some of Freud's conclusions, and on the other hand, his work has passed the test of time. Many of the concepts he proposed are still highly regarded by psychiatrists and psychologists. In addition, there are numerous branches of his original theory, all of which are in some close way related by the common thread of psychosexual development. Patients who suffer from various neurotic and/or psychotic behaviors have often been helped through the application of Freudian therapeutic techniques. Certainly no methodology is without its flaws or limitations. Behavioral therapists criticize the psychoanalytical technique as unscientific and not founded on empirical fact. They also claim that classical Freudian treatment of emotional problems takes too long. Whereas it may take a psychoanalyst several years or longer to treat a phobic patient, behavioral methods can accomplish the same result in a matter of months, quite often more effectively, and most often with less expense. Psychoanalysts retort that the behavioral therapist is treating only the symptoms and ignoring underlying causes. They claim that the behavior that was treated in such a mechanical fashion (see some of the behavioral methods described earlier) will recur in a different form. This is called symptom substitution. Clinically and experimentally there is no evidence that a well-applied behavioral course of therapy will lead to a recurrence of the dysfunction, or a symptom substitution. And so the debate continues. Behaviorists have experimental data and effective technique and results on their side, and classical analysts have tradition, longevity, and results on their side. Both techniques work. I for one have my personal bias. It is, however, my duty to present you with both sides of the coin.

Turning back once again to Freud's theory of psychosexual development, we will see why it is important to understand one's deep-rooted sexual feelings and conflicts. If, indeed, they influence our overt adult behavior, then we must be aware of their effects and consequences at all times. Perhaps we are engaging in a certain behavior that could be avoided were we to understand or have *insight* into the unconscious motivation. This is, to be sure, one of the key elements of classical analytical (and many other) theories. It is necessary to unlock pent-up feelings. It is necessary to dig deeply into the unconscious mind, probe the experiences and feelings, bring them into consciousness, experience them, and put them into their proper perspective. Some of the examples that follow will, no doubt, be deemed incomplete by those who are avowed followers of Freud. I cannot, however, do justice to the immense theory of this man within the limited amount of space available. I can, on the other hand, present sufficient information to provide many readers with insights previously not experienced. Other investors, not blessed with these insights, may be inspired to take up the study of Freud and his theories.

SEXUAL CONFLICT AND PROFITS

A trader has just experienced the greatest single profit he has ever made. He is elated that his trading system has functioned so well. Everything he did was correct–the profit was expected, he liquidated near the indicated objective, and the desired result followed. Several hours after his victory he begins to experience a gnawing feeling in the pit of his stomach. As the day grows later he becomes aware of his increasing anxiety. By evening he is extremely tense, jumpy, has a nervous stomach, and cannot get more than several hours of sleep. The thing that distresses him most is the fact that he cannot understand *why* he feels as he does. He should be pleased with the success, and yet he cannot enjoy it. But to add insult to injury, he soon begins to lose the money back. It takes several days of persistently poor trading, but he manages to achieve his goal and the money is soon gone. Now he feels a sense of relief. But at the same time he feels depressed. Within a matter of days he becomes anxious once again, this time because he does not understand why he lost the money back, why it did not make him feel good, why he is depressed, why he has undone his success, what he can do about it, and why he is so very confused. This is a classic case of sexual conflict. You may be surprised to see the word "sex" enter into the discussion at this point. After all, there has been no mention of sex throughout the brief story. How does it now enter into the picture?

This trader is suffering from an unconscious sexual conflict. Ideally, this one situation should not be removed from the total picture of his personality, but for the sake of example I will do so. Freud wrote a great deal about the feelings of "castration anxiety" and the sexual attraction of the male child to his mother. He theorized that a male child is attracted to his mother and a female to her father. The sexual attraction that is experienced leads the child to begin fear reprisal by the father (or mother for female children). Fear is related primarily to the body organ which experiences sexual pleasure, namely the genitalia. Armed with only a very elementary understanding of the world, the child begins to fear that his father, on learning of the attraction to mother, will remove the child's penis and/or associated parts as a punishment. In female children the feelings run in generally the same direction. They realize that they do not have a penis and feel that it has been removed as punishment for attraction to father. Both cause what is termed castration anxiety. But the fear does not stop here. As the child matures the feelings remain. In some cases, the fears are intense and buried deep within the unconscious mind. In other situations, there has been resolution of the fear through positive experiences between father and son or mother and daughter. When the child becomes an adult he is no longer aware of the basis for such feelings. All he knows is that he feels anxiety. During the course of his childhood the fear of castration becomes generalized into a fear of authority. Often the child begins to feel that if he is successful at conquering, or overcoming, a great task, this will bring upon him the wrath of his castrating father. Through the process of generalization, fear then becomes associated with any major achievement. The individual becomes anxious that he will be punished, or castrated, and this generally results in guilt, depression, and a series of losses. The losses are an unconscious way of repenting for the victory. It is as if the investor is saying, "Now that I have succeeded in conquering my mother, I had better undo the damage, give her back to my father, and hope that he will not castrate me."

SEXUAL CONFLICT IN DREAMS

Frequently the conflict may express itself symbolically in dreams. During his sleepless night subsequent to being victorious the sufferer may have a dream which, although he does not fully understand, feels to him as if it relates to the problem. An example of how such a dream might be related by the trader to his therapist:

I am riding in an automobile with my mother and father. We are on a mountain road and the climb is long and steep. My father is driving. I am sitting in the back seat. Suddenly the car begins to swerve. My father is injured as the car hits a large rock. For some reason or another we decide to put him in the trunk of the car (patient laughs) . . . that seems funny to me now, I wonder why we had to put him in the trunk . . . well actually . . . well it seems that there was some sort of a hospital in the trunk . . . sounds funny . . . but there was some first aid there. Can't understand why . . . but then my mother asked me to drive the car. Even though I was very young in the dream, I took the wheel and drove the car all the way up the mountain . . . my mother was happy . . . then I woke up.

There is some very deep symbolism in this contrived dream episode. The subject has injured his father, removed him from the picture by locking him in the trunk, and then he has assumed the "wheel" or control of the car, thereby making his mother happy. He has conquered the mountain, his mother, and his father, all at the same time. The dream expresses in symbolic, or unconscious, laughter how trader feels about his victory in the market. In fact, the dream might have continued with the father leaving the trunk and punishing the child for assuming control of the auto. In any event, the dream was created from the unconscious feelings of the individual. By understanding how the dream relates to his current situation the trader might gain some insight, thereby relieving his anxiety and castration fear.

SEXUAL INADEQUACY AND THE MARKET

There are many other situations in which sexual feelings might dictate market behavior. It should be said that market behavior is not the only thing affected by sexual conflicts. The entire personality can be shaped by these events, according to Freudian theory. Its effect on investment behavior is merely one aspect upon which I have chosen to focus. Here is another example of how sexual feelings can mediate or influence market behavior. Assume the following situation: an investor is very aggressive in the market. He seeks to acquire as much wealth as possible, within the shortest period of time. Meanwhile his attitude is one of self-centeredness, conceit, and blatent immodesty. He believes that he is the market Messiah (if there is such a thing). Not only does he trade actively and aggressively, but he seems to have no regard for caution, conservatism, or common sense. There are times that will be enormously profitable for such a trader, and there will be occasions that bring him to the brink of ruin. His overall behavior is one of a "chance taker." He is confident to a pathological extreme; so much so, that he ignores many of the realities in a situation. How can we understand his behavior from an analytical point of view?

In my opinion, such behavior is typical of one who is attempting to compensate for feelings of inadequacy. Most likely he feels that he has either been castrated and must compensate, or that his sexual equipment is inadequate to do the job. Such feelings typically arise from childhood experiences which either were threatening or instilled a sense of smallness and/or worthlessness in the individual. In adulthood there are several response styles that could have developed. In this case our subject overcompensated for his internal feelings of inferiority. Internally he most likely feels negative about himself, is afraid of the market, and does not believe he will ever succeed. This type of behavior is typical of many who suffer from the same feelings. Men who, for example, are extremely "macho," who are inveterate bachelors and women chasers, who feel that they are the Lord's gift to women, are often compensating for unconscious feelings of sexual inadequacy and, possibly, homosexuality.

LINGUISTIC CLUES AND SEXUALITY

There are, in addition, many popular expressions and attitudes relating to the market which reflect an unconscious sexual orientation. Freud was a student of behavioral symptoms that reflected underlying feelings. Not only was the dream important, but such things as associations, slips of the tongue, jokes, and daydreams were also taken to be symbolic of internal feelings. There is a tendency for most traders to relate to the market in a sexual way. This is reflected in their behavior as well as in their verbal expressions about the market. Based on a purely Freudian interpretation of what transpires on the floor of an exchange, or in the trading pit, we can see how sex might become a factor. For many years pit traders and floor specialists were primarily male. Fortunately, this is beginning to change and more women are participating actively. The competition that transpires relates very closely to the competition between father and son for mother's affection, or mother and daughter for father's affection. Hence many of the emotions aroused in the competitive act, whether on the floor or behind a desk, are seen unconsciously as sexual. A loss is not seen unconsciously as a loss but rather as castration. Those who have had serious traumas in early childhood are particularly subject to such feelings. Typically they develop neurotic disorders. Women are subject to many of the same feelings.

Considerably more evidence can be cited. The common expression "we really got 'screwed' in the market," although not necessarily reflecting good taste, is typical of the manner in which some investors view the market. They feel as if the market has taken sexual advantage of them. There is no objective reason to relate to the market in such a fashion. The only realistic explanation is the one that has been presented here as an overview of Freud's work. There are other popular expressions about the market that have sexual overtones; they will not be repeated here.

This chapter is only a small indication of the manner in which classical psychoanalytic concepts apply to the marketplace. Certainly there will be those who have other interpretations. There will also be those who feel that I have not provided sufficient coverage of the topic. Since this is only a general text I do not have sufficient time or space to delve into any one topic as deeply as might be desired. Those who wish to take the plunge, however, can find enough information at the public library to last a lifetime of study.

REVIEW

1. Freudian theory stresses the importance of psychosexual development as an integral part or aspect of adult personality.

2. The many feelings to which a child is exposed can help create various unconscious reactions and attitudes to sexual experiences.
3. Such feelings are generalized and in adulthood become part of overall behavior.
4. Dreams, jokes, expressions, slips of the tongue, and attitudes are all symbolic of underlying sexual attitudes.
5. By helping a patient understand these feelings, the therapist can effect a cure.

24 Using Psychology To Maximize Investment Success

I am, both by profession and attitude, interested in only one thing—*results*. All I have attempted to tell you, and all I have sought to teach you, both by example and by instruction, will amount to naught unless faithfully employed. Provided your investments are legal, the technique you have used does not matter so long as profits result. As indicated at the outset, my focus has therefore been not on the system but rather on the trader. Let us examine briefly where we have been, what we should have learned, what we can still learn, and how we can implement what has been expressed.

There lies a vast expanse of intellectual wilderness between education and expression. Lessons learned from a book will perhaps never be translated into action. Were we capable of internalizing and integrating all we have read and heard, many of our life's problems would be readily solved. Unfortunately our capacity to act on information is limited. There are, however, a number of proven psychological techniques that will help in the profitable implementation of what has been expressed here. Review, repetition, and reaction are the three R's of learning. Thus I advise you now proceed to review, in outline form, each chapter of this book. I suggest you treat it as a textbook. Make an outline of what has been discussed, study the outline, examine the review at the end of each chapter, and internalize the concepts. You need not agree with what I have said. You need only observe the market to see that what I have said is valid.

Next, repeat the process. Attempt to put yourself into the picture as much as possible. In so doing you will have personal contact with the concepts. You need not jump into the change process with both feet. Test some of the ideas on a limited scale. Acquire a feel for what has been presented, and see if it has potential. Certainly the market will let you know very quickly if you are correct. If an idea appears to have merit, then follow up and take further action.

Finally, react to the more specific sections of this book. Set goals, implement them, design your own programs, read some of the recommended texts, ask relevant questions, but above all, *act*. Don't be content to just sit there, losing money, making bad investments, feeling sorry for yourself, and being jealous of others' success. Put your ideas to work and they will work for you. They will bring you the investment profits you seek. But you will never know if you don't act.

I have said on many occasions that it is a relatively simple matter to determine whether a market will go up or down. It is yet another to implement, with success, what has been decided. It is fortunate that the rules which must be followed in attaining market success are so simple—otherwise many basically average investors, myself included, would never have achieved wealth. In fact, the personal rules for investment success are so (deceptively) simple that they could all be overstated on half of an 8½ × 11 inch piece of paper. We have all heard these rules over and over again. They do not bear repetition.

Let's step back and take a look at what has been discussed. First and foremost, the point has been repeatedly made that market prices are a function of supply and demand over the long run, but related to investor psychology over the short and intermediate term. The basics of market theory and psychology were discussed. Attention was given to the psychoanalytic versus behavioral methods as opposite ends of the continuum. An analogy was made between fundamentalist versus technician and medical versus behavioral models of human behavior. The basics of both major psychological theories were discussed with close consideration of their individual concepts relating to investor psychology. Sample programs for change were discussed along with key concepts such as interpersonal relationships, sex and the market, stress, the use of trading systems, losses and how to take them, broker-client relationships, the use of advisory services, and scheduling. A number of frequently asked questions were answered.

And now the rest is up to you. Within the limits of what I can transmit via the written word, I have provided you with many of the basics as well as directions to try in looking for answers. I would, in closing, leave you with several final suggestions I believe have merit in any trading program, for any individual, regardless of financial ability, and independent of experience.

Before investing in any market–stocks, commodity futures, options, real estate, or collectibles–make certain that the market you have chosen has the potential to lead you to the desired goal. If you seek the satisfaction that comes from social service, then you must not expect the market to bring you what you need. The market can only yield profit and the pleasure that accompanies being right. Expect more, and you will most likely be disappointed. Investments such as antiques, coins, or stamps can yield aesthetic satisfaction as well. Each avenue of investment, therefore, has its unique ability. You must make certain that your goals are realistic and, above all, within the scope of your selected area of endeavor.

After having decided where and when to invest, be certain to approach your program with all the seriousness of a neurosurgeon involved in a life-or-death operation. There is a tendency for many investors to be flippant, disorganized, casual, and unconcerned about their investments. This more often than not leads to losses. Investing, trading, speculating, forecasting, money management, and advising are serious businesses. Unless given total consideration their end result will not be positive. Dedication, persistence, thoroughness, and hard work are the keys to investment success.

Your most difficult task will *not* be prediction, but *rather* self-control. Expect to encounter some of the most difficult and frustrating personal experiences of your life. You will find that *you* are the most important element of the success equation.

In addition, you will rapidly discover, if you have not already done so, that attitude, state of health and emotion, interpersonal relations, stress, tension, and work environment will all have a market effect on your investment success. The more active your trading, the more susceptible you will be to these influences.

Keep investment goals firmly in mind at all times. Set new goals after current objectives have been attained.

In the coming years economists will continue to make advances in forecasting methodology. Trading systems will come and go. Computer technology has only recently made its mark in the area of econometric analysis and mechanical trading methods. But through it all the basic substance of price change will continue to be human emotion. Panic, fear, greed, insecurity, anxiety, stress, and uncertainty will endure as the primary forces of short-term price change. Success in the market is, in my opinion, not as complex or difficult as it appears to be. There are time-tested rules that if religiously applied, will lead to profits. It's as simple as that— and, at the same time, it's as complicated as that. The answer to investment success lies within.

25 Writings of the Masters

I maintain that the best and most meaningful lessons are learned from direct experience, yet there are ways in which we can acquire certain types of knowledge without suffering the attendant pain. One of these less painful methods of learning is through vicarious experience. Although indirect learning such as this in no way compares to the strength and power of direct stimulus–response–reinforcement, there are many behavioral cues that can reach us through the indirect route. By watching others trade we can learn a particular style and vocabulary. And by reading about how others have been successful in the markets, we can learn a great deal about our own technique.

My personal experiences have led me to the conclusion that all investors, traders, and speculators must include, as part of their market education, an intensive reading of works produced by the great "trading masters." To name but a few, these include the writings of Cutten, Pugh, Baruch, Livermore, Gann, and Wyckoff. Certainly there are many other individuals whose words of wisdom should be taken to heart. And there are many other texts of a technical nature which have made major contributions to the field. My concern is, however, with the psychological aspect of what has been experienced and recorded by those who have traded profitably through the years. If we can learn even one lesson from their experiences, if we can gain even one insight, or one inspiration, then the effort will have been well worthwhile. This is why I always recommend such reading as the first step in market education (or reeducation).

What exactly can we learn by spending time studying the masters' works? How can we apply their learning to our own? Is there a way in which we should approach the study of their writings? Have we indeed spent enough time learning from their errors? Should their teachings be read more than once? Here are some of my thoughts regarding these questions. I will attempt to give you some general rules of a psychological nature.

WHY READ WHAT THEY HAD TO SAY?

There are those who believe that the markets of today are not like the markets of yesteryear. There was less volatility in those days, there was more price manipulation, and there was considerably less volume. The fact remains, however, that investors and speculators were as much governed by their emotions as they are today. The common element in all great masters' writings is their repeated reference to psychological principles. Despite differences in technique, the net result of their achievements was almost exclusively a product of several key personality traits–patience, perseverence, determination, and rational action. These are all skills trading systems cannot teach us. They are all personal qualities that come with experience. And they are, in fact, the most basic and important tools a trader can possess. By vicariously experiencing the trials and tribulations of those who have been successful before us, we can gain the inspiration to help us carry on. We can acquire a general idea of the qualities that have helped others on the road to trading and investing riches. By reading what they had to say we can shorten significantly the discovery process.

In addition to the indirect learning that may result from such readings, the investor who seeks to acquire new trading techniques can be so inspired. Frequently one develops original ideas about the market while familiarizing one's self with the approach of others. The synthesis of many readings can help formulate what appear to be totally unique technical and/or fundamental approaches. Not only can new systems be created, but old ideas, which may not have worked for others, can be avoided. In reading about the losses resulting from the use of certain concepts, we can learn to avoid them, refine them, or study them closely before we implement them.

Last, and by no means least, the writings of successful investors can help encourage us when times are bad, and caution us when times are good. It helps to know that we are not alone in our struggle for success. It helps to know that others before us have experienced the same defeats and enjoyed similar successes. For the uninitiated, the rags to riches stories Jesse Livermore reports can provide goals and directions as well as comfort. When one realizes that the road to vast profits is a long and difficult one, any one profit or loss can be put in its proper time perspective. It is important to remember that most market wealth is acquired steadily over a period of years. This message will be clearly conveyed by the masters' writings.

READING FOR PLEASURE—READING FOR FACTS

There are many different ways in which your readings may be approached. For simple entertainment value, it is not necessary to maintain any organized study program. And there is certainly nothing wrong with reading for enjoyment! In fact, I strongly recommend that your first time through any market text should be primarily for enjoyment. Following this initial reading, return to the text for a more thorough, learning-oriented examination of the material. I suggest you use the following specific and time-tested method to achieve the maximum benefit from your reading:

1. Underline in the book. If you do not wish to mark in your book, buy two copies, one for the shelf and one for repeated use. By underscoring relevant passages, concepts, or observations, you will highlight their importance. After the reading has been completed you may wish to scan through the underlined sections as a quick review. It would also be a good idea to categorize the underlinings in different colors, according to topic. Technical trading rules might be underlined in blue, and psychological concepts in red, for example.

2. Make an outline. I suggest that you make a topic outline of the book. If you do not know how to do this you can consult almost any text on English grammar or composition to learn how. The object of this lesson is organizational. By having a topic outline of what you are reading you can gain some insight into the transitional events in the writer's life and experiences. This will provide you with a perspective and framework within which to evaluate your own experiences. Having an outline will also help you find key topics quickly when you wish to refer to them.

3. Make a list. List the ten most important psychological trading rules *you* have extracted from the text. These rules may not be the same for all individuals. They may, in fact, be different from the main points the author has stressed. The only important consideration should be their relevance and importance to you, the reader. Each book and author will have his or her own set of rules. I suggest you keep them close at hand for ready referral.

4. Make note of common rules. In your readings it should become obvious that some trading rules are common to most successful investors. It is especially important to indicate these on your list. In fact, I suggest you draw up a list of those rules or observations that are common to all or most traders whose works you have read.

5. Take referrals. If, in your readings, an author refers to another work of importance, note the reference and place it on a list of things to read. In so doing you will broaden your base of readings. I advise you to study as many of the works on your list as possible; at times they may be more helpful than the book you are reading. They will, in turn, lead you to other useful sources.

6. Review rules frequently. This will help "burn" the rules into your memory. It is no simple task to acquire a functional set of trading rules, and it is even more difficult to learn how and when to apply the rules. Constant exposure will keep them foremost in your mind. This will allow you to apply them frequently, which in turn will help you learn.

7. Your favorite author. As you progress in your readings you will begin to find favorite authors. Pursue your readings of these authors. Most likely you have identified with their experiences for a good reason. When you study their trading in greater detail, you may find additional reasons for your interest. Because you are attracted to what they have said and done, there is reason to believe that you either strive to duplicate their successes or strongly identify with their experiences. If you are especially intertested in a certain "master," then make it one of your goals to study his work intensively.

8. Look for similarities and differences. If you have a particular handicap or repetitive market error, attempt to determine how others have solved similar difficulties. This is perhaps one of the most efficient and effective ways of finding solutions to recurrent market problems. By drawing on the experiences of others you can save yourself time, and often money. Note also any large differences between your trading rules and those of successful traders. If there are too many radical differences, then you may be on the wrong track and a change could be helpful.

9. Reread them often. Although I have read most of the great works many times over they never seem to lose their appeal. And they never lose their instructive ability. It seems that there are new bits and pieces to be learned with each additional reading. It is for this reason that I recommend frequent readings. When I have suffered some losses in the market and feel my spirits getting low I read my favorite market book to help inspire me. And it does!

Like most traders I have my own ideas as to which market readings are best. I do not wish to impose my own bias on you. Nevertheless, my list is the result of considerable experience and investigation. Certainly there are many other writings. I would advise you to read all of them if you have the time. Let me make clear precisely what I mean when I tell you to read writings of the "masters." I am not making reference to the rash of *How to Make a Million Dollars . . .* books that have appeared on the market. I am referring strictly to the writings of those who actively traded the markets, with success, from the early 1900s through the mid-1950s. There have, indeed, been many capable traders since then.

I have found, however, that lessons learned in the early 1900s have more of an impact on the individual trader than those of recent years. Note also that I am not referring to texts that explain various or specific trading systems. The type of book I suggest you look for is autobiographical, and not trading-system oriented. There are too many trading systems each claiming to be better than the next. There are too few good traders to implement these systems.

In the pages that follow I have attempted to provide you with a brief overview of some "trading masters" whose works I suggest you read. I cannot do justice to the totality of their experiences or writings, but I believe that I can offer you some additional understandings of how important proper attitude and effective psychology can be in the overall attainment of success. In providing only brief coverage I have chosen to place virtually no emphasis on the trading system each individual employed. My orientation is, as you certainly know by now, almost purely psychological.

W. D. GANN

SUGGESTED READING: *Truth of the Stock Tape*
How to Make Profits in Puts and Calls
How to Make Profits in Commodities
45 Years in Wall Street

Available from: Lambert-Gann Publishing Co., Box 0, Pomeroy, Washington 99347.

Of all the well-known traders W. D. Gann was perhaps the most prolific writer and the most active researcher. His trading systems were detailed, innovative, extensive, and in some ways almost mystical. But more than technique itself, Gann recognized the overriding importance of psychology in the marketplace. Despite his considerable coverage of historical price behavior, methodology, and seasonality, his observations of human nature and its relationship to the market were not overshadowed or given a back seat. Even his closing remarks in *45 Years in Wall Street* were tinged with comment on the emotional state of traders and investors:

We cannot escape it [emotion] in the future. It will cause another panic in stocks. When it comes, both traders and investors will sell stocks, *as usual, after it is too late* or in the last stages of the bear market. . . . (1949, p. 94, emphasis mine)

We can learn a great deal about Gann's market psychology by examining his list of "24 Never Failing Rules" (1949, p. 16). The following are those rules that apply to investor psychology:

14. Never get out of the market just because you have lost patience or get into the market because you are anxious from waiting. . . .
16. Never cancel a stop loss order after you have placed it at the time you make a trade.
17. Avoid getting in and out of the market too often. . . .
23. Never change your position in the market without a good reason. When you make a trade, let it be for some good reason or according to some definite plan; then do not get out without a definite indication of a change in trend.

In addition to these specific rules, Gann commented extensively on the human element and his belief that it is the trader's greatest weakness. His basic belief is similar to what I have been telling you throughout this book. Simply and concisely stated his point is as follows:

Therefore, in order to make a success he (the trader) must act in a way to overcome the weak points which have caused the ruin of others. (P. 25)

Gann writes additionally:

When a trader makes a profit, he gives himself credit and feels that his judgment is good and that he did it all himself. When he makes losses, he takes a different attitude and seldom ever blames himself or tries to find the cause with himself for the losses. He finds excuses; reasons with himself that the unexpected happened, and that if he had not listened to some one else's advice, he would have made a profit. He finds a lot of ifs, ands, and buts, which he imagines were no fault of his. This is why he makes mistakes and loses the second time.

The investor and trader must work out his own salvation and blame himself and no one else for his losses, for unless he does, he will never be able to correct his weaknesses. After all, it is your own acts that cause your losses, because you did the buying and the selling. You must look for the trouble within and correct it. Then you will make a success, and not before. . . .

I can give you the best rules in the world and the best methods for determining the position of a stock, and then you can lose money on account of the human element which is your greatest weakness. You will fail to follow rules. You will work on hope or fear instead of facts. You will delay. You will become impatient. You will act too quickly or you will delay too long in acting, thus cheating yourself on account of your human weakness and then blaming it on the market. Always remember that it is your mistake that causes losses and not the action of the market or the manipulators. Therefore, strive to follow rules, or keep out of speculation for you are doomed to failure.

These words, taken from years of experience in stocks and commodities, are well worth the price of Gann's book. Bear in mind that Gann had extensive experience in the markets. Keep also in mind the fact that his main point was similar to what has been stressed throughout my writings as well. The speculator, trader, investor–the human factor–is the weak link in the chain. This alone is the instrument that can guide the trading system to success or failure.

I will close my commentary on W. D. Gann with some words from *How to Make Profits Trading in Commodities:*

Hope and Fear: I have written about this often in all my books, and I feel that I cannot repeat it too often. The average man or woman buys Commodities because they hope they will go up or because somebody advises them they will go up. This is the most dangerous thing to do. Never trade on hope. Hope wrecks more people than anything else. Face the facts, and when you trade, trade on facts, eliminating hope.

Fear causes many losses. People sell out because they fear commodities are going lower, but they often wait until the decline has run its course and they sell near the bottom . . . never make a trade on fear. . . . (1942, p. 17)

BURTON PUGH

SUGGESTED READING: *A Better Way to Make Money*
Mastering Cotton
Science and Secrets of Wheat Trading
Trader's Instruction Book

Available from: Lambert-Gann Publishing Co., Box 0, Pomeroy, Washington 99347.

Another "master" of the markets was Burton Pugh, who ran a successful market advisory service and pioneered many new technical market concepts. Although Pugh's work was highly technical, he also found it necessary to comment on the fallibility of man in the overall success of a trading program. In his 1948 publication entitled *A Better Way to Make Money* Pugh covers many trading techniques and commodity market indicators. His words are concise and his concepts specific. And his concluding "Epigrams and Observations" is rich in psychologically oriented trading rules. Here are a few of his observations:

Enter the market with the belief that you *will win.*

Surrender no advantage to the natural human indolence. Money is made by aggressiveness and determination. If in doubt, learn more about what you are doing. . . .

All the crop news and political events will be of little use. If it were possible to trade successfully by good and bad weather conditions, it would be unbelievably easy to make money. When the news filters through ten or twenty thousand minds interested in wheat, the major opinion may be quite different from the opinion of an individual. . . .

If a trader fails to come out right, the error will be found in the operator–not the market. . . . A loss makes one thoughtful. It is the losses that makes the operator studious–not the profits. Take advantage of every slip to improve your knowledge of market action. It will be found that, no matter how erratic the action of either stocks or grains, they are still conforming to the laws of market movements. Practice is a greater renovator. It enables us to discard wrong ideas. . . .

There is a very simple *philosophy of loss* in all trading.

The reason traders lose readily is because there is no one to make them accept a profit, and there *is* someone to make them take a loss–the broker. . . .

Success is the most desirable thing in the world, but it is an eliminating contest. The one who wins must try and try until he is able to pass the test. . . . (Pp. 299–303; emphasis in original)

JESSE LIVERMORE

SUGGESTED READING: *Reminiscences of a Stock Operator*

Available from: American Research Council, Larchmont, New York 10538.

A reflection of my fondness for the writings of Livermore is the frequency with which he is mentioned throughout this book. Most certainly the man had his own "trading system," as did other speculators. But his technique was not as much a part of his story as was his psychology. *Reminiscences of a Stock Operator,* written under the name Edwin Le Fevre, is perhaps the greatest single compilation of psychological market wisdom contained in one work. It is thought to be biographical although it is presented in a fictional format. Regardless, it is, in my opinion, a must on any serious investor's list of reading materials. The greatest justice I can do this work of art is to quote for you several of the significant passages. Others have been quoted extensively elsewhere in this book. I would not want to limit, in any way, the possible benefits and enjoyment that can be obtained through your independent reading.

In fact, I always made money when I was sure I was right before I began. What beat me was not having brains enough to stick to my own game. (P. 14)

I know from experience that nobody can give me a tip or a series of tips that will make more money for me, than my own judgment. It took me five years to learn to play the game intelligently enough to make big money when I was right. (P. 31)

Finally there came the awful day of reckoning for the bulls and the optimists and the wishful thinkers and those vast hordes that, dreading the pain of a small loss at the beginning, were now about to suffer total amputation–without anaesthetics. (P. 110)

A loss never bothers me after I take it. I forget it overnight. But being wrong–not taking the loss–that is what does the damage to the pocketbook and to the soul. (P. 118)

ADDITIONAL READINGS

In addition to the works of "great masters," many books contain a wealth of historical information about the markets. I believe that every investor, whether interested in stocks, commodities, bonds, real estate, or options, should have a firm knowledge of market history. A great deal can be learned from studying the action of investors in past bull and bear markets, fads, crashes, and panics. Such information will supplement much of what I have discussed in this book.

I therefore recommend you either purchase or, at the very minimum, read most of the publications described here.

BARUCH, B. M. *My Own Story,* New York: Holt, 1957.

Baruch was one of America's most outspoken and successful speculators. His writings are a must, particularly the one mentioned. More than most well-known investors, he recognized the importance of emotion in the market, and gave specific recommendations as to how it might be used to one's financial advantage.

SMITH, ADAM. *The Money Game*. New York: Random House, 1967.

This book is also a must for those who enjoy laughing at themselves. In a humorous and purportedly fictional series of tales, many of the markets' foolish goings-on are discussed.

There are also historical works that should be read, and possibly studied. The major bull and bear markets, as well as some of the well-known investors who helped make them, are discussed at length. Two important books are:

MOTTRAM, R. H. *A History of Financial Speculation,* Boston: Little, Brown, 1929.

THOMAS, D. L. *The Plungers and the Peacocks,* New York: Putnam, 1967.

In the general category of market books I advise the following:

LOEB, G. M. *The Battle for Stock Market Profits,* New York: Simon and Schuster, 1971.

SOBEL, R. *Inside Wall Street,* New York: W. W. Norton, 1977.

TEWELS, R. J., et al. *The Commodity Futures Game: Who Wins? Who Loses? Why?,* New York: McGraw-Hill, 1974.

For an overview of the many available publications in the commodity futures area you can consult the following:

WOY, J. B. *Commodity Futures Trading: A Bibliographic Guide,* New York: R. R. Bowker, 1976.

I have by no means covered all of the major works. Certainly there are many others that can provide the information necessary to successful investing. All things considered there are relatively few books in the investment area that are truly worthwhile reading. Those that focus on trading systems, techniques, and methodology are generally lacking in the area of investment psychology. The well-rounded investor should make it his or her goal to read every significant market work. In so doing, several favorite authors will emerge. I advise you to follow up on the works of the "masters" whose stories appeal to you.

SUGGESTED PSYCHOLOGY READINGS

In addition to the market texts recommended previously, I also believe you can find some guidance in the psychology texts listed in the references at the end of this book. There are several other sources you might find interesting. I have not used them as references for this book but recommend them as informational sources:

BERGSON, ANIKA and TUCHACK, VLADIMIR. *Zone Therapy,* New York: Pinnacle Books, 1974. (Physical therapy and relief of tension Ch. 16, 27, 34).

FREUD, SIGMUND. *The Interpretation of Dreams,* New York: Avon, 1965.

GELLERMAN, SAUL W. *The Uses of Psychology in Management,* New York: McGraw-Hill, 1960.

HARPER, ROBERT A. *The New Psychotherapies,* Englewood Cliffs, N.J.: Prentice-Hall, 1975.

ORNSTEIN, ROBERT E. *The Psychology of Consciousness,* New York: Penguin, 1972.

REVIEW

1. Every investor should be familiar with the experiences and philosophies of those investors who have been successful.
2. Most of the market masters had their own psychologically based trading rules.
3. Many of the opinions and philosophies of famous investors are similar, even though they had different backgrounds and experiences and traded at different times.

4. By reading what they had to say about the emotional side of the market, and their experiences with it, we can help limit some of the losses that might be part of the learning process.
5. Several readings of each book can yield a wealth of information. Notes should be taken to maximize the learning process.

Bibliography

Altman, L. L. *The Dream in Psychoanalysis.* New York: International Universities Press, 1969.

Binet, A. and Simon T. "Le Dévelopment de l'Intelligence Chez les Enfants." *L'Anée Psychologique* **14** (1908): 1–94.

Brenner, Charles. *An Elementary Textbook of Psychoanalysis,* Garden City, N.Y.: Anchor Books, 1974.

Caplan, Ruth B. *Psychiatry and the Community in Nineteenth Century America.* New York: Basic Books, 1969.

Capra, Fritjof. *The Tao of Physics.* Boulder, Colo.: Shambhala Publications, 1975.

Dollard, J. and Miller, N. E. *Personality and Psychotherapy.* New York: McGraw-Hill, 1950.

Eriksen, C. W. *Unconscious Processes.* In M. R. Jones, ed., *Nebraska Symposium on Motivation.* Lincoln: University of Nebraska Press, 1958. Pp. 169–227.

———. "Discrimination and Learning Without Awareness: A Methodological Survey and Evaluation." *Psychological Review* **67** (1960): 279–300.

Escalona, S. K. "The Use of Infant Tests for Predictive Purposes." *Bulletin of the Meninger Clinic* **14** (1950): 117–128.

Ford, D. H. and Urban, H. B. *Systems of Psychotherapy–A Comparative Study.* New York: Wiley, 1965.

Franks, C. M. and Wilson, G. T. *Annual Review of Behavior Therapy: Theory and Practice.* New York: Brunner/Mazel, 1974.

Freud, S. *The Interpretation of Dreams. Collected Works.* Vols. 4–5. London: Hogarth, 1953.

———. *Three Essays on Sexuality: II–Infantile Sexuality. Collected Works.* London: Hogarth, 1957.

Gann, W. D. *Truth of the Stock Tape*. Pomeroy, Wash.: Lambert-Gann, 1923.

———. *How to Make Profits in Commodities*. Pomeroy, Wash.: Lambert-Gann, 1942.

———. *How to Make Profits in Puts and Calls*. Pomeroy, Wash.: Lambert-Gann, 1943.

———. *45 Years in Wall Street*. Pomeroy, Wash.: Lambert-Gann, 1949.

Gesell, A. and Amatruda, C. S. *Developmental Diagnosis*. New York: Harper, 1962.

Gibson, Elanor J. *Principles of Perceptual Learning and Development*. New York: Crofts, 1967.

Gittelson, Bernard. *Biorhythm—A Personal Science*. New York: Arco, 1976.

Goldberg, F. H. and Fiss, H. "Partial Cues and the Phenomenon of Discrimination without Awareness." *Perceptual Motor Skills* **9** (1959): 243–251.

Henry, William E. *The Analysis of Fantasy*. New York: Wiley, 1956.

Laffal, Julius. *Pathological and Normal Language*. New York: Atherton, 1965.

Le Fevre, Edwin. *Reminiscences of a Stock Operator*. Larchmont, N.Y.: American Research Council, 1965.

London, Perry. *Behavioral Control*. New York: Meridian, 1977.

Marx, M. H. and Hillix, W. A. *Systems and Theories in Psychology*. New York: McGraw-Hill, 1963.

McCleary, R. A. and Lazarus, R. S. "Autonomic Discrimination without Awareness: An Interim Report." *Journal of Personality* **18** (1949): 171–179.

Meyer, William J. *Developmental Psychology*. New York: Center for Applied Research in Education, 1964.

Mikvlas, William L. *Concepts in Learning*. Philadelphia: Saunders, 1974.

Mounier, Emmanuel. *The Character of Man*. New York: Harper, 1956.

Packard, Vance. *The Hidden Persuaders*. New York: Pocket Books, 1961.

Pavlov, I. P. *Conditioned Reflexes*. Oxford: Clarendon Press, 1927.

Pötzl, O. "The Relationship Between Experimentally Induced Dream

Images and Indirect Vision." *Psychological Issues* **2**(3), Monograph 7 (1960): 41–120.

Pugh, B. *A Better Way to Make Money*. Pomeroy, Wash.: Lambert-Gann, 1948.

Secord, P. F. and Backman, Carl W. *Social Psychology*. New York: McGraw-Hill, 1964.

Selye, H. *The Physiology and Pathology of Exposure to Stress*. Montreal: Acta, 1950.

Skinner, B. F. *Science and Human Behavior*. New York: Free Press, 1953.

Watts, A. W. *The Book on the Taboo Against Knowing Who You Are*. New York: Vintage, 1972.

Watson, J. B. "Psychology as the Behaviorist Sees It." *Psychological Review* **20** (1913): 158–177.

———. *Psychology from the Standpoint of a Behaviorist*. Philadelphia: Lippincott, 1919.

———. *Behaviorism*. New York: Norton, 1924.

Watzlawick, Paul, et al. *Pragmatics of Human Communication*. New York: Norton, 1967.

Wiener, M. and Schiller, P. H. "Subliminal Perception or Perception of Partial Cues." *Journal of Abnormal Social Psychology* **61** (1960): 124–137.

Wolman, Benjamin, ed. *Handbook of General Psychology*, Englewood Cliffs, N.J.: Prentice-Hall, 1973.

Index